Race Migrations

Race Migrations

Latinos and the Cultural Transformation of Race

Wendy D. Roth

Stanford University Press
Stanford, California

Stanford University Press
Stanford, California

Printed in the United States of America on acid-free, archival-quality paper

Library of Congress Cataloging-in-Publication Data

Roth, Wendy D., author.
  Race migrations : Latinos and the cultural transformation of race / Wendy D. Roth.
    pages cm
  Includes bibliographical references and index.
  ISBN 978-0-8047-7795-7 (cloth : alk. paper) — ISBN 978-0-8047-7796-4 (pbk. : alk. paper)
  1. Hispanic Americans—Race identity. 2. Hispanic Americans—Social conditions. 3. Dominican Americans—Race identity. 4. Puerto Ricans—Race identity—United States. 5. Race—Social aspects—United States. 6. United States—Emigration and immigration—Social aspects. 7. Dominican Republic—Emigration and immigration—Social aspects. 8. Puerto Rico—Emigration and immigration—Social aspects. I. Title.
  E184. S75R695 2012
  305.868'073—dc23
                              2011045213

Typeset by Bruce Lundquist in 10/14 Minion

Contents

Illustrations

Photographs discussed in interviews appear after page 22

Acknowledgments

As a native New Yorker, I am always a little surprised when people go out of their way to help me. I never expect to rely on the kindness of strangers, much less to experience significant acts of generosity at their hands. Conducting this research was a transformative experience in that sense. I was deeply touched by the amazing warmth and kindness of the people who helped me in many different ways, from opening their homes and sharing their experiences with me, to making practical suggestions about the fieldwork, to reading drafts of my work. This book could not have been written without those many acts of kindness.

I am particularly grateful for the guidance of Mary Waters. I am awed by her ability to see the big picture and to help me communicate it in my work. With her tremendous skill as a teacher, a presenter, and a researcher, she is a role model for the scholar I hope to be. More than this, she is a role model for the person I hope to be. I am indebted to her for her empathy, her compassion, and for illustrating how to be a superlative academic and a superlative human being at the same time. Peggy Levitt broadened my intellectual perspective and helped me rethink the theoretical foundations of my work. She was incredibly generous with her time, her contacts, and her ideas. Working with her was always a pleasure, and I have grown considerably under her guidance. Prudence Carter offered exactly the kind of direction a young scholar needs. She challenged me to push the envelope, and to develop my own voice. Her comments always helped me see the path more clearly and left me energized to improve my work. Kathy Newman amazes everyone with her motivation and unsurpassable mentorship. I consider myself especially fortunate to have benefited from that mentorship on so many projects. I have learned from her to be a better writer and a more ambitious scholar. I am also extremely grateful to those who read complete drafts of this work and provided invaluable guidance on how to frame and focus the material: Richard Alba, Nancy Foner, Neil Gross, Tomás Jiménez, and Robert C. Smith, as well as the anonymous manuscript reviewers. My writing group—Catherine Lee, Ann Morning, and Alondra Nelson—was a tremendous source of support, sanity, and good advice. Many of their suggestions improved this work immensely.

I owe a strong debt of gratitude to my research assistants: Carla Abreu, Laura Bauzá, Edwin Marrero, Carmen Ortiz, Pedro José Perez Rivera, Angela Ramírez Guzmán, Nelida Iris Rivera, Cecilia Zambrano, and Amalia Zarranz. Their commitment, dedication, and patience in hunting down respondents and traveling to any corner of the city at a moment's notice were truly exceptional. I am especially grateful to those who were my cultural tour guides as well as my assistants. I also want to thank the people who transcribed and translated the interviews: Michael Chiappa, Adrian Gómez, Mayobane Gómez, Sandy Jiménez, Robert Julian, Andrea Lawson, David Lebron, Marisela Morales, Stephanie Nieto, Kathy Paez, Enrique Prieto, and Lee Soto. I appreciate all your comments and reflections on the interviews, as well as your skill in your work. Thanks also to Alana Busby, Will Goldbloom, Xela Korda, and Miguel Angel Ruz Pérez for their research assistance.

While in the Caribbean, I was fortunate to be a visiting scholar at two wonderful research institutes. I still feel a part of the family at the Instituto de Estudios del Caribe at the University of Puerto Rico in Rio Piedras. For this, I am exceptionally grateful to Pedro Rivera-Guzmán and to Ana Fabián, Delia Figueroa, Humberto García, Jorge Giovannetti, Vivian Iglesias, Juan Luís Martínez, Felix Ojeda, Minerva Pérez, Mildred Santiago, and Ovideo Torres. A number of other scholars offered me advice and guidance during my time in Puerto Rico as well. I am particularly grateful to Jorge Duany for his suggestions, support, and ideas. I also want to thank Ineke Cunningham, Isar Godreau, David Hernández, and Milagros Iturrondo. In Santo Domingo, I was fortunate to be welcomed at the Facultad Latinoamericana de Ciencias Sociales (FLACSO), where I received tremendous assistance from Eddy Tejeda and from Tracy Beck-Fenwick, Pilar Corporán, Duleidys Rodriguez Castro, Adrivel Ruiz, and Rubén Silié. I would also like to thank Agueda Bonilla, Thelma Camerena, Wilson Castillo, Dagoberto Ortiz Tejeda, Johanna Vidal, and Karin Weyland for their help and advice. I am also grateful to Brandy Case-Haub and the students at FLACSO for listening to my ideas and sharing their experiences with me.

In New York, I received invaluable assistance from Jennifer Holdaway, Philip Kasinitz, and John Mollenkopf at CUNY Graduate Center. Also from CUNY, I would like to thank Diana Hernández, Joseph Pereira, Belkis Suazo-Garcia, and Rafael Torruella. Several other scholars took the time to talk with me and gave me useful advice and contacts. I am particularly grateful to Anthony de Jesús, Ramona Hernández, Solangel Maldonado, Nicole Marwell, and Sheridan Wigginton. I would also like to thank Wendy Morales for sharing her experience and insights.

Many other people helped me to locate respondents by referring me to potential candidates or spreading the word about my research as far as their networks would carry it. For this, I send my deepest thanks to Sacha Delgado at Instituto Internacional Euskalduna; Eduardo V. Genao of the Dominican Administrators of Schools; Jim McGowan at Centro de Lenguas y Cultura; José A. Santos at the Association of Dominican Engineers; Joe Semidei of the Committee for Hispanic Families and Children; the Professional Engineers Association of Puerto Rico; and all the members of the Dominican-American Professional Alliance, especially Winston Hernández and Felix Sención; Hector Bird-Lopez; Daisy Braverman; Victor Chen; Judy Gallo; Amy Kover; Ali Marin; Jo Ann and Bill Rosen; Miriam Shelef; and Tommy Taveras and Karen Wallman. I also want to thank the Dominican contingent at 270 Riverside Drive for giving me my earliest and most enduring taste of *la dominicanidad*: Leandro Cruz, Claudio Hernández, Carlos Jiménez, Rodolfo Ovalles, and Tony Rivera.

My education in Puerto Rico and the Dominican Republic would not have been complete without the kindness of those who welcomed me and showed me different corners of their societies. I am thankful to Margarita Baguero de Reid, Omar Bautista González, Jacqueline Bello, Alejandra Bird, Rosa Hernández, Ana Teresa and Ani Martínez and their family, Blanca and Braulio Rodríguez, Lili Rodríguez, Sandy Rodríguez and Axel Berrios, Ida Salusky, Lincoln Sampong, Emily Schlotka and Beato Coronado, David Kearns Smith, Veronica Toro-Ruiz, Miguel Urdaneta, Sylvaria Vazquez and Edna, Arbuste Victor, and many others. I want to extend my deepest appreciation to Doña Milagros Polanco de Cabrera and Mariluz for providing me with a home away from home.

I was very fortunate to receive outstanding support from the wonderful faculty, students, and staff at Harvard University. I want to thank Larry Bobo, David Gibson, Jennifer Hochschild, Sandy Jencks, Michèle Lamont, Stanley Lieberson, Vivian Louie, Orlando Patterson, and Carola Suarez-Orozco for their guidance and suggestions. Susan Eckstein of Boston University showed me the forest of my arguments when I was lost in the trees. Many graduate students also provided invaluable feedback, including Patricia Banks, Melissa Barnett, Irene Bloemraad, Barry Cohen, Felix Elwert, Helen Marrow, Monica McDermott, María Rendón, Miguel Salazar, Kyoko Sato, Van Tran, and Natasha Warikoo. Pamela Metz, Cheri Minton, and Lauren Dye were also unfaltering sources of support. Cynthia Verba reviewed numerous drafts of my proposals over the years, and her advice has improved my writing as well as helped me to finance it.

The Department of Sociology at the University of British Columbia has given me more support in working on this manuscript than I could ever have anticipated. Jennifer Chun, Amy Hanser, David Tindall, and Rima Wilkes gave me helpful comments on pieces of this work, and I have benefited from the discussions and seminar comments of the entire department faculty. I'm particularly indebted to Neil Guppy for proactively looking for ways to facilitate my writing and improve my scholarship.

This research was made possible by grants from several institutions, including the National Science Foundation (#SES-0221042 and #98070661), the Weatherhead Center for International Affairs, the David Rockefeller Center for Latin American Studies, Harvard University, and the University of British Columbia. I am very grateful for their generous financial support.

I am also extremely grateful for the excellent support I received from Stanford University Press, particularly from my wonderful editor, Kate Wahl. Many thanks also to assistant editor Joa Suorez, production editor Carolyn Brown, and copy editor Jan McInroy. Their assistance and dedication has made this an ideal publishing experience in practically every way.

Perhaps most important, this work would not have been possible without the people who volunteered to be interviewed for this project. Their generosity with their time and their willingness to open up to a stranger were truly remarkable. Their views have certainly influenced my own, and I hope I have done justice to them here.

Finally, no one could have offered me more personal support and understanding than my parents, Marcia and Stan Roth, and my husband, Ian Tietjen. Not only did my parents make the ultimate sacrifice in allowing me to live with them for nine months of my fieldwork, but they have supported my every step with unquestioning love and belief in my ability. Ian provided the calm, the sanity, and the perspective to help me get through this immense challenge. He has been with me every moment, has read countless drafts and listened to endless talks, and has been the energy source behind all my powers. Ian and my parents have sustained me in the best of times and the worst of times, and I dedicate this work to them.

1 How Immigration Changes Concepts of Race

SITTING ON THE FRONT STEPS OF HIS STUCCO HOUSE IN SANTO DOMINGO, Agustín is sur-rounded by the bustle of activity.[1] His house serves as an informal gathering place for neighbors, his teenage children, and volunteers for the various po-litical activities he organizes. The group huddled around him today, awaiting direction for the latest campaign event, looks like a cross-section of the Do-minican population: there are people with light skin, dark skin, African fea-tures, European features, and almost every mixture in between. Later, Agustín confidently describes the racial categories that exist in the Dominican Republic:

> Here there's a mix of *negro* and *blanco*—that's the majority, the ones that are
> *mulato*. There are some that are a minority, which is a minority that almost
> doesn't exist, which are the *sambos*.... The ones they call *sambos* are Indian
> and *negro*.... You can find some in some regions of Yamasa, around there,
> and Sabana Grande de Boya, some individuals that have Indigenous and *negro*
> characteristics.

He concludes that there are primarily three races in the Dominican Republic today: *mulatos*, *blancos*, and *negros*. In the past, there used to be *mestizos*, those who are a mixture of White[2] and Indigenous, as well as *sambos*, but these races barely exist now because the Indigenous race was wiped out by European colo-nizers. The vast majority of Dominicans today—more than 80 percent of the population, he estimates—are *mulatos*.

A 53-year-old man with dark skin and African features, Agustín places him-self within that *mulato* majority. He explains, "I understand that I'm a mix of *blanco* and *negro*, of Spanish and African origin.... [I'm] *mulato*, ... not totally

1

negro but instead a mix." For him, the term *mulato* represents any mixture of White and Black heritage, and so it incorporates people with a wide variety of appearances. In fact, without hesitating, Agustín classifies the people around him as *blanco*, *negro*, and *mulato*. But almost everyone, whether light or dark, he labels as *mulato*. "Dominicans are a mix of races," he claims, and anyone who has any visible evidence of racial mixture can be considered the same race.

. . .

Raquel was born in the Dominican Republic and moved to New York when she was a young adolescent. Now in her mid-30s, she is an assistant principal in the Dominican enclave of Washington Heights. Amid the cinder-block walls and fluorescent lighting of her small high school office, Raquel's decorations—a screen saver of a tropical beach with clear blue water and palm trees, and paintings of the flowering red *flamboyan* trees common in the Dominican Republic—allow her to dream of escaping from her urban routine. Raquel has pale, light skin, straight black hair, and looks mostly European. At first glance, many people in New York would probably see her as White. Yet Raquel identifies her race as Black. She explains how she came to understand what race means and how to classify herself and others:

> There was a confusion, at least for [me] . . . about what race is, what ethnicity is, what nationality is. So, for me, it was an experience like an epiphany one day when I found out that there are only three races . . . and you have to decide which you belong to. So not only by the color of the skin, but there are a lot of other factors. . . . There would be your ancestry—you need to look at your grandparents, your great-grandparents. You need to look at the shape of your mouth, the size of your ears, how your nose is, the texture of your hair. There are a lot of other things: the color of your eyes, the color of your hair, all those things. But in the Dominican Republic, as soon as you're a little light or medium light, already, you can't say that you're Black. No, that's like a sin. So, after you educate yourself and after you accept that there are either three or, if you want to be more specific and talk about the Indigenous people . . . then there would be four [races], but you need to choose one of these three or four. You can't invent a new one. So I don't have any other option than choosing Black because I'm not White or Asian. So I must be whatever is left.

> *Q: Could you say a little about your epiphany? How did that happen? . . .*

> I was in college . . . taking a sociology class. I was reading in the book and it said that there were three races: Asian, White, and Black. I kept looking for my

race because there wasn't a race for me. And I was talking with my teacher and so, during the conversation, he explained it to me. Sincerely, I tell you, with all the experience that I had, before that day it was one thing and after that day is another.

Before this experience, Raquel might have identified her race as White. But because she feels that the texture of her hair and some of her features reveal some African heritage, she realized that she did not have the option of choosing White. Now she sees others this way too, even people back in the Dominican Republic. Through her experience in college, Raquel now adopts a more historically "American" way of classifying race—that anyone with any Black ancestry should be seen as Black.

. . .

Isandro, a 38-year-old Puerto Rican man with medium-brown skin, works as an income tax auditor in San Juan. He identifies his race—and that of practically everyone around him in Puerto Rico—as Latino:

> To me, I'm Latino. A lot of people say that Latino doesn't exist as a race. In case that one day it's defined or it's excluded [as a race], then I'd be Black. But I understand that I'm Latino because I'm . . . neither White nor Yellow. I'm Latino.
>
> Q: And what is the Latino race? What does it include?
>
> Okay, the Latinos, I think . . . they're not Whites, but they would be something like the mix of maybe White and Black. They tend to usually be shorter in height than the Whites. They tend to have features . . . that are more lengthened, features that are finer than those of Blacks. . . . If someone asks me what I am, I say that I'm Latino . . . because I don't consider myself Black or White, or Chinese, I mean Oriental. And so I understand that the fourth option would be that one.

Isandro has never lived outside of Puerto Rico, but he has so many relatives and friends in the mainland U.S. that he is always aware of what's happening *allá* (over there). His father moved to New Jersey when Isandro was three, shortly after divorcing his mother, and married a Mexican American woman. He now has several half siblings born in New Jersey, as well as a brother who moved there seven years ago and married a woman from Ecuador. Isandro estimates he has between fifty and a hundred relatives in the mainland U.S., and he talks with someone there at least every month. These connections have influenced his view of race. Isandro admits that as a child he used to identify as

Black, but now he hears everywhere about how Latinos are a different group from Blacks and Whites:

> My family has commented that they've noticed the difference. . . . Over there the issue about race is . . . like the extremes, [you're] either too *blanco* or too *negro* or *trigueñito*[3] [a little brown] and Latino. And that's where the Latinos fall. Which is actually another [reason] why I think that maybe we're a race, because we aren't either with the Whites or with the Blacks, but in the middle.

In conversations with his relatives, in news reports and movies—much of it coming from the United States—Isandro frequently hears the word "Latino" used to describe a separate group. As a racial category, "Latino" is not very useful for distinguishing one person from another in Puerto Rico. But Isandro's classifications are not meant to reference only Puerto Rico; they are very much in dialogue with the society at the other end of a migration path.

. . .

How does immigration affect the way people think about race and classify themselves and others? That is the question at the heart of this book. These three cases illustrate many of the central themes I explore to answer that question. First, there are many different ways of classifying race. *Mulato*, Black, and Latino are three different ways that Agustín, Raquel, and Isandro, respectively, think about the same racial mix. Different nations and cultures often have their own ways of dividing the world into racial categories and deciding how to assign people to each one. Second, as the experience of Raquel shows, individuals can change which set of categories or rules for sorting people they use, and while there are many factors that may influence this change, immigration is a significant one. Do immigrants to the United States come to adopt an "Americanized" way of viewing race? Or do they change American notions, like a racial melting pot, to create new concepts out of the immigrant experience? Third, the question of how immigration shapes concepts of race is one that affects many people whose lives are touched by immigration, whether they have moved to a new society or not. Isandro's case shows that even someone who has never immigrated can be influenced to think of race in a new way by the experiences of those who have. How, then, does immigration change concepts of race for the immigrants, for their host society, and for those who stay in the countries they left behind?

For decades, people who study immigration have focused on whether or not immigrants assimilate to the culture of their new society. This type of cultural assimilation—what is known as acculturation—focuses on whether immigrants adopt the language, dress, and traditions of their new country. But beyond basic issues of outward appearance and practices, acculturation is also about immigrants' ways of behaving and interacting every day, their strategies for how to act in different situations. We expect immigrants' behavior to change over time as they become more accustomed to their environs and pick up new ways of understanding social patterns such as gender roles, family dynamics, or workplace interactions. Ultimately, immigrant acculturation is an issue of cultural change, something that should be of interest to scholars of culture.

Race is also an aspect of culture. Just as different societies have different ways of understanding race and different ways of determining what races exist, concepts of race are one aspect of the cultural change that immigrants may experience in a new society. We can think of the example of Raquel above as a case of *racial acculturation*. In the Dominican Republic and other countries of the Hispanic Caribbean, many believe that the category "Black" is reserved for those whose ancestry is only African, with no racial mixture. The United States, by contrast, has long had a history of a "one-drop rule," a principle of hypodescent, which allows African ancestry to trump everything else and lead to a Black designation, regardless of how distant that ancestry may be.[4] Raquel's shift is not just about her own identity; it is also about her way of seeing the world and other people in it. It is a cognitive shift that affects who she feels a connection to and how she behaves toward others. Recently, scholars have called upon researchers to integrate theories of race and culture.[5] In this book, I consider how we can think of race within a cultural framework to better understand how it is transformed by the process of immigration.

These issues are especially relevant because of current debates about how Latin American immigration is changing the United States and the centrality of race in those discussions. The Latino population has grown tremendously in the last few decades, due in large part to immigration. In 1950 less than 3 percent of the U.S. population identified as Hispanic or Latino; in 2010 that percentage had increased to more than 16 percent.[6] The Latino population had a growth rate more than four times that of the U.S. population as a whole in the 1990s.[7] In 2003, headlines trumpeted an important shift in American demographics: Latinos were now the largest U.S. minority group, surpassing Blacks for the first time.[8]

Accompanying these demographic shifts has been a range of policy initiatives, political debates, and public concern over the growing Latino presence in America. In 2004 Harvard political scientist Samuel Huntington described large-scale Latino immigration as a cultural threat to the nation in his book *Who Are We? The Challenges to America's National Identity.* Warning that Latino immigration could "change America into a country of two languages, two cultures, and two peoples,"[9] Huntington saw Latino immigrants as essentially unassimilable because of fundamental differences between their culture and an Anglo-Protestant American identity. In 2006 and 2007, the U.S. Senate voted on amendments to immigration legislation to designate English as the national language.[10] English-only policies are seen to target, and predominantly affect, Spanish-speaking communities.[11] In 2010 Arizona passed a controversial immigration law, SB 1070, allowing police to detain anyone they suspect of being in the country illegally.[12] Should the law survive its court challenges, it will likely require American police officers to judge who "looks illegal," or in other words, who "looks Latino."

These events reflect a perception—and sometimes a fear—that Latino immigration is transforming American society, and some of that fear is racial. In many of these discussions, Latinos are treated as a race, one that can be visually picked out on the street. Latinos are seen as changing the racial character of the nation, a sentiment captured by Richard Rodríguez in his description of "the browning of America."[13] Predictions that within a few decades minority groups will be the majority of the population can produce a sense of racial group threat, a fear that rapidly growing groups like Latinos will challenge the privileges that others have long held.

All of these issues, present every time we pick up a newspaper, involve judgments about race—who is Latino, who is White, and so on. These are the types of judgments we make every day, and they reflect our understanding of racial classifications in the United States. That understanding has been shaped by American history, and it has produced a racial structure that has traditionally been divided into White and Black. Latinos, though, seem to challenge that division. What is central, if often unstated, in these political debates and media coverage, is the question of how Latinos fit into the U.S. racial structure. The Office of Management and Budget (OMB), the department responsible for setting standards of federal data collection, such as the U.S. Census, stipulates that Latino or Hispanic is not a race but rather an aspect of ethnicity. According to this "official" classification system, Latinos may be of any race—meaning the ones the OMB enumerates in federal data: White, Black, Native American, Asian, or Native Hawaiian or Pacific Islander. Yet many Latinos do not see themselves fitting within these official classifications; on the 2010 Census, 37 percent of Latinos identified themselves as "Some other race."[14] Many scholars interpret this response as indicating a Latino or Hispanic racial identity and a rejection of the existing racial categories of the United States.[15] Others note that the majority of Latinos identify themselves as White, and suggest that they should be considered White rather than as members of a racial minority.[16]

Accordingly, scholarly debates over where Latinos will fit into the U.S. racial structure in the future have offered several differing predictions. Some see Latinos forming a new racial group of their own, separate from White and Black and falling hierarchically between the two.[17] Others argue that Latinos are socially closer to Whites—they tend to live near them and to intermarry—and suggest that the definition of Whiteness will expand to include Latinos, just as it did for Irish, Jewish, and other ethnic groups in earlier times.[18] A third prediction holds that a tri-racial stratification system will emerge, with a "pigmentocracy" that ranks groups and individuals based on their skin color. While some assimilated White Latinos will join the privileged White group, most light-skinned Latinos will remain in an "honorary White" middle tier, and those with dark skin will join a collective Black category at the bottom of the racial hierarchy.[19] To get a handle on these possibilities, it is crucial to understand how Latinos see themselves fitting into American racial classifications, and how they are seen by others. And since approximately 40 percent of Latinos are born outside the mainland U.S.,[20] that brings us back to the question of how migration from Latin America affects the way people—both Latinos and non-Latinos—think about and classify race.

In this book, I set out to address these questions, drawing on an in-depth study of Dominicans and Puerto Ricans, both those who migrate to New York and those who stay behind in Santo Domingo and San Juan. Often when people think of large-scale migration from Latin America, they think first of Mexicans and South Americans. But the experiences of people from the Hispanic Caribbean offer a particularly useful window into issues of racial classification and acculturation. The slave trade was especially developed in these former colonies, and widespread racial mixing between European colonizers, African slaves, and the Indigenous Taíno group produced a contemporary population that spans a continuum from White to Indigenous to Black.[21] While there are some Afro-Latino populations in Mexico and South America, especially in certain regions,[22] a less advanced slave trade there has resulted in a population whose range of appearances more commonly spans from White to Indigenous.[23] Many Dominicans and Puerto Ricans have remarked on the experience of arriving in the mainland U.S. and being seen as Black, a less common experience among Mexicans or South Americans. Because Puerto Ricans and

Dominicans fall on both sides of the Black-White divide in the United States, scholars have long asked whether skin color will lead some to be seen as White or Black while those who do not fit clearly into either category become seen as racially Latino.[24] The position of these groups, straddling existing racial categories, gives us particular analytical leverage to consider how appearance, or immigrants' visual "fit" with existing categories, influences how these Latinos are seen and see themselves in the United States.

Puerto Ricans are often excluded from research on immigration, and thus tend to be under-studied.[25] As U.S. citizens by birth, they are usually not considered immigrants. Puerto Rico has been part of the United States since it was annexed as a protectorate in 1898, and in 1952 the island nation was established as a Free Associated State. In English, Puerto Rico is frequently called a Commonwealth, but this nomenclature is misleading. Legally, as well as culturally, Puerto Rico is a separate country, albeit one "associated" with the United States.[26] For this reason, some claim that the label "immigrants" is appropriate,[27] although their affiliation with the United States also makes their resettlement resemble internal migration within a country.[28] On a social and cultural level, however, Puerto Ricans' integration experiences are quite similar to those of Dominicans and other immigrants. Most Puerto Ricans consider their island a distinct nation and distinguish themselves culturally (and racially) from *los americanos*.[29] First-generation Puerto Ricans in the mainland U.S., especially those from lower-class backgrounds, often have limited English abilities. I include Puerto Ricans here because my focus is primarily on social and cultural integration, and I refer to both Puerto Ricans and Dominicans who have moved to the mainland U.S. as "migrants."[30]

Comparing Dominicans and Puerto Ricans

Because Puerto Ricans are overlooked in immigration studies, they also tend to be excluded from comparative research. In some ways their experiences are unique among Latinos; they are the only group that does not need a visa to move to the United States. Yet in other ways, Puerto Ricans and Dominicans make an ideal comparison for a study of changing concepts of race. Their colonial histories, populations, and cultures resemble one another in many ways. Only about 75 miles apart, both societies were populated by the Indigenous Taíno people when colonized by the Spanish conquistadors, at approximately the same time.[31] Although the slave trade was more widespread in the Dominican Republic, leading to a more prominent African influence in the contemporary population there, both colonies experienced widespread miscegenation and a blending of Taíno, European, and African roots. Under Spanish rule, the nations came to share a common language, religion, and customs that blended together the cultures of these three origin groups. In particular, both societies recognize a continuum of racial types, adopt a complex terminology to describe them, and employ these terms in similar ways in their everyday lives.

Puerto Ricans and Dominicans are also the two largest Latino migrant populations on the East Coast of the United States, and migration from both societies has historically been concentrated in the same receiving city: New York.[32] The vast majority of Puerto Rican and Dominican migrants over time have settled in New York City, which has become the primary site of the communities' political and social institutions in the mainland U.S. Even as the communities begin to disperse geographically to other parts of the country, New York remains the largest concentration of each group at the start of the twenty-first century. There are sometimes tensions between these nationalities both in New York and in San Juan, where a large number of Dominicans have also settled. But many also recognize their shared cultural heritage on a broader level.[33] Culturally and socially these societies have much in common.

The two groups are also united by a similar experience of transnational migration. Transnationalism is "the processes by which immigrants forge and sustain multi-stranded social relations that link together their societies of origin and settlement."[34] Puerto Ricans and Dominicans do not simply settle in their host society and immerse themselves in a new way of life. They actively link their home and host societies through a range of involvements and continued participation in the societies they left behind.[35] The geographic proximity of their home countries to New York, the availability of inexpensive transportation, and improved technology and infrastructure all facilitate back-and-forth movement, frequent communication, and continuing involvement in the political, economic, and civic life of those communities.

Migrants' continued involvement changes their sending societies, not merely through the financial remittances they send back but also through new concepts that they communicate to the people who have never left.[36] Part of understanding how immigration affects concepts of race and classification, then, is understanding how transnational activities, ties, and the general globalization that often accompanies such international connections affect those concepts. Just as migrants' lives are increasingly spanning national boundaries, processes of identity formation are also shaped by the cyclical give-and-take as ideas are exchanged. Concepts of race and ethnicity are challenged and re-created in this transnational space, as new ideas about race that migrants adopt or create are communicated back to non-migrants. As migration continues, it creates an on-going cycle, in which new migrants arrive having already incorporated—pre-migration—concepts of race that have been created by the experiences of earlier migrants. Dominicans' and Puerto Ricans' transnational lifestyles thus help to reveal how race and ethnicity can be transformed by migration simultaneously in both sending and receiving societies.

Puerto Ricans and Dominicans also differ in important ways that may shed light on processes of identity formation. Most significantly, they differ in their political status. Puerto Rico's affiliated status creates strong institutional ties with the United States and allows its citizens to move freely between the island and the mainland. The U.S. government and private capital have also played a significant role in the development of the Dominican Republic, but Dominican migration is restricted by immigration laws, and many Dominicans enter the country illegally. Although the privileges of citizenship have not necessarily eased Puerto Ricans' socioeconomic integration, they do permit ease of physical movement in and out of the mainland U.S., which may affect what the immigrants communicate to those who stay in Puerto Rico.

Puerto Ricans' and Dominicans' identifications on national surveys may reveal how they see themselves fitting into American racial structures. In the mainland U.S., Puerto Rican migrants are about equally likely to identify as White or Other race (Table 1). That pattern did not change much, even as they

Table 1. Racial identification of Latinos in the mainland U.S.

	White, alone	Black, alone	Other, alone	White and Black	White and other	Black and other	N	% of all Latinos
1990								
Puerto Rican	45.8	5.9	47.1				2,632,326	12.1
Dominican	28.2	27.3	43.2				516,891	2.4
All Latinos	52.2	2.9	43.2				21,836,851	100.0
2000								
Puerto Rican	47.2	5.9	37.9	0.8	3.9	1.3	3,400,527	9.7
Dominican	22.7	8.9	58.4	1.1	4.0	2.2	796,724	2.3
All Latinos	47.8	1.8	42.6	0.2	4.2	0.5	35,204,480	100.0
2006								
Puerto Rican	45.9	5.3	41.1	1.1	2.5	1.3	3,985,058	9.0
Dominican	24.0	7.3	63.9	1.5	1.4	1.0	1,217,160	2.7
All Latinos	52.3	1.4	41.2	0.3	2.0	0.3	44,298,975	100.0

SOURCES: 1990 Census 5% PUMS; 2000 Census 5% PUMS; 2006 American Community Survey. PUMS data compiled by Steven Ruggles, Matthew Sobek, Trent Alexander, Catherine A. Fitch, Ronald Goeken, Patricia Kelly Hall, Miriam King, and Chad Ronnander, *Integrated Public Use Microdata Series: Version 4.0* [Machine-readable database] (Minneapolis: Minnesota Population Center [producer and distributor], 2008). Available at http://usa .ipums.org/usa/.

were allowed to mark more than one race starting with the 2000 Census. Puerto Ricans' identification patterns roughly resemble those of all Latinos in the mainland U.S., although they are slightly more likely to check "Black" than are Latinos overall. By contrast, Dominicans were much more likely to identify as Black in 1990. Specifically, 27.3% of Dominicans checked "Black" as their race, compared to 5.9% of Puerto Ricans and 2.9% of all Latinos. This is particularly striking because the Dominican Republic has systematically deemphasized its African heritage, in part to distinguish itself from neighboring Haiti. In the country of origin, most Dominicans reject a Black label and government institutions promote the view that Dominicans are a non-Black population.[37] In the 1980 Dominican census, only 11% of the population was classified as *negro*, while 16% was classified as *blanco* and 73% as *indio*—or mixed.[38] On their national identification cards, Dominican government officials classify 90% of the nation as *indio*.[39] Despite rejecting a Black label back home, it would seem that many Dominicans in 1990 felt they should check "Black" in the United States.

Dominicans' racial identifications have also changed dramatically in a relatively short period. The proportion that identified as Black alone decreased from 27.3% in 1990 to 8.9% in 2000 and 7.3% in 2006. Meanwhile, the proportion that identified as Other alone increased from 43.2% in 1990 to 58.4% in 2000 and then 63.9% in 2006. Some of this pattern undoubtedly reflects changes in the order and wording of the questions. But it is unlikely that this shift is entirely a matter of questionnaire effects, because no similar change occurred across Latino groups. The context in which such a change occurred, and what factors contributed to it, is part of what this comparison will explore.

Compared to Dominican migrants, Puerto Rican migrants are much more likely to identify themselves as White. But compared to those back in Puerto Rico, Puerto Rican migrants are much more likely to choose "Other" as their identification. In 2000, the first time a race question was asked on the island of Puerto Rico in 50 years, 80.5% of those in Puerto Rico identified as White, while 8.0% identified as Black and only 6.8% identified as Other.[40] These simple survey questions cannot capture the full range of complexity in how people understand race or even their own racial identity. But they do suggest that, as a general pattern, migrants' experiences in the United States lead each nationality toward checking the "Other" box, albeit to different extents. By exploring their experiences at home and abroad, this research can help us understand why. The similarities as well as the differences between these groups make for a particularly revealing comparison of how widespread movement to a new society can shape not just individual identities but also a cognitive mapping of race.

Racial Schemas

In the past, race was seen as a given—something objectively defined and obvious. As concepts of race have moved away from seeing it as a biological reality and toward viewing it as a way of dividing up and stratifying individuals, it becomes more important to focus on the process of racial categorization and classification. I define race as a cognitive structure that divides people into hierarchically ordered categories on the basis of certain physical or biological characteristics, commonly revealed in appearance, that are believed to be inherent. Although biological characteristics are referred to in delimiting a racial group, deciding which characteristics define the race—whether skin color, eye color, height, or any number of other features—is a social rather than a biological construction.[41] It is also something that societies, each operating with different cognitive structures, may do differently.

As scholars have moved toward viewing race as socially constructed, there has been increased recognition of the cognitive processes—including perception, memory, and judgment—that go into determining a person's race or ethnicity.[42] Around the same time, sociologists have focused attention on cognitive approaches to the study of culture. Paul DiMaggio has written that "individuals experience culture as disparate bits of information and as schematic structures that organize that information."[43] In this book, I try to provide the third link in this triangle: that race and ethnicity are aspects of culture.[44] We can view race as a cognitive process that is part of a shared culture in a society.[45]

Schemas are among the central concepts in cognitive science. These are mental structures that represent knowledge and process information. Schemas are not just groups of categories, but a complex of information about the relationships among them. They involve rankings of the categories, leading some to be treated as subordinate to others. They also guide perception and recall when faced with a new experience that must be interpreted. Like a set of mental rules that help people recognize and process new people, events, or stimuli, schemas treat such information as new instances of an already familiar category.[46]

I focus throughout this book on the concept of *racial schemas*—the bundle of racial categories and the set of rules for what they mean, how they are ordered, and how to apply them to oneself and others. The categories within racial schemas are relational—they inhere in their relationship to one another, in who is defined as inside or outside the group and what that means for how those people are treated within a society.[47] Racial schemas are necessarily cognitive phenomena, because they are mental processes that shape our knowledge. But they are also cultural. There are different concepts of what racial categories exist and how they are ordered in the United States, Latin America, and other regions around the world. There are also differences within nations and communities in the racial schemas that people use. Their racial schemas may not match official classification systems in each nation, since people often develop their own taxonomies for everyday use or bend the meanings of official categories in unofficial directions.[48] Understanding the variations in racial schemas, how migrants and others affected by migration acquire new schemas or cease to use old ones, and what circumstances or situational cues invoke different schematic understandings are among the central concerns of this study.

Most sociological research on race and immigration focuses on racial identity—for instance, how immigrants identify their own race and whether this changes over time. Recently, prominent sociologists have called for a move away from a narrow focus on identities.[49] The term "identity" is used so broadly that its meaning is often ambiguous and it loses a sense of who is doing the identifying. It also tends to be treated in scholarly work as an end in itself, rather than a process that leads to sociologically relevant outcomes. Racial identity is an important aspect of racial categorizations, and it can be helpful in revealing the nature of the schemas that people use. But it says less about people's understanding of what races are and which ones exist, which is central to understanding race as an aspect of culture.

Racial schemas, like all cognitive schemas, do not exist just within people's heads. They are shared representations that are partly independent of individuals' beliefs;[50] this is why there is overlap between those held by different people. In part, they are publicly shared because of the way that schemas and classifications are institutionalized. Institutions like the state, schools, workplaces, families, social movements, and bureaucracies of various kinds play a role in creating and conveying racial schemas.[51] Studying how racial schemas are used helps us connect what happens at the individual level to what happens at the macro level, or how individuals share and are influenced by a common culture of race.[52]

An important advantage that comes from thinking of race in terms of cognitive schemas is the recognition that people can hold multiple racial schemas at any given time. People acquire new schemas throughout their lives, some of which are inconsistent. But some schemas are more salient and available than others, which leads individuals to activate them more easily and frequently.[53] We typically have more racial schemas than we use at any given time. The multiple racial schemas that people know about and can access are stored within a cognitive *racial schema portfolio*. Like an artist's portfolio, this is where people mentally store the different racial schemas within their repertoire, selecting and activating different ones in different contexts, when cued by triggers in particular situations.

A racial schema may seem to some like a core concept—something people would use consistently—especially in the United States, where race so fundamentally structures many aspects of life. And for those who have little interaction with other cultures, that may be the case. But immigration is a social process that adds new racial schemas to societies' cultural repertoires. As immigrants interact with others in their host society, they typically learn new racial schemas that predominate there.[54]

Viewing race as an aspect of culture to which immigrants may assimilate reframes our understanding of racial acculturation. From this perspective, what racial acculturation really means is not that immigrants entirely drop an old racial schema associated with their country of origin and replace it exclusively with a new one representing their new country. Rather, it is a change in the frequency and facility with which they use a set of new racial schemas as opposed to others. Old schemas are rarely lost; they may still be used in some situations. But immigrants who are most acculturated use the schemas associated with their new society most often and in most contexts, while their old schemas atrophy and fade into the far recesses of their minds from disuse. Acculturation in general resembles a cognitive rewiring, leading people to choose new concepts and strategies more easily and more often.

Immigrants can also reinterpret new schemas, blending them with old concepts, or infusing them with new meaning. How they use racial schemas, and the variants they create, may also influence the native-born around them. The very presence of large populations of newcomers may lead the native-born to reconceptualize some of their existing schemas to account for and position those new groups within a shifting racial hierarchy. This "melting pot" scenario views immigrants and the host society as changing one another, adding new racial schemas to the society's cultural repertoire. When enough people follow suit, this process creates macro-level changes in racial repertoires, and native-born Americans, like the immigrants, have access to additional schemas as well.

A more challenging issue is how and why *non*-migrants' use of racial schemas changes. These, after all, are people who do not move to a new society, who do not interact with a new culture on a daily basis. To the extent that non-migrants in the sending societies also access new racial schemas, it is because transnational migration practices, and the globalization processes that typically accompany large-scale mass migration, produce a cultural diffusion of racial schemas. Culture, including concepts of race, is diffused in large part through social networks, the mass media, and institutions.[55] The diffusion of racial schemas does not mean that non-migrants necessarily enact those concepts. It simply adds a new understanding and categorization of race to their portfolios, which they can select and activate for different purposes.

Many studies assume that culture is organized around nations or subgroups within those nations, and is enacted in similar ways across different types of situations.[56] In fact, as I hope to show, it is not. At the macro level, at any given moment, there are multiple racial schemas within a society. There are existing schemas, new schemas brought in by immigrants, amalgams as immigrants change existing schemas, and so on, all of which make up the society's racial repertoire. There are also official classification systems and the bundle of knowledge, rules, and hierarchies that they invoke. And there are more unofficial schemas as many people simultaneously, through their everyday usage, challenge and reinvent those official systems. Within each society these various schemas are distributed across individuals, who may be more or less likely to evoke a given schema on a somewhat regular basis because of the different situations they tend to find themselves in.[57] The processes of immigration, transnationalism, and globalization that I detail in this book change which racial schemas individuals use more frequently than others. And as migrants, their host society, and non-migrants more or less simultaneously begin to use these new forms of race more and more often, a macro-level cultural change occurs in both sending and receiving societies.

Measuring Racial Schemas

Assessing how immigrants and others conceptualize race is a methodological challenge. One approach is to look at how Latinos self-identify their race on the census or other surveys to determine if they are adopting an American concept of race—i.e., by checking "White" or "Black"—or are rejecting American notions of race by checking "Other." The problem, though, is that some people in Latin America do think of themselves as *blanco* or *negro*, although not necessarily the same people Americans would see as White or Black. Are the Latinos who check "White" on the U.S. Census adopting an Americanized understanding of race or a Latin American one? We cannot tell from their self-identifications alone.

To shift the focus away from self-identification and toward racial schemas, I use photo elicitation. I developed a set of photographs representing the range of racial appearances that is typically found in the Hispanic Caribbean (see images following page 22). I asked respondents to identify the race of the person in each photograph in open-ended terms—whatever terms they would normally use. I gave no other instructions about the kind of categories they should use; instead, I allowed the photographs to evoke a set of categories that respondents employ in their daily lives.[58] To move beyond the categories and toward the relations between them, I used respondents' classifications of the photographs to initiate an in-depth discussion of how they decide what labels to apply, what those categories mean, how they relate to one another, what implications they have for daily life, and how the respondents understand race more generally. Such topics are often awkward and difficult to evoke in an interview setting, yet the exercise of identifying the photographs opened the door to discussing the respondents' thought processes.

Because the photographs depict real people, they allow respondents to think about how they would classify individuals they might actually see during the course of their day and to choose for themselves what to focus on in attributing race.[59] Also, unlike open-ended racial self-identification questions, the photographs let all subjects classify the same objects—rather than having each person identify a different object (herself)—and thus permit comparison across different samples and sub-samples.

Of course, respondents' classifications of the photographs reveal only one racial schema. It may not be the schema that each person uses most often across different settings, but the interview provides a standard context to compare the schemas that different respondents use in this one setting. I also asked respondents to classify the race of the friends they listed in their social network, again with no guidance as to the racial categories they should use. This exercise again allowed them to apply their own labels, but with more context for who these people are and how they have thought of them in the past.

To examine respondents' knowledge of and use of additional racial schemas, I asked more directed questions during the interviews about their understanding of different racial terminology, and how race is understood in the U.S. and their society of origin. For example, the scholarly consensus maintains that race in Puerto Rico and the Dominican Republic is understood as a continuum, with a wide range of terms like *trigueño, indio,* and *moreno* describing different racial types. Late in the interview, I asked respondents to recall all the terms like this that are used in their home society, and then I showed them a list of these terms (see table on page 19) and asked them to define those that are used there. If they had not already used these terms to identify the photographs, I asked them to go through the photographs a second time, using terms from the list or other similar terms used in their country to classify the people in the photographs. I also asked respondents how they would identify themselves using such terms, and several follow-up questions about what these categories mean, when they are used, and how they relate to one another. Combining opportunities for open-ended and closed-ended classifications provides a rich exploration of the range of schemas that respondents maintain within their racial schema portfolios; it captures not just the schemas they use, but also the bits of cultural knowledge that they have internalized but may not use.[60]

Mapping the Racial Schema Portfolio

If people operate with a number of different cognitive schemas of race, then what are the different racial schemas used by the Dominicans and Puerto Ricans in this book, both those who migrate and those who do not? Much of the literature on the Hispanic Caribbean and Latin America depicts a particular understanding of race: what I call the continuum model, which views race as a fluid continuum of racial mixtures between Black and White. However, many people in these countries also use a schema based on a racialized concept of nationality or regional origins, and some are also influenced by the common concepts of race used in the United States. I identify three general types of schemas based on these cultural models of race[61]—what I call the *continuum racial schema*, the *nationality racial schema*, and the *U.S. racial schema*—as well as some of the variants within them (Table 2). These schemas, applying to the range of phenotypes between Black and White,[62] dominate the range of ways that both Dominican and Puerto Rican migrants and those who remain in their countries of origin talk about race.

Although people in a given society may use one schema more often than others—creating the idea of an American or a Latin American concept of race

Table 2. Variants of racial schemas

Continuum racial schema	Includes intermediate racial terms between Black and White, such as those in Table 3 (e.g., *trigueño, indio, mulato*)
Nationality racial schemas	
Basic nationality schema	Includes only nationalities and ethnic groups (e.g., Puerto Rican, Dominican, Italian, American)
Panethnic nationality schema	Includes nationalities and ethnic groups, as well as the panethnic terms Latino or Hispanic
U.S. racial schemas	
Binary U.S. schema	Includes only the categories White and Black, with any racial mixture classified as Black
Hispanicized U.S. schema	Includes the categories White, Black, and Latino/Hispanic

as part of that society's culture—even within that society people differ in the schema they use in a given context, and may switch between schemas in a single conversation. Rosaria provides an example of how this occurs. A middle-aged Puerto Rican woman with dark skin and a fourth-grade education, she lives in public housing in a barrio on the outskirts of San Juan and does temporary clerical work at the local school. While we talk at the table of her small apartment, she seems to switch between different sets of categories when talking about race. She describes her own race and those of her daughters as "*negra*" and insists, "for me there are only two races . . . *blanco* and *negro*. Well, I am *negra* [laughs]. They tell me, 'no you are brown*cita* or *trigueña*,' but the *trigueño* is a *negro* race." Asked to describe the race of various friends and acquaintances in her social network, she identifies them all as *blanco* or *negro*. But when I ask her to classify the race of the people in the set of photographs, she switches to different categories and identifies them by their nationality. She classifies each one as Mexican, Dominican, Puerto Rican, or Cuban, referring to their facial features and the "look" of each person. Later on, I ask her to view the photos again, but this time I say, "If I told you that all these people are Puerto Ricans and if you saw them here on the street, how would you describe their race?" Rosaria switched her classifications again, this time identifying the same individuals as *trigueñito, clarito, prieto, jincho, blanquito,* and *jabao.*

An initial reaction might be that Rosaria is confused or does not understand what race means. It seems inconsistent to say that the only races are White and Black, but to later use a variety of other categories. Yet subsequent discussions with Rosaria reveal that she understands all these labels in racial terms. They are simply different types of schemas that she uses in different ways. The context of the interview, including my presence as an American, and the different ways that she is prompted to think about race throughout our conversation, are the stimuli that trigger which racial schema she evokes. Although these stimuli influence her answers, no one schema that she uses is more "right" than another, tapping into what she "really" thinks about race. The context and the way questions are asked affect the answers, but for Rosaria and others, these contexts trigger different schemas of race, all of which are used in different ways in their daily lives.

Racial Continuum

Scholars describe race in much of Latin America, including Puerto Rico and the Dominican Republic, as a continuum from Black to White.[63] Harry Hoetink characterized this model of race in the Hispanic Caribbean as "an interweaving of European, African, and Amerindian strands. These multiple influences were reflected in a local conceptualization in which physical traits ranged from 'dark' to 'light,' different 'types' of which could well manifest themselves within a single family. 'Pure' types gave way to a racial continuum."[64] The continuum model includes a wide variety of labels, assigned to the numerous points along the racial continuum. In an ethnographic study of a San Juan neighborhood, anthropologist Jorge Duany identified at least nineteen different racial categories commonly used in Puerto Rico (Table 3).[65] Many of these same terms are used in the Dominican Republic, although there are regional differences.[66]

In the United States, while people typically focus their daily classifications on indicators like appearance, dress, or accent, the historical basis underlying racial distinctions is knowledge of a person's racial ancestry, for which appearance serves as a proxy. For instance, a person who looked White but whose parents or grandparents were Black would traditionally have been considered Black.[67] In the continuum model, however, the basis for racial distinctions is not ancestry but phenotype and social factors. A child of a Black and White

Table 3. Racial terms used in Puerto Rico and the Dominican Republic

Term	Approximate meaning
Negro(a)	Black
Azulito(a)	Blue-Black; very dark with African features; used primarily in Dominican Republic
Prieto(a)	Dark skinned; usually derogatory
Grifo(a)	Dark-skinned with kinky hair; usually derogatory
Moreno(a)	Dark-skinned; usually dark mulatto
De color(a)	Euphemism for Black; usually meaning Black
Cenizo(a)	Literally, ashy; skin that looks gray or faded, traditionally from deposits due to bathing in river; used primarily in Dominican Republic
Mulato(a)	Mixed-race, frequently the mixture of Black and White
Trigueño(a)	Literally, wheat-colored or brunette; usually light mulatto; most common in Puerto Rico
Mestizo(a)	Mixed-race; traditionally the mix of White and Indian but also used as the mix of any two races
Indio(a)	Literally, Indian; brown-skinned with straight hair; widely used in the Dominican Republic
Piel canela	Literally, cinnamon skin; tan or brown-skinned
Café con leche	Literally, coffee with milk; tan or brown-skinned
Blanco(a) con raja	Literally, white with a crack; white with some visible black features; used primarily in Puerto Rico
Jabao(a)	Fair-skinned with curly or kinky hair
Colorao(a)	Redheaded, reddish skin
Rosadito(a)	White, with rosy cheeks or skin tone
Rubio(a)	Blond
Cano(a)	Blond or gray hair, fair-skinned
Jincho(a)	Pale-skinned, lacking color; may imply illness or unattractiveness
Blanquito(a)	Literally, little white; figuratively, elitist, upper-class
Blanco(a)	White

Adapted from Jorge Duany, *The Puerto Rican Nation on the Move: Identities on the Island and in the United States* (Chapel Hill: University of North Carolina Press, 2002). Used by permission of the publisher.

interracial couple who appears White would probably still be classified as Black in much of the United States, whereas in Latin America, scholars describing the continuum model claim, the child would be considered White.[68] Phenotype considerations include not just skin color but also hair texture and color, eye color, and facial features. The classification of full siblings reveals the distinction between the U.S. model based on racial ancestry and the continuum model based on phenotype: in the United States, siblings have the same racial classification, reflecting their parents' races; in Latin America, full siblings often have different races.

Social considerations also influence racial classifications in the continuum model. Greater socioeconomic status, prestige, or social networks can lead to a lighter classification, giving rise to the common expression that "money whitens." In his study of prominent Puerto Rican families in the 1950s, Raymond Scheele asserted that "[a]nyone who is accepted into the upper class is considered non-Negro, despite his physical appearance."[69] Some claim that a Black person in Puerto Rico can become White by achieving the friendship of Whites.[70] Rather than racial roles being ascribed at birth, in the continuum model they can be achieved, or changed by accomplishments later in life.

These racial terms are relational, based on interactions and implicit comparisons. Someone who is dark or has African features may refer to a man of medium skin tone as *blanco*. But that same man might be described as *trigueño* by someone of light color who has European features. In both Puerto Rico and the Dominican Republic, it is common for a child to be nicknamed *la blanquita* or *el negrito*, not because she or he is objectively White or Black but because she or he is the lightest or darkest in the family. Similarly, the same person may identify a woman as *trigueña* at one moment and as *morena* at the next, even in a single conversation, based on the context or the implicit comparison.[71]

Specific racial terms can also have different meanings when used in different ways. The same racial label can be used as a term of endearment, an insult, or a sexualized come-on. Racial terms may serve as euphemisms, to avoid negative associations; the terms *indio* and *trigueño*, for example, are often used to avoid describing someone as *negro*. A darker person might be called *trigueño* out of deference, but in an argument or brawl he might have the epithet "Dirty *negro!*" hurled at him. Terms are often selected, perhaps even subconsciously, according to the meaning a person wishes to convey. Much like the semantic distinction between using the informal *tú* or the formal *usted*, racial continuum terms can be used to treat people with respect or disrespect, to create solidarity, to include or exclude.[72]

The continuum model implies a hierarchical structure for the various categories. People toward the lighter end of the continuum enjoy the greatest status and rewards and those at the darker end, the least. A normative value system is apparent in the racial terminology, with lighter and more European traits considered more desirable. European hair is considered "good hair," while African hair is "bad"; a European nose or mouth is described as "fine," while African features are "ordinary." Young men and women are routinely pushed by their families to "improve the race" by marrying someone lighter.

Those who use a continuum racial schema assign racial categories to individuals on the basis of this concept of race. In identifying the race of the people in the photographs, they apply some intermediate categories between Black and White, based on an assessment of various aspects of appearance. Inés, a non-migrant who hails from a prominent family in Santo Domingo and has some college education, does exactly this:

Q: [Now] I have an experiment. One of the segments of this study is how people classify the race of others. There is no right or wrong or answer. It's more to learn how people make the classification and what are the categories used. I have a group of photos of different people; could you please tell me how you would classify the race of each person? Please say the number of each photo first, and then the race.

(1) . . . The race, more or less finer, the race is less *negro* . . . it's a mix. He's not *blanco. Mulato,* [or] more *blanco* than *mulato.* (2) *Mulato.* (3) *Negra.* (4) More or less *blanco.* (5) She's not *blanca. Trigueña.* (6) *Negro.* (7) *Indio,* what we call *indio.* (8) *Blanco.* (9) *Negra.* (10) A mix. She's not *blanca,* she's like *india,* these people that are neither *blanca* nor *negra.* Her nose is very ordinary. She has blue eyes, but she's not *blanca,* she's not fine. (11) This one is more *blanca* than fine, than the one with the light eyes (10) . . . You know why? Because of the features, right?

Q: Which features? . . .

[She's] *Trigueña,* more or less. . . . She has curly hair, she has "good" hair, right? . . . *Trigueña.* (12) She's not *blanca.* This one is *negra.* (13) *India, india . . .* (14) This one is very pretty but she has "bad" hair . . . *Negra.* (15) *Negro.* (16) Not *blanca.* Like *mestiza* or *trigueña.* (17) Neither. . . . Not *blanca,* she is . . . what do you call that, because she's neither *blanca* nor *negra,* she's *clara* [light], she has "good" hair, a wide nose, she has Black race hanging from the back.[73] *Trigueña.* (18) *Moreno.* (19) *Blanca,* but she has mixed race. (20) *Negro.*

Q: And 19, would you say that she is blanca?

I don't see her as *blanca* because of the hair. [Pause, reconsidering] She's *blanca*, yes.

Q: And when you decide what you say for each person, for each photo, what do you base it on?

For the race? If she's fine, if she's light. Well, I understand that it could be because of the features, the color, the hair. But it really needs to have everything to be *blanco*, because if there is a *blanco* with the large ugly nose, he can't be *blanco*. . . . Not purely *blanco*, there's a mix, maybe between *negro* and *blanco*.

Q: And if a person has dark skin but his features are fine [European], is this person negro?

He's not *negro*, but he does have *negro* race [in him]. (Dominican non-migrant, beauty salon owner)

There are several things to take away from Inés's identification of the photos. First, the facility with which she can talk through the process of determining and classifying other people's races is striking. The ease with which respondents could all decide who was what race shows just how commonplace this activity is in their lives, even if they are unaware of it. Second, the example illustrates how classifying the photographs reveals the type of racial schema the person is applying. In this case, Inés adopts a set of categories and a conception of race that correspond to the continuum model. She also reveals the particular aspects of appearance that she's drawing upon for her classifications—eye color, nose, hair type, as well as skin color. All of these features are considered to determine how much Black or White is in people. Third, Inés reveals her definitions for who is White and who is Black. To be White, a person must have little to no Black or African influence. She also reserves the category Black for those with little or no mixture, a one-drop rule in reverse. By selecting as Black those whose features reveal little mixture, she distinguishes between someone who "is Black" and someone who "has Black" in their ancestry. Finally, her discussion demonstrates how she relates these categories to one another. Whiteness and the categories that are closer to White are ranked higher within a racial hierarchy. The language she uses to describe characteristics—African features as "ordinary" or "bad" and European features as "fine" and "good"—highlights the implicit ordering of these racial categories along the continuum.

Photographs discussed in interviews

(1)

(2)

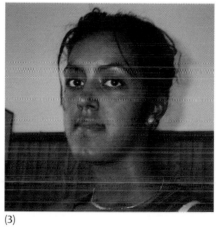
(3)

(4)

(5)

(6)

(7)

(8)

(9)

(10)

(11)

(12)

(13)

(14)

(15)

(16)

(17)

(18)

(19)

(20)

The number of categories, and which ones are used when, vary among respondents using a continuum racial schema. While Inés used a range of terms such as *mulato, negro, blanco, trigueño, indio,* and *moreno,* Gisela, another woman in Santo Domingo, also used a continuum race schema, but with a more limited range of categories: just *blanco, mulato,* and *negro.* Regardless of which terms are used, what unifies this conception of race is the idea of a continuum that includes one or more mixed-race categories.

Race as Nationality

Although from the scholarly literature we might expect the continuum model to be the predominant way people conceptualize race in the Hispanic Caribbean, another model was much more prevalent in my interviews—one that associated race with nationality.[74] I call this way of classifying race a nationality racial schema. Gregorio, a taxi driver in Santo Domingo who left school in the tenth grade, reveals this type of racial schema as he classifies the photographs:

(1) Well I think he can be Dominican. (2) I would consider him like Puerto Rican. (3) looks Dominican. I think. (4) I also see him like, physically like the Dominican, I don't know. (5) She also seems to me, I see the physical [appearance] like from our country, Dominican. (6) Looks like, I don't see him like a Dominican, but, by the color more or less, I figure him to be from Haiti, the race you see, by the physical appearance. . . . Yes, Haitian . . . (7) Looks like Colombian, the physical appearance seems to me like a Colombian. (8) I believe, he's American. (9) Looks Mexican. (10) Looks Venezuelan. (11) Looks Mexican, too. (12) Looks like from the countries, like Asian, like China or more or less around there. (13) Looks like Peruvian. (14) I would say, she could be like Puerto Rican. (15) Looks like he could be Dominican. (16) Looks Dominican too. (17) I think he could also be Dominican. (18) I don't know. I consider him like Dominican too. (19) I believe she could be like Spanish, or something like that.

Q: Does that means that she lives in Spain or that she could live here?

I mean, she could be from over there, but I don't know, she could live here too. I mean, it could be that she was born there. . . . (20), Looks like, I believe he's Dominican. . . .

> Q: *And how do you decide what to say for each person? How do you decide who's Dominican, who's Puerto Rican, or Mexican? On what aspects of the person do you base it?*
>
> Well, on the physical appearance. Because each person from each country has their physical appearance . . . the features, not so much the color, because sometimes you can be American or North American and you can be *negro* just as you can be *rubio*. At least by the physical, by the shape of the face and things, it's how you distinguish it more. (Dominican non-migrant, taxi driver)

Gregorio uses an entirely different racial schema from Inés. His concept is based on where people are from, and on his perception of what typical people in those places look like. This way of conceptualizing race in terms of people's nationalities was the most common approach to identifying the photographs among both the migrants and the non-migrants I interviewed. Gregorio uses what I call the *basic nationality schema*—he uses only national origin groups or ethnicities as racial categories. Because the photographs portray mostly people who are of Latin American origin, it was particularly common for respondents to use a basic nationality schema to distinguish among Latino groups. However, some also incorporated ethnicities from outside Latin America, such as Irish, Italian, Jamaican, Jewish, Haitian, or American.

Another variant, the *panethnic nationality schema*, combines nationality terms with the panethnic labels Latino or Hispanic. For many people, these panethnic labels have become racialized so that they are now treated as racial groups in their own right. But when respondents use both specific Latin American nationalities and a Latino panethnic label to identify people, the panethnic terms are frequently used as placeholders because respondents are unsure of the individual's nationality. This usage is illustrated by Nilda, a Puerto Rican migrant and customer service representative living in the Tremont section of the Bronx. She assigns nationalities—mainly Latin American ones such as Puerto Rican, Colombian, Honduran, and Dominican—for each of the photos until she gets to one she cannot place. She then says, "I don't know. (11) Looks like a *hispana* but I can't identify from which country. [I'll classify her as] Latina, I don't know." In the panethnic nationality schema, panethnic labels serve as an acceptable answer when the respondent cannot determine the nationality of the individual.

Most scholars do not think of nationality and panethnicity as races, but if we take an interpretivist approach and try to understand the perspectives and worldviews of respondents, it becomes clear that this is how many of them conceptualize what race is. Where does the association of race with nationality come from? Is it merely a difference in translation, with the word *raza* meaning something different in Spanish than "race" in English? Some scholars claim that national identities are more important than racial ones among Latin American populations, leading some people to substitute the more salient national identities when asked about race.[75] Are respondents, following this logic, simply confusing race and nationality? Others suggest that national identities become seen as races through the experience of Latino migrants living in the United States. By interacting with racially differentiated populations, groups like Puerto Ricans and Dominicans were increasingly racialized into separate categories as Americans came to see them as something other than Black or White.[76] Are concepts of a "Puerto Rican race" or a "Dominican race" born from migrants' experiences abroad and then communicated back to influence the racial concepts of non-migrants?

I maintain that processes of racialization in the United States do support an association between race and nationality, and that these concepts do filter back to the sending societies. But I also argue that the reason migrants' concepts have such resonance for those in the Hispanic Caribbean is that this notion of race as nationality already existed there. Migrants' experiences of being racialized in the United States—as part of the "Puerto Rican race," "Dominican race," or "Latino race"—are consonant with this existing concept of race as nationality, so that these ideas reinforce one another.

A concept of race that is more closely associated with nationality has long existed in Latin America, side by side with others. Because American scholars have distinguished between race, ethnicity, and nationality on the basis of American definitions and models of race relations, this alternative way of understanding race has largely been marginalized from their discussions. But anthropologist Julian Pitt-Rivers argues that there are two distinct uses of the term *raza* in Latin America: one that is biological in meaning, referring to either appearance or modern concepts of genetics, as with plants, and another that is based on a notion of descent that is social, and associated with social groupings such as tribe, community, or nation—the groupings that distinguish people in their social life.[77] In Latin America, the mixing of populations like the Europeans, Africans, and Indigenous groups kept a social or cultural concept of race relevant. According to Pitt-Rivers, people were not classified by their physical appearance, but their phenotype became an indication of the culture and behavior that one could expect from them. In this way, the two senses of the word *raza* often came to correspond to each other: people from Indian tribes tended to look Indian, which maintained the image of what an Indian was. The concept of *raza* contin-ues to be used in these two distinctive ways: to indicate both physical/biological characteristics and cultural characteristics.

This second, cultural conception of race has long been present in much of Latin America, and especially in the Dominican Republic. Since at least the late 19th century, the word *raza* has sometimes been used synonymously with "na-tion" or "people."[78] In 1894, José Ramón López published an essay on nutrition that spoke of the Dominican people as "a race."[79] In public speeches, Domini-can leaders like Joaquín Balaguer frequently used the words "race" and "nation" interchangeably to emphasize the connection between them and to distinguish the Dominican people from their Haitian neighbors.[80] Dominicans often refer to the *raza dominicana* as their sense of themselves as a people, a concept that combines race, nationality, and culture.[81] Throughout Latin America, the cul-tural concept of a race as a "people" is maintained in calling October 12, the day celebrating Christopher Columbus's arrival in America, *el día de la raza*— the day that brought these distinct groups into contact to form a new "race" or people.[82] In Puerto Rico, the word *raza* is less commonly heard used in this way, but similar constructs abound.[83] The importance of racial mixing, or *mestizaje*, between European colonizers, African slaves, and Indigenous Taíno groups, in national founding myths constructed a racialized concept of Puerto Ricans as a mixed-race people. Key written works that contribute to popular discourses on Puerto Rican identity convey this construct.[84] Contemporary research has also found evidence of widespread belief in a Puerto Rican race, and of people on the island identifying racially as "Puerto Rican."[85] Of course, the view of Puerto Ricans or Dominicans as distinctive mixed-race peoples is also related to broader discourses elsewhere in Latin America of *mestizaje* creating a new race. Most prominently, Mexican philosopher José Vasconcelos argues that Latin Americans have become "*la raza cósmica*," from their mixture of all the races in the world.[86]

This cultural understanding of race—as a nation, tribe, or a cultural "peo-ple"—is closely related to what American and European scholars consider to be ethnicity. I define "ethnicity" as a cognitive structure that divides people into groups, often hierarchically ranked, that have common ancestry, memories of a shared history, and a cultural focus involving symbolic elements that define their peoplehood.[87] Pitt-Rivers's first, biological concept of *raza* corresponds more directly to my definition of race.

Because the cultural concept of race resembles American scholars' defini-tions of ethnicity, this concept tends to be marginalized from scholarly discus-sions of race, which overlooks the way subjective interpretations of race have developed in Latin America, and the way nationality is often racialized. As social processes, race-making and ethnicity-making are remarkably similar. Both are cognitive processes that involve dividing the world into groups by constructing symbolic boundaries to separate one group from another. What distinguishes race and ethnicity is whether groups are formed on the basis of cultural characteristics or physical/biological ones—criteria that themselves often overlap.[88] Anthropologist Frederik Barth argues that the content of those groups—the characteristics that they share and that distinguish them from others—is much less important in defining the group than the boundaries that separate them.[89] These observations have led some scholars to argue that it is not useful to treat race, ethnicity, and nation as essentially different and that we should focus on the process of creating race ("race-making") rather than on racial groups.[90]

While I agree that it is important to focus on processes of race-making, I nevertheless contend that it is useful to retain the distinction between race and ethnicity, even while recognizing the similarities in how they are constructed. It is particularly valuable in a U.S. context, where this has become a socially meaningful distinction in practice. Racially defined groups tend to suffer greater disadvantages than ethnically defined groups, which generally have less difficulty achieving social mobility and integration.[91] While this may be only a matter of degree, it is important to recognize the way race and ethnicity are treated in order to understand why some groups are more able to improve their social position than others are. This is the very reason why one of the most intriguing questions for sociologists is whether Latinos will emerge in the United States as a racial or an ethnic group. The distinctions between race and ethnicity are less meaningful in Latin America, and in many contexts the constructs of race, ethnicity, and nationhood are almost synonymous. Such national differences are part of what comparative research is valuable in revealing.

My goal is to both interpretively understand how my respondents understand what "race" means and analyze the different types of meaning they apply to that term. To do so, I rely on distinctions between race and ethnicity that come from an American scholarly tradition, distinctions that the respondents themselves may not make. This approach gives me the flexibility to reveal when respondents are using the term "race" in different ways. Even among those who use the same schema of categories, some may understand those categories as being based on different characteristics. Respondents' widespread use of a *nationality racial schema* reveals that there is a complex association between race, ethnicity, and nationality in these countries, and a need to pick apart the many different meanings that are all bundled under the rubric of "race."

Americanized Race

In the United States, a unique way of classifying race emerged: a "one-drop rule," meaning that people with any trace amount of Black ancestry were classified legally and socially as Black. During much of the era of slavery in the United States, the prevailing logic did not consider Mulattoes (offspring of Blacks and Whites) to be Black, but defined them as a racially mixed group between Black and White. By the 1850s, however, as fear of abolition and slave insurrection created increased hostility toward miscegenation, Southern Whites revoked Mulattoes' relatively privileged, in-between classification. By the 1920s, the one-drop rule came to be uniformly accepted in the United States.[92]

By the logic of the one-drop rule, most Dominicans and Puerto Ricans—and indeed most Latin Americans—would be classified as Black. While there are some high-status families of European descent within each country that avoided racial intermarriage, the vast majority have at least some African heritage. Indeed, many early Puerto Rican and Dominican migrants to the United States complained of their discriminatory treatment and frustration at being labeled Black when they arrived. In his memoir, *Down These Mean Streets*, Piri Thomas describes growing up as a Puerto Rican in 1940s East Harlem, when Italian kids looking for a fight would call him "Black" and "nigger."[93] Dominican poet Chiqui Vicioso famously said, "Until I came to New York, I didn't know I was black."[94]

I call the variant of the U.S. racial schema based on this tradition of hypodescent the *binary U.S. schema*. It includes only the terms "White" and "Black," with people of any racial mixture being classified as Black. Raquel uses precisely such a schema to identify the people in the photos:

> I think that (1), (2), and (3) fall under the Black race. (4) Could be White. (5) and (6) Black. (7) It's possible that he's White. Could be. (8) White. (9) Black. (10), (11) White. (12) Black. (13) I don't know. (14), (15) Black. (16) White. (17) I don't know. (18) Black. (19) White. And (20) Black. . . .

> Q: *A lot of people say that. . . . Hispanics are all a mix of different races: Indians, Whites or Europeans, Africans. Do you think that if the majority of Hispanics are a mix, that you would classify them as Black?*

> It depends on the country. . . . If you ask me "How are Uruguayans?" Maybe in my life I've had contact with 2 or 5 Uruguayans. But if you ask me more about the people in Puerto Rico, the Dominican people, the Cuban people, there I could tell you a little more. And, in the Dominican Republic, the great major-

ity falls under the classification of "mixed." *Mixto, mestizo, mezclado.* And all that, in the end, is Black. . . . And in Puerto Rico, I think the pattern looks a lot like the Dominican Republic. (Dominican migrant, assistant principal)

The racial schema Raquel uses here is a manifestation of the one-drop rule, applied to Latin Americans.

However, while the federal standards for U.S. data collection maintain that "Latino" is not a race, a popular discourse has emerged that treats "Black," "White," and "Latino" as mutually exclusive categories. Everything from newspapers, television news and Web sites to academic articles treats these categories as if they did not overlap, with "Black" and "White" implying non-Latino.[95] Such sources rarely specify that these are racial categories per se or claim that they are mutually exclusive. But by separating these groups, the popular discourse implies a racial differentiation that has taken on a reality of its own in the public mind. There is considerable evidence that today both Latinos and non-Latinos consider "Hispanic/Latino" to be a race.[96] Even some government agencies use this classification system, complicating what is seen as official and popular levels of discourse.[97]

I call the variant of the U.S. schema that classifies individuals racially as White, Black, and Latino/Hispanic the *Hispanicized U.S. schema.* Pedro, a Dominican migrant who lives in Washington Heights and works as an assistant librarian, uses this schema to identify all the photographs as White, American *Moreno* (a Spanish expression for African American), and Hispanic. "White" and "Black" are typically used to refer to non-Latinos.[98] In the interviews, only a few Puerto Ricans or Dominicans adopted the U.S. schema in its binary form. Many of those who had migrated to the mainland U.S. were convinced that Americans saw their race not as Black or White, depending on their color, but as Latino.

. . .

The racial schemas described here are ideal types, specified to demonstrate different ways of understanding and using race. In practice, some individuals combine aspects of different schemas or introduce unique variants within these themes.[99] One combination form was especially common: a hybrid of the U.S. and the nationality race schemas. In this variant, the respondent uses the categories Black and White, usually to refer to people thought to be American or non-Latino, and nationality categories are used for everyone else—typically people thought to be Latino. Panethnic labels like Hispanic or Latino may also be used along with the list of Latino nationalities. Raul, a Puerto Rican migrant who works as a deputy manager in a city government office, uses this hybrid schema by racially classifying the photographs as Dominican, Cuban, Colombian, Black, White, Puerto Rican, Peruvian, Filipino, and Jamaican. His classification reserves the White and Black categories for Americans, while Latinos and other immigrants are defined outside the U.S. framework and are classified by nationality.

Such hybridization of schemas represents one way that concepts of race get slowly transformed. Migrants who arrive in a new society primarily using one racial schema may begin to pick up aspects of a new one and blend them together. Non-migrants who are influenced by the new racial constructs that filter back to them from their migrant ties may also begin to combine these concepts. We might, in fact, expect such hybridization of racial concepts before the full-scale replacement of one concept with another. The fusing of concepts is a form of cultural change, and the blending of new and old ideas about race points to how cultural change is spurred by migration.

Focus of the Research

To address the themes of this research, I conducted qualitative interviews with 120 first-generation Puerto Rican and Dominican migrants in New York City and non-migrants in San Juan, Puerto Rico, and Santo Domingo, the Dominican Republic, as well as participant observations during nearly a year and a half of fieldwork in these locations. I interviewed migrants who were old enough to have formed ideas about race in their home society before they migrated, yet who had spent sufficient time in the United States for those ideas to be influenced. To avoid any possible confounding influence of living in other locations, I excluded those who had lived anywhere besides the mainland U.S. and their country of origin, as well as those who had returned to their home country for more than six months after migrating. Although I am interested in how these migrants' lives are transnational, my focus is not on the experience of return migration but rather on how those transnational connections are maintained by individuals who live full-time in the United States. For the non-migrants, my main concern was to capture the views of those who had never lived abroad, and whose concepts of race were developed wholly within Puerto Rico or the Dominican Republic.

In each of the four samples, I sought variation in the characteristics that I expected would influence the process of racial identity formation—namely age, sex, occupational status, and skin color. For the migrant samples, I also sought variation in respondents' age at arrival in the mainland U.S. and the amount of time they had lived there. The sample is therefore not representative of Puerto Ricans or Dominicans in a statistical sense; rather, I used quota sampling across these characteristics to provide insight into a variety of experiences, particularly among individuals of differing racial appearances.

I generated the samples by combining several methods, including seeking referrals from people who participated in a random survey of second-generation Puerto Ricans and Dominicans in New York; posting advertisements and passing out flyers in public places; knocking on doors; talking to everyone I met in restaurants or shops; seeking personal referrals, usually through a widely forwarded e-mail message; and contacting professional organizations. Together, these methods helped me fill the various quotas for my sample distributions, and I did not interview more than one person referred by any source or group.

The interviews were conducted in person, at either the home of the respondent, an office, or a public location. They were conducted in Spanish. Both a native-Spanish-speaking research assistant, usually from the same ethnic group as the respondent, and I (a White American) were present, and we alternated leading the interviews. Further details of the sample and research methods are described in the Appendix.

Racial categorization and racial schemas matter because they shape how people see the world, how they treat one another, and what other groups they align themselves with to demand rights, resources, or power. Immigration is a major factor that is reshaping the racial composition of the United States, but the experiences of all those affected by it can also reveal the mechanisms of how racial concepts change, within individuals and within societies. The racial schemas that immigration transports and transforms reveal where groups like Latinos will fit within the racial structure of the United States.

2 Beyond the Continuum

Race in the Dominican Republic and Puerto Rico

BEFORE MIGRANTS EVER SET FOOT IN THEIR NEW SOCIETIES, they acquire an understanding of race from their country of origin. Their concepts of how to classify people racially are not simply formed on the plane trip to their new location. Yet scholars of immigration and race rarely investigate the conceptions that migrants bring with them.[1] This background provides a crucial starting point, a way to understand what the new racial schemas acquired in the host society are competing with in a migrants' racial schema portfolio and what is changed by the process of migration.

This chapter examines the racial schemas that Dominicans and Puerto Ricans who remain in their countries of origin use and recognize in different contexts, and how they conceptualize what those categories mean. In addition to comparing the two nations, I focus on differences within each population, primarily along class lines, that influence the type of schema respondents use in a given context. Different individuals also sometimes use the exact same categories, but understand them in very different ways, depending on the definition of race that they adopt.

The racial schemas that people select in different circumstances often reflect the symbolic boundaries that they draw. Symbolic boundaries are conceptual distinctions that we make between people, things, and practices. By constructing and sustaining symbolic boundaries—or conducting "boundary work"—people create collective identities and draw on common traits and experiences and a sense of shared belonging to differentiate themselves from others.[2] Symbolic boundaries are embedded within each racial schema's categories, and situational cues often trigger particular boundaries rather than others, influencing which schema is chosen from a racial schema portfolio.

Institutions, particularly educational ones, also influence how people conceptualize racial categories. They construct symbolic boundaries through what they teach or the terms they use, which also affects the salience of different racial schemas in different scenarios. In this chapter I focus on local influences, and in Chapter 5 I turn to the transnational and global forces that also influence concepts of race in these sending societies.

Racial Schemas in a Single Context

The way participants in the study classified the photographs I showed them revealed a racial lexicon that was relevant in their lives and in how they related those terms to one another. I found meaningful patterns in the racial schemas that non-migrant respondents used on the photos, based on their level of education. Education and social class turned out to be a primary dividing line in how respondents classified and defined race.[3] While I also examined gender, age, and color, I found no differences in the predominant racial schemas that respondents used along these lines. Across non-migrant respondents, the nationality racial schema was the most commonly used on the photographs, by Puerto Ricans with both higher and lower levels of education[4] and by most Dominicans with a lower level of education. Although the continuum racial schema is most consistent with the literature on race in Latin America, it was primarily used on the photographs only by Dominican non-migrants with higher levels of education.

Of course, the racial schema that respondents use on the photos is unlikely to be the only one they use in all situations. In the particular context of classifying the photos, respondents choose a particular schema from their racial schema portfolio—the one that seems most appropriate in that setting. The same individual who uses a nationality racial schema to classify the photographs might use a continuum racial schema when chatting with friends in her home. While their ratings of the photographs need to be understood in this light, the ratings nonetheless reveal how the schemas that people use differ relative to those used by other people in the same situation.

In addition to using nationality labels for the photos, many respondents declare their own race to be Dominican or Puerto Rican. While my primary focus is how they classify others, respondents often refer to their own identity to explicate how they understand the nationality racial schema in general.

What does it mean when non-migrants say someone's race is Puerto Rican or Dominican? In fact, it can mean quite different things for different people who are using the same categories. When non-migrants with lower levels of education, among both Puerto Ricans and Dominicans, adopt a nationality racial schema, they are adopting a cultural definition of race, which conceptualizes race in terms of nationhood, tribe, cultural traditions, and a sense of descent that is tied to a physical location or the people who populate it. In applying national origin terms to the concept, these Puerto Ricans and Dominicans are employing a different understanding of what "race" means than do most American scholars. We can think of this pattern as the *nationalization of race.*

By contrast, Puerto Rican non-migrants with higher education, who also primarily use a nationality racial schema, adopt a biological definition of race and actively racialize national origin categories by extending racial meaning to those categories. The biological concept that they associate with race, however, is rooted more in genotype than in phenotype; what it means to be Puerto Rican for them is less about particular skin colors or features and more about a biological notion of descent. This pattern amounts to the *racialization of nationality.*

Dominicans with higher education adopt a continuum racial schema, and would seem to lend some support to the continuum model described in the scholarly literature. They employ intermediate categories between Black and White, although the number of categories they use is quite limited; their functional schema involves only a few core terms. However, they define racial categories not by phenotype but by the genetic mixture of specific racial groups. Categories typically correspond to the "original" races that populated the island—White, Black, and Indigenous—and the first-level mixtures between them. Thus, while college-educated Dominicans and Puerto Ricans use different schemas for racial classification, both groups understand race as based on knowledge of racial descent. This concept of race more closely resembles the model applied in the United States than the phenotypic construction associated with the continuum model.

The Racialization of Nationality:
Puerto Ricans with Higher Education

Dulce is a 60-year-old non-migrant with a master's degree. When I asked her to classify the race of the people in the photos, she was initially unsure what type of racial categories she should use, revealing her use of different racial schemas.

She first asked if she should say, "*Blanco* race, *negro*, *indio* . . . ?" and when I responded, "Whatever you would say in your daily life," she began to identify the photos using a panethnic nationality schema—mostly as Puerto Rican, American, and Latino. She also identified her own race in terms of nationality. Although her light-colored skin and straight hair lead many people to see her as White, she does not identify herself this way but as the mixture of races that she calls "Puerto Rican."

> Many Puerto Ricans consider themselves . . . [a] mixture of *blancos*, *indios*, and *negros*. . . . I consider myself a mixture of *blanca*, *negra*, and maybe *india*. . . .
> I don't consider myself *mulata* because *mulato* is *blanco* and *negro*. I consider myself Puerto Rican, and the Puerto Rican is that.
>
> Q: *Puerto Rican is* blanco, negro, *and* indio?
>
> Yes. I don't know if I have *indio* race and I don't know if I have *negro* race but if I look at myself in the mirror I think that, although I have, look, straight hair and I'm more *blanca* than *negra*, but I'm a Puerto Rican. There is no way that I'm not Latina. (Puerto Rican non-migrant, arts administrator)

Dulce believes that racial mixture is evident in one's features—in her case, her nose, which is slightly wider, and her lips, which are slightly longer and fuller than most Europeans' noses. When Puerto Ricans with higher education levels identify Puerto Rican as a race, they racialize that nationality label, attributing it to the particular type of racial mixture they see as characterizing their national population—the mixture of White Spaniards, Black Africans, and Indigenous Taínos. The three groups have intermixed so much over the generations, respondents like Dulce claim, that it is impossible to know how much heritage any Puerto Rican derives from each of them. As a result, this particular racial mixture is best described as simply "Puerto Rican."

Multiple popular expressions capture the idea that Puerto Ricans are a mixed-race people, and non-migrants evoke these sayings in explaining why they associate the category "Puerto Rican" with a race. Dulce cites some of these expressions in explaining why she assigned a Puerto Rican race to several of the photographs:

> Q: *When you say this person is of Puerto Rican race, does it mean that she has this mixture [of blanca, negra, and india]?*
>
> Well, we have a popular expression that says "*Y tu abuela, ¿dónde está?*" [And your grandmother, where is she?] and that [means] that in some way you

have [her] race. Or the *mancha de platano* [plantain stain], that is . . . the plantain, when you cut it . . . it leaves a stain on you. That stain turns dark and they say "This one has a plantain stain or has his grandmother hidden" because in some way there is something. (Puerto Rican non-migrant, arts administrator)

The common expression "*Y tu abuela, ¿dónde está?,*" from the poem by Fortunato Vizcarrondo,[5] refers to the person who, in trying to pass for White, hides her darker grandmother so as not to reveal her own Black ancestry. Although it intends to challenge Puerto Ricans' tendency to deny their Blackness, respondents frequently use it to talk about the presence of racial mixture in general, or the inability of light-skinned Puerto Ricans to claim that they are truly White. The expression touches on the concept of "passing" more frequently associated with the United States. But even a Puerto Rican who looks White, Dulce notes, still carries traces of her grandmother's race. Such cultural constructs challenge Puerto Ricans' claim to Whiteness and act similarly to American notions of the one-drop rule. Even those who look White are not *really* White if they have a grandmother who is not.

This conception draws on a notion of race as based on ancestral inheritance, regardless of phenotype, although many respondents believe that their mixture is frequently revealed in their appearance. Several Puerto Rican respondents mention the "plantain stain," referring to the staple of the Puerto Rican diet, to note that something in their appearance—a somewhat darker skin tone, perhaps—distinguishes them as racially Puerto Rican. Teresita, a woman in her early 20s with light brown skin, describes her own color as marked by the plantain stain. After using a hybrid of a nationality schema and a Hispanicized U.S. schema on the photos (Latino, Puerto Rican, White, and Black), she explains that she could identify who was Latino in part by their "plantain stain," a color that characterizes many Puerto Ricans.

Q: *And [in the photos], how can you say who is Latino and who isn't?*

By the facial features. . . . Curly hair, plantain skin color . . .

Q: *Plantain color?*

Exactly. . . . In Puerto Rico this color [referring to her own color] is called the plantain stain. . . . I'm not *blanca-blanca* [*really* White or "pure" White]. I'm also not African American, *negra* color. [I'm,] well, plantain. (Puerto Rican non-migrant, college student)

Earlier in the day when setting up our interview over the phone, Teresita had described her appearance so I would know how to recognize her. She described her shirt and euphemistically described herself as of large proportions (which was untrue). And she described her skin color as "well, Puerto Rican color." The racial mixture that makes her color neither completely White nor Black is represented with a Puerto Rican label, here racialized as a specific color.

Jaime works as a professor at a technical school toward the outskirts of San Juan. Only in his late 20s, he obtained a master's degree at an early age. Jaime used a basic nationality schema for the photos, listing nationalities such as Puerto Rican, Dominican, Cuban, Venezuelan, and Honduran to classify people's races. Later in the interview, he explained that he considers Puerto Ricans, like himself, to be a mixture of Black, Spanish, and Indigenous:

> We are a mix of three races, but we're already so mixed that if we were dogs, we'd be mutts instead of a specific race.[6] The pedigree has been lost. . . . And I consider that, for example, there are things in the Black race that are in me, but there are also things in the Spanish race that are in me. . . . And [there are things] from the natives, . . . the Indigenous, which I also know are in me. (Puerto Rican non-migrant, professor)

With medium-brown skin, Jaime falls right in the middle of the racial spectrum from Black to White. The racial mixture of Africans, Spaniards, and Indigenous fundamentally defines Jaime's sense of Puerto Ricans as a people, and his perception of who he believes to be racially Puerto Rican. In choosing to describe that mixture, he uses not an intermediate racial term such as *mestizo* or *trigueño* but a term denoting national origin   to him, that particular mixture is quintessentially "Puerto Rican."

Phenotypically, respondents insisted, the Puerto Rican race is not "defined"; in other words, it cannot be characterized by any one physical description. There are too many colors and appearances that are recognizable as part of the "Puerto Rican race"; what unites them all is that practically no one is pure White or Black. This concept of racial purity is often conveyed through repetition: *blanco-blanco* implies someone who is completely White, while *negro-negro* indicates someone who is completely Black.[7] These expressions can refer to phenotype—someone whose features reveal no mixture—or to ancestry— someone whose family has not mixed. Diana explains:

> There isn't anyone *negro-negro*, there isn't anyone *blanco-blanco*. There isn't anyone completely *mestizo* because there could be someone whose complexion

is less dark but whose features are a little different. . . . [Here] you can find any guy or girl around who is *blanco* with [African] features. At the same time you can find a person who has completely refined features, with features like a thin nose, small lips, very marked eyes, and so since there's been a mix of races and of colors, [we're] very different. . . . The Puerto Ricans can't be defined with any specific color. (Puerto Rican non-migrant, librarian)

The Puerto Rican race is characterized by the fact of racial mixture, rather than by any particular appearance or phenotype.

And yet, while the Puerto Rican race is not "defined" in a given set of characteristics, many maintain that it can be differentiated from the race of other nations, even those nearby that are also characterized by a similar racial mixture. According to Daniel, a college graduate in his mid-20s, the populations of each nation mixed in different proportions to create different "races." Daniel explains why "Puerto Rican" is a race:

Puerto Rican is a race at least in the sense that . . . I believe the race differentiates itself [from] one of any other place because of the origins. When the island was colonized, the Spaniards arrived. . . . They killed the *indios* . . . after mixing. . . . Also . . . the *negros* that they brought . . . mixed. So this race has mixed basically with the passing of time, left and right [all over]. There wasn't too much exclusivity, with the exception of some regions . . . but in general terms there is like a mix. The mix is exclusive of Puerto Rico. And I believe that that is enough to constitute a Puerto Rican race. For example, it is differentiated very easily from the vicinity, from Santo Domingo, Haiti, Jamaica.

Q: And would you say the Dominicans, the Cubans are of a different race than the Puerto Ricans?

. . . Definitely. The Puerto Rican race is easily differentiable because there is like a mix. . . . It is easily differentiated from . . . the nearby islands, and from the U.S. A native race was created. (Puerto Rican non-migrant, medical technician)

The contemporary Dominican population is also descended from the mix of Spaniards, Africans, and Taínos, yet Daniel believes that the mixtures that resulted, many generations later, are distinguishable. Some respondents emphasize the racial commonalities between the nations of the Hispanic Caribbean, claiming that they look more alike than different, but most feel that there are distinct types of racial mixtures that cause someone to look Puerto Rican, Dominican, or Cuban. This contributes to the construction of the nationality racial schema. Those who use this construct racialize not only Puerto Ricans but other nationality groups as well.

A few highly educated respondents are reluctant to give the Puerto Rican label a racial status, even as they use it to identify others' races. For example, Jaime claims that using the term "Puerto Rican" is merely a shorthand to represent the racial mixture that is "undefined." Although he used the Puerto Rican label to identify the race of many people in the photos, he claims that he does not think of it as a race but as the only term available to express his concept of Puerto Ricans' mixed racial origins.

> *Q: Before, with the photographs, you said "the Puerto Rican race," and "the Dominican race"* . . .

> Yes, yes . . .

> *Q: And so do you think there is a "Puerto Rican race"?*

> No, I said it to generalize. I mean, when you say you're Puerto Rican then you maybe understand that the Puerto Rican has the mix of the three races and that you say the place of origin. For example, you [don't hear]. . . "Look at the three-race-Spanish-African-Indian." . . . No, they'll call you Puerto Rican. And so you already understand that by being Puerto Rican you have such [heritage]. (Puerto Rican non-migrant, professor)

Even if nationality labels are used as shorthand to avoid spelling out the particular racial mixture that they represent, the very act of doing so imbues those labels with racialized meaning. As people use national labels in this way, they stop being a shorthand and take on the complex meaning that people use them to represent. Respondents may differ in their opinions of whether "Puerto Rican" constitutes a race, but their use of the term in this way helps it to become one.

For those who racialize nationality, what it means to be racially Puerto Rican and what it means to be ethnically Puerto Rican are intertwined. The three groups whose mixture forms Puerto Rico's heritage represent distinct races as well as cultures. Thus, in descriptions of Puerto Rico's origin myth, the Spaniards are often referred to as *los blancos*, just as African slaves are *los negros* and the Taínos are *los indios*. Puerto Ricans' sense of themselves as a people derives from both the cultural and the racial imprints that this mixture left on the population. Being Puerto Rican thus becomes an ethnic category and a racial category at once.

The Nationalization of Race:
Puerto Ricans and Dominicans with Lower Education

Puerto Ricans and Dominicans with lower levels of education also predominantly use nationality labels as races, but they adopt a cultural definition of race. Many use a nationality racial schema, associating race with where they were born and with the cultural heritage of their nation. They do not racialize those terms, however, to see Puerto Rican or Dominican in terms of phenotype or biological characteristics. Instead, they understand them—and race in general—as the identity that best captures who they are, and of what "people" or cultural group they are a part.

The comments of Ofelia represent those of many Dominicans with lower education. An attractive woman in her 20s with very dark skin, Ofelia is a domestic worker in Santo Domingo. Pregnant at a young age, she left her child with her parents in her hometown to live and work in the capital. In describing the photographs, she uses a basic nationality schema with Dominican, *estadounidense* (U.S. American), Cuban, and Puerto Rican as racial categories. Although she identifies her own race as Dominican, she does not associate this identity with a group defined by physical or biological characteristics.

> Q: *Could you explain to me why Dominican is a race?*
>
> That's because if they are Dominicans, [their] race is Dominican. For example, you're American, your race is American. Now if your mother was Dominican or your father, you come from both sides, so you're Dominican and also American.
>
> Q: *. . . And are there Dominicans of different races?*
>
> Well, yes, there are Dominicans of different races. . . . If your mother is Dominican and your father is American then it's different, you have two types [of races]. (Dominican non-migrant, domestic worker)

She goes on to explain that if I were born in the Dominican Republic, my race would be Dominican. When she uses the term "race," Ofelia is employing a concept closer to nationality or ethnicity.

Puerto Rican non-migrants with lower education levels understand race similarly. Most describe their race as Puerto Rican, but view this in cultural or national terms rather than physical or biological ones. Rosaria uses a basic nationality schema to identify the race of the people in the photographs as

Mexican, Dominican, Puerto Rican, or Cuban. But when pressed for a definition, she is not really sure what "race" means:

Q: For you, what does "race" mean?

[Pause]—Race, for me, means—what you are.

Q: And what is it based on? [pause] Is it based on appearance, or color—or where you come from? [long pause] Or culture? Or language?

—What you are.—And on language.—And customs, culture.

Q: And does it have to do with appearance or color?

Not for me. (Puerto Rican non-migrant, temporary clerical worker)

Rosaria uses nationality labels to describe people's races, but like many respondents, she has not thought much about what race means. As she considers the meaning of race, she is fairly certain it does not refer to physical characteristics, and instead strikes upon a cultural definition. This cultural identity fits because it is Rosaria's most essential expression of "what she is." This is an example of nationality labels being used because they are the more important sources of identity.

Many of these respondents have never left their country; thus if they are asked about their own race, their response occurs within the context of Puerto Rico or the Dominican Republic. Why would they choose to say their race is Puerto Rican or Dominican in their own country, where these nationalities are likely presumed and the label does not differentiate them from most people around them? The use of a nationality racial schema, for oneself and others, is reinforced by the symbolic boundaries that these non-migrants construct. Even within these sending societies, people of other nationalities are part of their consciousness, whether through in-migration, tourism, political relations with other societies, or people they see on the increasingly globalized mass media. Gregorio, who has light skin and a tenth-grade education, explains that in his experience when people classify or distinguish individuals, they use nationality terms.

Q: Could you tell me what race you consider yourself to be?

Well, from the country, I mean, Dominican. Dominican.

Q: Okay. And would you say that Dominican is a race?

Yes, I believe so. Yes, because each country has its origin. Each country has its race of origin. . . . I'm Dominican and everywhere you go, you say, "What country [are you] from?" or "what race?" Well, you say, "Dominican." (Dominican non-migrant, taxi driver)

Gregorio claims it is because he meets people of other nationalities within the Dominican Republic that he identifies his race as Dominican, but further probing reveals that he actually meets very few. His only real contact with non-Dominicans is one Mexican reporter he frequently sees on television and sometimes picks up in his cab, and the many other Latin Americans he feels he has gotten to know from watching them on television programs. Gregorio exaggerates the extent to which he personally is asked about his race or nationality; but the salience he gives to such interactions reflects his understanding of how people are classified by others.

While he declines to discuss it, Gregorio likely does interact locally with non-Dominicans in the Haitian minority living in the Dominican Republic. Estimates of the Haitian and Dominico-Haitian population living in the Dominican Republic have ranged from 500,000 to 1 million, in a country of 9.8 million.[8] Dominicans' efforts to differentiate themselves from Haitians, both at the individual level and at the state level, have helped to create a strong national Dominican identity.[9] Puerto Rican non-migrants in San Juan similarly interact with a sizable Dominican minority population in their own society. In both cases, daily interactions may be limited, as these minority groups are economically marginalized and residentially segregated. Many are undocumented migrants and tend to be socially excluded. Yet their presence highlights the salience of the symbolic boundaries based on nationality, allotting to the majority a privileged status and greater rights within the country.

Even as various interactions help to make nationality categories salient for these respondents, this particular cognitive construct is situationally triggered. What makes these respondents identify themselves and others in terms of nationality labels in this particular context is most likely my presence as an American. Even in interviews that were led by my Puerto Rican or Dominican research assistants, my presence and their awareness that this was a study being done at an American university likely triggered a mental frame that reached beyond their own society, toward their awareness of how they are seen by Americans and on a world stage. One of my Puerto Rican research assistants,

Roberto, explained why a Puerto Rican respondent would be less likely to use racial categories like White and Black in the interview: "When it comes to his mind, he's going to think the *blanco* race and he's going to compare it with the *blancos* of the United States or the English or French. And when he says *negro*, he's going to [think of] . . . Africans from the United States." The context of its being an American study may lead a respondent to visualize race in terms of how it is seen internationally, and how people are classified in an international context—one that for many Latinos is dominated by the experience of living in the United States. This may not be how people regularly talk about and classify race within the context of their own society. But this racial schema is no less "real" to them because it is triggered by a particular environmental cue. The fact that so many respondents adopt a similar set of categories when asked to identify the race of strangers suggests that this is a schema that has meaning for them and reflects salient symbolic boundaries in their lives—the boundary between themselves and Americans or those outside of their own society.

A Limited Continuum: Dominicans with Higher Education

In some ways, Dominican non-migrants with higher levels of education have a concept of race similar to that of higher-educated Puerto Ricans. They, too, recognize that they live in a fundamentally mixed-race society, and that their mixed racial origins are revealed in the appearance of practically all Dominicans. Like the Puerto Rican group, college-educated Dominicans claim their race is "defined" not by a given set of physical characteristics but by the fact of their racial mixture. Yet where Puerto Ricans conceptualize these ideas by racializing nationalities, Dominicans take a different approach.

Most Dominicans with some college education use a continuum racial schema to classify the photographs. But rather than using a wide range of intermediate terms between Black and White, they typically restrict their identifications to just a few categories. Most of these respondents use only the terms *blanco*, *negro*, and *mulato*, with *mulato* by far the most prevalent. Others use terms like *blanco*, *negro*, *indio*, and *mestizo*. A few Dominicans in this group employ a wider range of terms, including *jabao*, *moreno*, and *trigueño*. Practically none of those with any college education believe there is a "Dominican" race.

Many Dominicans with higher education have very clear definitions of what they see as "official" racial categories: the three "original" races and additional categories that represent the mixture of two specific original racial groups. Agustín, the small-business owner introduced at the beginning of the book, defined *mulato* as the mix of Black and White, *mestizo* as the mix of White and Indian, and *sambo* as the mix of Black and Indian. But he used primarily the categories *mulato, blanco*, and *negro* for the photos, with the vast majority identified as *mulato* because he believes the mix of Black and White is most prominent in the Dominican Republic today. Federico, a light-skinned business owner in his 50s who attended college for several years, explains that *mulato* can be "the mix of *blanco* with *negro*, in the first, second, or third generation." He too uses the term *mulato* to describe most people in the photos, including those with light skin and dark skin and a variety of facial features.

Other respondents with higher education use somewhat different labels to represent the same mixtures of races. Some claim they know there is a term for the mixture of Black and White, but cannot remember exactly what it is, sometimes calling it *mestizo* or *trigueño* instead of *mulato*. Others choose a different term to represent the mixture of Black and White for symbolic reasons. For example, Alicia objects to the origins of the term *mulato*. An elementary school English teacher in her 40s, Alicia spent several years studying for her bachelor's degree as a young woman, and has recently gone back to college. With light skin and mostly European features, she would probably be considered White in the United States because of her appearance. Alicia could easily have claimed a White identity, yet she identified her race on the U.S. Census question as *mestiza*. As she marks her answer, she explains how she defines this term:

> [Reading aloud:] "What is the race of this person? Mark with an X one or more races. . . . " Let's see, how is it that they call this race, my race? I don't want to put *mulata* because I don't like it. . . . Let's put it as *mestiza*. *Mestiza* [said definitively].

> *Q: . . . And why don't you like* mulata?

> Because. . . . The mule . . . is an animal that is a mix of a horse and . . . a donkey. . . . Those of us who are mixed—my father is *negro* and my mother is *blanca*—they called us *mulatos*. . . . *Mulata* . . . comes from *mula* [mule], because the mule is the animal you get from the donkey and the horse, from breeding them. It's an animal that looks very much like the donkey, but it's smaller, weaker. So perhaps from the fact that it is a mix of two races, they call it like that.

> *Q: And* mestiza *for you means the same thing but without this origin? It means the mix between* blanco *and* negro?

> Exactly. *Mestiza* is *blanco* and *negro*. (Dominican non-migrant, teacher)

Alicia claims that everyone in the photos, and in fact all Dominicans, are *mestizos*, the mixture of Black and White by her terminology. Thus while there is some flexibility in the precise terms people use, many agree that racial categories denote the mixture of particular racial ancestries rather than a specific physical appearance.

The term *indio* is commonly used in the Dominican Republic. Many claim it serves as a euphemism to avoid calling dark-skinned Dominicans Black, and was deliberately fostered by Rafael Trujillo, the country's dictator from 1930 to 1961, to emphasize Dominicans' Indigenous heritage and to differentiate them from their Black Haitian neighbors.[10] Yet few non-migrant respondents with higher education use this as a racial category. In fact, most of them reject the label outright, insisting that the category *indio* does not really exist but was created by Trujillo to deny Dominicans' (and Trujillo's own) African heritage. Agustín explains why many Dominicans say their race is *indio*, but he rejects the idea:

> Q: *Here a lot of people say that their race is indio, right?*

> Well, that was an invention of our tyrant to soften [our race]. "We are *indios*," the color. We aren't *indios*. *Indio* is not a race. That's a deception. . . . [It's] a Dominican idiosyncrasy that that was created . . . [to say] "we aren't *blanco* or *negro*, we are *indio* because of our color." [Pointing to his own skin color]. . . . That was the government. It was something that deepened more in Trujillo's era, the tyrant. . . . He liked to [use] that more than saying *mulato*. He was a *mulato*. He didn't like it [the word *mulato*] or *negro* either. (Dominican nonmigrant, small-business owner)

Dominicans with higher education believe that the term *indio* refers not to descent from the Indigenous population, but to a brown skin color. Many, like Agustín, reject this concept and deny it is a racial identity because it refers only to "color," or phenotype, something they distinguish from race.

Like their Puerto Rican counterparts, Dominicans with higher levels of education adopt a biological view of race. They claim that race is determined by ancestry. Because racial categories represent for them a particular mixed-race heritage—the combination of ancestors of specific races—it is not revealed in aspects of phenotype such as a particular skin color or a defined set of features, as the continuum model maintains. Usually characteristics are visible that reveal the combination of those racial origins, but which characteristics reveal that mixture will differ across individuals.. Thus, someone with light skin but some African or mixed facial features could be considered in the same racial category as someone with dark skin but European or mixed facial features (e.g., photos 19 and 3). But even someone whose appearance does not reveal that mixture could still be considered *mulata* if her ancestry were known—very much like the one-drop rule in the United States.

In both Puerto Rico and the Dominican Republic, cultural and biological definitions of race coexist, with class differences in how they are used. Non-migrants with lower levels of education primarily subscribe to a cultural view of race, while those with higher education generally adopt a biological view that refers to genetic inheritance more than phenotype. Even within a single society, and within a single context, multiple ways of viewing and understanding race are evident.

Constructing Race through Institutions and Boundary Work

Although they tell a similar story about their mixed racial origins, these Puerto Rican and Dominican non-migrants with higher education classify race in quite different ways. What explains their distinct approaches to a similar situation, and why does their education level influence the way they understand race? Here, I examine the role of educational institutions and symbolic boundaries in race-making for those with higher educational levels.

Education plays an important role in national constructions of race. It gives people the skills to process, evaluate, and sometimes challenge messages they hear about race from a variety of sources. But from an institutional perspective, it also plays a direct role in shaping the messages that are communicated to the population about who they are. Ever since Michael Omi and Howard Winant's racial formation theory identified the state as the preeminent site of racial contestation, scholars have been looking to states and their institutions in analyses of race, in both the United States and Latin America.[11]

One way that the state realizes its racial projects—its efforts to construct racial meaning—is through educational curricula about the country's origins and its racial and cultural heritage.[12] In both Puerto Rico and the Dominican Republic, national approaches to teaching race shape the racial schemas adopted by non-migrants with higher education.[13] In Puerto Rico, the national discourse on race, communicated through school curricula and echoed in literature, poetry, and many forms of popular culture, is consistent with the tendency to group the mix of different races under a "Puerto Rican" umbrella label. Puerto Rican respondents recall being taught in school that Puerto Ricans are defined by the mixture of Spanish, African, and Indian. It is a short leap from there to a racialized understanding of "Puerto Rican" as denoting this mixture.

Like many other Puerto Rican non-migrants, Sofía drew upon her experiences in school as an important influence on her racial identification and classifications of others. A college student in her early 20s, Sofia has bronze-colored skin and mainly European facial features. Her appearance, closer to White than to Black, could have led her to adopt a White identity, but she identifies her race as Puerto Rican, although she did not always do so. She explains what influenced this change:

Q: Would you have ever said that your race is different than the one you say now?

Yes. Because when I was younger I used to say I was *blanca*. And after you grow [up], well, you understand that no, that you're not *blanca*. That there are more things out there [besides *blanco* and *negro*]. . . . Here, at least, I believe in the majority of the schools what they teach you from when you are small is that the Puerto Rican is the union of African, Spanish, and Indian. I believe that that is what they teach you since. . . . I'd say, you believe all your life that you're a mix of three races. . . . And they ask you, and you can answer it like a poem. "What race are you?" "I am a mix of three races: Indian, Spanish, and African." (Puerto Rican non-migrant, college student)

Although Sofia had been taught this lesson in school from a young age, it was not until she was in high school that she began to feel that her race was not really White. By this time, she had read more broadly and had enough intellectual maturity to reflect on the meaning of her identity, and came to embrace "Puerto Rican" as the term that best described her race. She was not told directly by her teachers that Puerto Rican is a race; the lessons were never so explicit as that. But this association made sense, given what she had always been taught and what she believed about the mixed racial origins of all Puerto Ricans.

In the Dominican Republic, too, respondents with higher levels of education draw upon their school lessons as the basis for their racial schema. In this case, the lessons were more explicit, teaching that each mixture of two racial groups is a different category. Higher-educated respondents recall being taught this, even if they cannot always remember the particular names that were assigned to those categories. Many remember textbooks in grade school that had a genealogical chart connecting each pair of races to its offspring. Gustavo, a Dominican teacher and school principal, explains that he knows what the different racial categories are because they are specified in the textbooks used in his school.

Mulato is a mix of various races. . . . It comes from Spanish and *negro*. There is a division in the [text]books that gives you that very nice explanation. That's why

I'm telling you [these racial categories], since they're already terms from the books but what's specified there is that formula. When we [finish the interview], I'll show it to you. . . . With a picture even. . . . There's an arrow that indicates each of these things. (Dominican non-migrant, teacher and school principal)

After the interview, Gustavo showed me a social studies textbook used for the third grade in his school with this genealogical chart (Figure 1).[14] Gustavo was surprised that the diagram did not also include a "*sambo*," the descendant of a Black and Indigenous couple, and assured me that there were other books with similar types of diagrams, perhaps used for different grades, which did include it.

The text accompanying this diagram instructs students about the racial character of the Dominican nation. It explains:

> The Taínos of our island have died off. This was due to the bad treatment they received from the Spanish and the hard work they had to do.
>
> Because the Taínos died quickly and their race disappeared from our island, only the White Spaniards and the Black Africans were left. That is why we say that the majority of Dominicans are *mulatos*, that is, the mixture of Whites and Blacks.[15]

Higher-educated Dominican respondents frequently cited these lessons in explaining why they classified race as they did, and particularly why they viewed most Dominicans as *mulatos*.

Figure 1. Dominican textbook image of racial *mestizaje*. Reprinted by permission of the Secretaría del Estado de la Educación.

Very few Dominican respondents with lower education mentioned their school lessons as influencing their views or recalled specific details of those lessons when asked about them. Gustavo perceives an educational divide in how Dominicans understand their race, saying, "A lot of Dominicans will not answer *mulato*. They don't understand this very well. It depends on the person you interview, their intellect. Because there are normal people that may not understand what *mulato* is." He believes that it is mostly those with higher education that use the term *mulato*, because they understand what it means. Dominicans with lower education, Gustavo concedes, would probably say that the mixture of White and Black is *indio*, or try to claim this identity for themselves, reflecting their belief in the false narrative that Trujillo constructed about their indigenous origins. Gustavo and others see this classification as "wrong" and view themselves as having learned the "right" way to understand race through their education, which is why they proudly refer to their memory of those lessons as explaining what the racial categories are in the Dominican Republic.[16]

In referring to their school lessons and dismissing as "wrong" the classifications used by those of lower status, better-educated Dominicans construct class-based symbolic boundaries that serve to highlight their superiority over lower-status Dominicans. They are quite critical of those who use a nationality racial schema and they insist that "Dominican" is not a race, but a nationality or ethnic origin. They perceive any discussion of the "Dominican race" as ignorance about the difference between these terms rather than a shifting understanding of what race means to people. Magdalena, a dark-skinned Dominican who received a bachelor's degree, used a continuum racial schema on the photos, choosing the terms *blanco*, *negro*, *mestizo*, and *mulato*. She said that those who say their race is "Dominican" just do not know what race means.

> Q: In the interviews, a lot of people say that their race is "Dominican." Can you explain why people here think that that's a race?

> Yes, yes, yes. . . . There are some of us that have certain [lower] levels [of education, intelligence] and we don't deal with other information. I understand that being Dominican is a Hispanic group, like being Ecuadoran. Simply, it's a name that we're given, invented by the Spanish and everybody that came here. . . . But it isn't a race. I'm clear on that. . . . We have everything here: *negro*, *mulato*. So I say that it is a total of all the races. That is what Dominicans are.

Q: And do you think that people here say that Dominican is their race because they don't know what race is or because they have other reasons for wanting that to be their race?

I think that it's because of ignorance, so not knowing what a race is and what a country is. Basically, that's ignorance. Even if they've studied, it's ignorance. (Dominican non-migrant, engineer)

Dominicans with higher education complain that the Dominican Republic is still a country with many illiterate people, people who do not have access to books or the means to learn. They recognize that many in their society do refer to the Dominican race or to other nationalities as races, yet they create symbolic boundaries to situate themselves above those offering such interpretations by claiming to have an exclusive knowledge of what racial categories "really are." Their understanding of what race is and which schema they use thus becomes a means of distinguishing themselves from less-educated, generally poorer individuals. Racial classification serves to reinforce those symbolic boundaries along class lines and to position these Dominicans, in their eyes, above the masses using nationality labels.

For Puerto Ricans, racial schemas based on nationality reflect symbolic boundaries distinguishing them from Americans, yet these boundaries are not class-based. Because Puerto Ricans with higher and lower education levels use the same racial categories, the different meaning that those with higher education attribute to such categories does not become a salient means of class differentiation. Accordingly, highly educated Puerto Rican respondents rarely criticize the race concepts of those with lower education in the way that Dominicans do.

Lessons about racial origins and classification are taught in elementary school, and thus all those attending public school should have been exposed to the same state constructions. Indeed, exactly as Sofia described, Puerto Rican interview respondents of all education levels did recite their Spanish, African, and Indian origins like a poem, much as they had been taught. But it is not simply learning these lessons in school that influences non-migrants' conceptions of race. Rather, some respondents reflect further on the meaning of racial identity and draw on these lessons as formative experiences. Higher education provides the opportunity for such reflection, and many college-educated respondents cited college courses, books, or discussions with college professors as the moment when they reexamined these earlier ideas and drew them into a coherent framework. Education also provides them with the skills to analyze and question prior beliefs, such as the belief that they are White, or that any Puerto Ricans or Dominicans can be White given the *mestizaje* in their country's history. And to some degree self-selection plays a role, as respondents who pursue a college degree are likely to have more intellectual curiosity and accordingly are more likely to reexamine those early school lessons as they deliberate on the meaning of race. Yet in the Dominican Republic, where rates of college completion are low, the process of achieving a higher social status through education reinforces symbolic boundaries around class, giving those who have attended college more reason to differentiate themselves through their use of racial schemas.

Because non-migrant respondents with lower education typically do not reflect on these school lessons in the same way, they are more influenced by alternative messages about classification—popular usage, popular culture, and ideas communicated by their migrant ties. A cultural connotation to the word *raza* is conveyed in public discourse, reinforced by media representations and migrants' experiences in the United States, where nationality labels are frequently used to classify individuals. These American classifications are conveyed by migrants to people back home, supporting notions of a Puerto Rican or Dominican race; non-migrants tend to repeat and adopt them. In Puerto Rico, the nationality labels that they hear and use are consistent with those adopted by higher-educated respondents to denote a conception of genetic racial mixture, and this consistency of terminology, if not meaning, bolsters the classification systems of those at all education levels. The difference in meaning that they attribute to the same terms is not always clear, even to them. In the Dominican Republic, popular messages from the diaspora are inconsistent with those used by higher-educated non migrants, leading respondents with varying levels of education to use different racial schemas.

The way race is taught in school is only one locus of state control over the shape of racial discourse, yet it is a particularly important one for constructing not just the categories that people recognize but their understanding of what those categories mean. However, these conceptions are not consistently adopted throughout the population, which leads to the proliferation of multiple systems of classifying and understanding race within a society.

The Context of a Continuum Schema

Whether respondents delimit race with nationality labels or with categories representing specific combinations of racial groups, their racial schemas generally do not represent the fluid continuum that characterizes the academic literature on race in Latin America. However, this is not to say that non-migrants do not use the continuous range of terminology that many scholars have observed, for indeed they do. The terms came up at various points in the interviews and during my observations in San Juan and Santo Domingo. Respondents also referred to how they use the terms outside of the interview context. In doing so, they revealed that they maintain this additional schema within their portfolio, but the context of classifying the photos was not one that activated it.

Many respondents used continuum terms during the interview, often to describe a photo they had just classified using a different schema. Others used the terms to refer to themselves or their friends and relatives. For example, Pablo, a Puerto Rican billing clerk who is studying for his master's degree, used a pan-ethnic nationality schema on the photos, employing such terms as "American," "Puerto Rican," and "Latino." But later in the interview, when I asked him to identify the race of each person he listed in his social network, he switched to a continuum racial schema, using terms such as *trigueño*, *blanco*, and *prieto*. Respondents often adopted a continuum schema when the interview question or context referred them to how race is classified specifically in their own society, among people they knew or might see in their daily interactions.

I asked respondents to recall all the racial terms that are used in their country, and then showed them a list of continuum terms and asked them which ones were used in their country, and to define the ones they knew. Practically all the respondents, even those who did not voluntarily use continuum terms earlier, were able to define most of these terms, often in fine detail, and explain how this schema is used, showing that the continuum schema also exists in their racial schema portfolio.

Why, then, did most respondents not use a continuum schema to identify the photos? Respondents claimed that these terms are used colloquially, as an informal argot. Lucio, a Puerto Rican surgical technician, explained that you would tend to use these terms "[w]hen you're talking in a vulgar way, of street slang, something like that . . . in jokes or in our regular way of talking. Not in the correct way." He described it as the language "of the people." It is very common to use aspects of appearance to refer to people. In both countries, people on buses, in restaurants, and in every other type of social interaction, use continuum terms to get one another's attention or explain to whom they are referring. On a bus in Santo Domingo, to get the attention of the *cobrador* (fare collector), a woman called out, "Hey, *negro*, this is my stop." In a café on the campus of the University of Puerto Rico, the owner yelled, "*Moreno*, come here," to call her employee back to the kitchen. Such physical descriptions have entered the culture as an informal means of expression. But respondents and my research assistants agreed that they were not the kind of language people would use in a formal situation like an interview.

In a study in Brazil, anthropologist Robin Sheriff distinguishes two ways that these continuum terms tend to be used. The first is a "descriptive discourse," in which the labels are used to literally describe someone's appearance. But the same terms can also be used in a "pragmatic discourse," to convey a particular relationship or treatment of a person. Much of the variability in which labels are used to describe a person can be attributed to the different discourses and the ways one individual intends to treat another.[17] Thus, referring to a woman as *triguena* at one moment may be using a pragmatic discourse to be polite and show respect, while calling her *morena* later on may be a more objective description of her appearance.

In Puerto Rico and the Dominican Republic the continuum terms are used both in descriptive discourse—to literally describe appearance—and in pragmatic discourse—to convey a manner of treating someone.[18] In descriptive discourse, people often use the terms to describe the person they are referring to or to describe a situation to others. Leandro, a Puerto Rican factory supervisor, explained, "Let's say that I get to a place and there are five [guys] and I say that there are two *negros* or two *blancos*. Or there are two *triguenitos* and a *mestizo*. It's like part of our language, our way of expressing ourselves. It's a cultural issue. It's not to offend or to make separations. It helps us to describe the person that is there." The terms are also frequently used to get someone's attention when his or her name isn't known.

In pragmatic discourse, the terms are used in a variety of ways to indicate one person's attitude toward another, or to convey the nature of the relationship one wants to establish. Some respondents feel that they are often used euphemistically—not to describe appearance but to be polite, for example calling someone *trigueno* or *indio* instead of *negro*, which has negative connotations. They may also be terms of endearment for family members or as *piropos* ("come-ons"). Although I have dark brown hair, Dominican men on the street sometimes tried to get my attention by calling out "*Rubia! Rubia!*" Technically, the word means "blond," but in this situation it is simply used as a compliment because being blond is considered attractive. On another occasion, the word was used in precisely the same way toward an African American woman with very dark skin who was studying in Santo Domingo. Men across the street called out "*Rubia! Rubia!*" to her, and when she did not respond, they tried another tack, calling out "*Morena! Morena!,*" thereby switching from pragmatic discourse to descriptive discourse. Color terms can also be used as insults.

One day in Santo Domingo, a small traffic incident led to a heated exchange of words between drivers—one with dark skin and African features and the other somewhat lighter, although not *blanco-blanco*. Both drivers yelled at each other from their cars, until the lighter man called the other "*negro*." Immediately, the confrontation escalated, with the darker driver getting out of the car to try to physically retaliate against the other. It was not inaccurate to refer to the second driver as *negro*; his features made such a label within the range of possibility. But the circumstances made it clear that it was issued as an insult. Social interactions such as these provide situational cues that trigger the continuum schema as opposed to others.

Race or Color?

Although the scholarly literature has long described the continuum model in terms of race, more recently scholars have begun to question this attribution, arguing that these labels and the concepts that drive them should instead be viewed as color. Robin Sheriff, for instance, claims that these labels are too imprecise and context-specific to be treated as a static system of racial classification. The terms are not mutually exclusive, and they tend not to lead to group-based identities.[19] The expression "color" should be interpreted broadly to include other aspects of appearance besides skin color, such as facial features, hair texture, hair color, and eye color—or phenotype in general.

Some respondents do use a continuum schema when asked to classify people's race, or say that the continuum terms I showed them represented races, even if they did not use those categories on the photos. But many respondents, both Dominicans and Puerto Ricans, said that these terms were not race, but only "color," a distinct concept that represents to them how they appear but not, fundamentally, who they are. This is another reason why many do not offer these terms when asked to classify race.

Respondents who used a nationality racial schema often insisted that the continuum terms are not races. Eduardo, a 22-year-old Dominican with a high school education, gave a typical response. Describing the list of terms, he explained, "They've taught us that this is color . . . for me, they're only skin colors." For him, "color" is firmly located in physical appearance in a way that race is not. Rosaria, the Puerto Rican temporary clerical worker, also insisted that these terms are not racial categories: "No, they're not categories. They're names that people have given in order to say, 'Oh, he's a bit lighter, but he's not *blanco-blanco*.' . . . Since there's such a mix, it's like a term that's been given to describe people." Color exists at the level of description, the phenotypical descriptions associated with the continuum model in the literature. For many respondents, the term "race" evokes more essentialist notions of a person's inner identity, something that surface-level appearances cannot represent.

For Puerto Ricans with higher education, what it means to be of Puerto Rican race is determined by ancestry. While this heritage is often revealed in one's phenotype, that is not always the case. Sometimes a racial imprint is latent, hidden within one's "blood," but nonetheless determines racial classification. Jaime locates the essence of the Puerto Rican race in an ancestral inheritance that may not always be expressed.

> If . . . you're Puerto Rican, [and] you have the races, Spanish, Indian, and African, then that's your race. And it doesn't matter if you're more *blanco*, or if this one is more *negro*, and they got married, the son still has the race. You see? Because the race isn't lost, the pedigree isn't lost, you know, you carry it (Puerto Rican non-migrant, professor)

Whether someone appears whiter or blacker in color, that person does not lose the ancestral mixture that defines a Puerto Rican. This is why Jaime asserts, "I don't think that the color defines a race."

For those who adopt a biological definition of race, the distinction between race and color mirrors that between genotype and phenotype. While race is something internal, buried within their makeup, color is what appears on the surface. This view reifies race as something essentialist, a truer indication of one's nature, while color is frequently described as misleading, masking aspects of oneself that are present, but hidden. Pablo also conveys this sense in describing how his family's racial mixture may be expressed even generations later. A dark-skinned man with predominantly African features, Pablo claims, after looking at the list of continuum labels, that these terms, like *trigueño*, cannot be considered races.

> I couldn't say that *trigueño* is a race. Because I turn out *trigueño* depending on who the heck I've mixed with. For example, . . . my brother . . . he's a very handsome *prieto*. . . . My brother married . . . a girl who was very *blanca*. . . . My nephews, the boys, they turned out *trigueñitos*, but the girl turned out just like her mother, *blanca, blanca, blanca*! With dead [straight] hair, beautiful! . . . She could live very happily denying her origins, she could mix with these people who are very *blanco*, beautiful. But she's going to be on the lookout because her children could turn out with characteristics from their grandmother, or from their grandmother's father, who were *negros*. So the fact that I can have at some point some skin tone doesn't classify me in a race . . .

Q: And that's the reason why you wouldn't say that these terms are races? Because they only have to do with physical appearance and not with the ancestry or genes they have?

Exactly . . . I can look completely *blanco*, but at some moment I'm going to have something that isn't within the features, because I have something from *negro* that wasn't in sight. But it's there, latent—hidden, but latent. And that it can be projected later on. And I can't control that. (Puerto Rican non-migrant, billing clerk)

The Whiteness of Pablo's niece is problematic because of her latent non-Whiteness, which may be revealed in future generations. Her *blanca* skin tone thus cannot classify her race, which Pablo claims can only be understood as Puerto Rican. The very notion that every Puerto Rican has a hidden grandmother who will reveal his or her racial heritage challenges the view that Puerto Ricans classify race on the basis of appearance alone.

Dominicans with higher education, who use a limited continuum schema on the photos, also define race in terms of racial ancestry. Yet they, too, distinguish between race and "color," for instance when they use a term like *mulato* to identify the races of many people whom they see as varying considerably in color. Alicia explains that someone can be *blanca* in color and still be a *mestiza* (the mixture of Black and White, according to her terminology), as is the case with her sister.

I believe that we are all *mestizos* here. . . . I'm going to give you the case of my sister. . . . She is very *blanca*, has blue eyes and yellow hair . . . because my mother has Spanish and European relatives so it seems like a gene got in through there. But I consider her a *mestiza*. She's mixed. My father is dark, *negro-negro*. . . . My father is like . . . number 20. . . . Exactly like that. The color of the skin is the same. The type of hair that is wavy but not kinky. Here we call it *indio lavado* [washed Indian]. . . . I think that race does not have to do with the appearance . . . because there are people who are mixed and come out a different color. . . . I think that the race does not have to do with the color of skin.

Q: And do you believe that there are White Dominicans or no, all Dominicans are mestizos?

There are very *blanca* people, with heritage of, here there were many Italians, Chinese, immigrants. But definitely they have mixed with the Dominicans.

That is, we cannot point out anyone pure from here. (Dominican non-
migrant, teacher)

Despite her sister's *blanca* appearance, her mixture of White and Black heritage makes her *mestiza* by Alicia's definition. Their shared parentage implies
that if Alicia is racially *mestiza* then her sister must be too. Respondents frequently invoke siblings' variations in appearance to illustrate how they understand race and color. Despite the efforts of academics to represent race as
a social construction, popular conceptions still associate it with something
essential and biological—a primordial quality that people must have in common with their brothers and sisters. Although siblings' colors may vary, their
race does not.

Even though Dominican non-migrants with higher education use a continuum racial schema that incorporates some of the terms in Table 3 (in Chapter 1),
they differentiate between what they see as "official" race categories and more
colloquial terms that indicate phenotypic notions of color. Alicia explains that
many of the color terms are synonyms and therefore cannot be race categories.

> What happens is that categories are exclusive, one excludes the other. [You
> have the] *blanco* category, the *negro* category. The *blanco* excludes from the
> *negro*, the *negro* excludes from the *blanco*. The one that is *blanco* cannot
> be *negro*. So here [on the list] there are like many things together. For example
> *negro*, *prieto*, *moreno*, *mestizo*, *mulato* are referring more or less to the same
> racial category, but with different terms. (Dominican non-migrant, teacher)

Alicia says that the only categories, as she sees them, are *blanco*, *negro*, and
mestizo, while the continuum terms I showed her are merely "pigmentations
of the skin and hair." For her, race categories are mutually exclusive, while the
terms that represent the continuum model are subtle distinctions in color,
or synonyms that fit within the "official" categories of respondents' racial
schema.

Some of the terms highly educated Dominicans consider "official" race categories—like *blanco* and *negro*—are also used as informal color colloquialisms,
but others are not. *Mulato* is one of the categories most frequently used by
higher-educated Dominicans on the photos. Yet they distinguish it from the
descriptive terminology one hears in social interactions, as Agustín explains:

> *Mulato*. . . . it's not used often here. It's an expression that is used little here,
> [as in] "Hey, *mulato*!" *Negro* and *prieto* are used more often. . . .

Q: You used the word mulato *a lot with the photos.*

Yes, but it was to define their race. It's not a term that I used as in, "Hey, *mulato,* come over here" as you use "Hey, *negro.*" (Dominican non-migrant, small-business owner)

The term *mulato* is an "official" term, something professionals would use but is not part of the popular language. Gustavo agrees. "A sociologist will talk to you about *mulato,* . . . " he jokes, referring to me, "but it's not common on the street." He asserts that the color terms are not found in the dictionary, emphasizing their informal, colloquial nature. The racial category *mulato* has long been taught in the school system, and its official status as a racial classification is further institutionalized by its use in the Dominican census and on recent Dominican identity cards. Such distinctions help Dominicans distinguish between categories of racial classification and a more informal language representing a continuum of appearances.

It is important to understand how groups like Dominicans and Puerto Ricans interpretively view the continuum terms and the difference between race and color. But from an analytical perspective, it is equally important to examine how these concepts function to shape society. There is a great deal of overlap between how color and race function in a cross-cultural comparison of the United States and the Hispanic Caribbean. Color is a racialized physical attribute that is often used in Latin America in ways similar to how North Americans use race—to stratify and structure society and to value particular racialized bodies over others. Some scholars refer to the continuum taxonomy as "race-color" to illustrate the similarity in the concepts used in North America and Latin America, respectively.[20] Although Sheriff and others argue that the continuum classifications do not represent race because they are not static or mutually exclusive and tend not to lead to group-based identities, these are not necessarily inherent properties of race. Increasingly, even in the United States with its rising multiracial population, people are recognizing that racial classifications need not be mutually exclusive or static, and they do not always lead to group-based identities.[21]

Certainly, phenotype plays a more important role in stratifying the populations of Dominicans and Puerto Ricans in their home countries than do racial classifications that use nationality labels. Color has real consequences for social outcomes in the Caribbean just as it does in the United States. Social status and color are closely related in both the Dominican Republic and Puerto Rico, leading some to describe those societies as pigmentocracies.[22] Undoubtedly the greater scholarly interest in the continuum model than in subjective interpretations of race stems partly from its association with social inequalities.

If color in the Hispanic Caribbean plays a role similar to that of race in the United States, then a cross-cultural comparison of the regions needs to recognize how these concepts resemble each other as well as how they differ. The continuum model, whether viewed as race or color, is one of several cognitive structures that lead Puerto Rican and Dominican societies to organize people into hierarchically ordered categories on the basis of socially designated physical or biological characteristics. This is my analytical definition of race, even though my respondents sometimes adopt other ones. When we are freed from the notion that people operate with one and only one schema of race, it is possible to recognize the continuum schema as a type of racial schema, one of many that can exist within a racial schema portfolio.

A Portfolio of Multiple Schemas

Puerto Ricans and Dominicans who remain in their home societies maintain a range of different racial schemas that they use in different contexts, both throughout the interview and in informal interactions. In addition to the nationality schema and continuum schema, some respondents in San Juan and Santo Domingo also at times use a U.S. racial schema—either in its binary form of just White and Black or in a Hispanicized version of White, Black, and Latino. For example, Matilde, a Puerto Rican secretary in her 60s, classifies the race of everyone in the photographs as Black, White, and Latino, while she identifies the race of the people in her social network as only White and Black.[23]

Respondents reveal distinct patterns in how they switch between schemas when classifying the images of people they do not know in the photos and classifying the race of people they do know in their social network. Puerto Rican respondents were more likely to switch between schemas on the photos and the social network than were Dominicans. Among Puerto Ricans—both those with higher and lower levels of education—most respondents used different racial schemas across these contexts; some switched completely among nationality, continuum, or U.S. schema, while others created a hybrid combining one they had used elsewhere with one of the others. Some also switched between different variants of the U.S. or nationality schema. More of the Dominican respondents maintained a particular schema between the photos and the social network. Those with higher education were particularly likely to use their limited continuum schema for both. But many of the Dominicans also changed or used a variant of their earlier schema. Puerto Rican respondents seemed to have greater fluency with more of the schemas, not simply recognizing them but actively using them across situations. If we think of Puerto Rico as culturally more influenced by its long-standing institutional connections to the United States, a greater flexibility between cultural constructs of race makes sense. Dominicans, especially those with higher education who had a firm sense of how racial categories were defined, were more likely to use that as their predominant system of cognitive organization across situations.

These two contexts—classifying photographs of unknown individuals and classifying people they know personally—trigger different cultural frames, the global and the local. While we might have expected people who have always lived in a certain society to look at a set of photos and place them within the context of that society, the reality of life in these migrant sending societies is a constant awareness of the world beyond their own borders, and particularly the society to which they are linked by mass migration networks. Even the presence of an American foreigner and a formal interview under the auspices of an American university would not have caused them to switch their cognitive frameworks if they did not have a preexisting conception of what race means from a global perspective. The geographical context of the photographs was ambiguous; respondents generally did not know what societies the people depicted were in or where in the world they lived. This very ambiguity cued respondents to think of categories that would differentiate people from different parts of the world, rather than local frames that would be used within their own society.

The opposite was true when classifying the race of people whom respondents knew personally. Those who switched to a different schema on the social network all switched to either the continuum schema or the binary U.S. schema. For people they knew, respondents tended to use terms they might have used in interacting with these friends, such as the continuum terms they might use as joking nicknames or ways to call their friends' attention. Both continuum terms and the Black and White categories of the binary U.S. schema serve to distinguish their friends from one another, particularly in comparison to nationality terms, as most respondents' friends were of the same nationality as themselves.

Knowledge of origins is also relevant when respondents switched between different variants of the same schema. Those who did so typically used a panethnic nationality schema or a Hispanicized U.S. schema on the photos and switched to a basic nationality or binary U.S. schema to describe their social network. Effectively, this meant using the terms "Latino" or "Hispanic" for the photos but not for their networks. For those using a nationality schema, a panethnic term served as a place filler on the photos when respondents were unsure of the particular nationality; for their friends, they knew the nationality. For those using a U.S. schema, a Hispanicized U.S. schema on the photos indicated that many of these individuals were seen as Latino in an international frame, by people outside their own societies. For their social networks, they described the people they knew as White or Black, since they were practically all Latino.

It is tempting to view the different racial categories that people use at different moments as inconsistencies, perhaps reflecting an uncertainty about what race means. Yet there is method in the madness; when respondents explain why they believe Puerto Rican or *mulato* is a race, they reveal a way of seeing the world and a framework for constructing particular kinds of social comparisons and distinctions. That framework can shift when an awareness of one type of social comparison—an international one versus a local one, for instance—is triggered rather than another. But respondents are not switching randomly between different schemas. The patterns in who uses which schema, and which ones they switch between when classifying people they know and do not know, reveal that these changes are not just inconsistencies but a logically ordered cognitive process reflecting different racial comparison groups at different moments.

Of course, just because there are multiple competing racial schemas does not mean that they all have the same social and structural significance for how societies are hierarchically organized. This, too, varies by the social context. The continuum schema, representing color, is more important for stratifying society in Puerto Rico and the Dominican Republic than is a nationality schema. Some might argue that the reverse is true (or at least that these schemas are equally significant) in the United States. Yet while these classification systems may not have the same structural impact in each society, people's awareness and use of them reveal the extent to which those people are not simply living in one local society. Even if they have never lived outside their home society, their world can be shaped by social influences and structures elsewhere. And adopting multiple concepts of race facilitates the process of cultural change.

3
Migrant Schemas
Race in the United States

AFTER MIGRANTS HAVE MOVED TO A NEW SOCIETY and lived there for several years, how do their conceptions of race come to differ from those of non-migrants who stay behind?[1] Do they adopt the racial schemas of their host society, experiencing a type of racial acculturation? How do migrants learn these new schemas and, particularly, where their own group fits within these classification systems in the eyes of the dominant host population? I explore these questions in this chapter, with Puerto Ricans and Dominicans who have migrated to New York.

Cultural assimilation means learning how a society is organized and how to behave within it according to its rules, norms, and expectations. Those who are most acculturated are those who regularly adopt such understandings and patterns of behavior, even if they also retain their old cognitive structures from their home society. Racial acculturation, then, involves adopting and using conceptions of race that predominate in the new society and structuring one's behavior and interactions according to the implied relations between racial groups.

A difficulty with this perspective, however, is the frequent assumption that the "culture" of the host society is homogeneous—that if migrants have internalized that society's culture they will view the world in one particular way and behave accordingly. Culture is rarely so one-dimensional. It changes over time, is internally contested, and usually comprises multiple subcultures. In immigrant receiving societies, a great deal of that change and contestation comes from immigration itself. Immigrants change their host society by bringing ideas and practices with them that sometimes influence the dominant groups.

Such cultural heterogeneity is clear with regard to concepts of race. Scholars often talk about a single U.S. system of racial classification—represented in the binary U.S. schema based on the one-drop rule. This model has been codified in law and has traditionally shaped race relations in the country.[2] In its treatment of Latinos, it is reflected in the federal Office of Management and Budget's declaration in 1977, and confirmation in 1997, that "Hispanic/Latino" is not a race and Latinos should be classified racially as White, Black, or another racial category.[3] Social scientists often give primacy to the OMB directive, and the census categories that follow from it, as constituting an "official" U.S. concept of race. Yet few have considered whether individuals, who may see the census once a decade or be unaware of the OMB directive, are influenced by these categories in their daily lives.

Alternative constructs of race compete with the OMB directive and the binary U.S. schema. The large-scale presence of Latinos, who bring their own conceptions of race with them, challenges this model and has created an alternate classification system, represented by the Hispanicized U.S. schema, that treats Black, White, and Latino as mutually exclusive racial categories. This alternate model has also been de facto reinforced in a variety of "official" forums, including the U.S. Department of Education and the Equal Employment Opportunity Commission. The EEOC instructs employers to identify their employees as White, Black, Hispanic, Asian or Pacific Islander, and American Indian or Native Alaskan.[4] The DOE collects data on Hispanic/Latino origin and race separately, but it reports Latinos of all races together and mutually exclusive from all other racial groups, which are restricted to non-Latinos.[5] Even academic writing and sociological surveys frequently divide people into White, Black, and Latino. These classifications have also been widely adopted in public media, from TV shows and films to news broadcasts and music labels. They appear regularly in reputable news sources like the *New York Times* and the *Washington Post*, which lay readers may view as an equally "official" representation of American classifications as the options listed in the census, yet which they likely see much more often. While these sources do not describe Hispanic/Latino explicitly as a *racial* category, that is often what people infer from seeing the category distinguished from other racial groups, particularly from White and Black, the very ones with which it is supposed to overlap.

There is a great deal of confusion in the United States about whether Latino is a race or an ethnicity. Scholars have debated the costs and benefits of its being treated as one versus the other, with some suggesting that it is preferable to regard it as an ethnicity because groups classified as ethnicities have experienced more socioeconomic integration and mobility than those classified as races.[6] Others have suggested that it is both at once, an ethnic group that has become racialized.[7] The reason that Latino is treated alternately as an ethnicity and as a race, I argue, is because of the different schemas that are simultaneously used in the same society. Under the binary U.S. schema, the Latino category is treated as an ethnicity; under the Hispanicized U.S. schema, it is treated as a race. With both of these schemas in the U.S. cultural repertoire, and competing within American culture, the position of Latinos will be ambiguous until one of these two models becomes culturally dominant.

I believe that the Hispanicized U.S. schema—which treats Latino as a race—is winning out in U.S. culture. Not only is this schema increasingly dominant in this country's media, public discourse, and now even some government reporting standards, but more importantly it has come to dominate in everyday language, as used by Latinos and non-Latinos alike. Although not everyone uses a Hispanicized U.S. schema in every situation—indeed, many of the working-class migrants I interviewed do not—public conceptions of where Latinos fall within U.S. racial structures are influenced by this discourse that treats Latinos as a separate racial group.

I find that migrants' use of racial schemas in the United States, like that of non-migrants who remain in Puerto Rico and the Dominican Republic, is shaped by their education level and social class. While some racial acculturation does occur, it is primarily among college-educated migrants. Those with lower educational backgrounds tend to use a nationality racial schema, much as their counterparts in their home countries do, while college-educated migrants are more likely to use a U.S. racial schema. This is because migrants learn about Americanized racial schema primarily through structural assimilation—the adoption of primary relationships with the host society by entering into its clubs, cliques, and institutions.[8] Through these institutions and substantive interactions with non-Latino Americans, college-educated migrants come to learn both the binary and the Hispanicized U.S. schemas. While they primarily use the Hispanicized U.S. schema because it better reflects the reality of their lives, these migrants, unlike their less-educated co-ethnics, are at the forefront of this cultural conflict, forced to negotiate the changing concepts of race in America that are brought about by Latin American migration. Yet all respondents believe that they are viewed as a distinct group by Americans; they may see their racial classification in the United States as Puerto Rican, Dominican, or Latino, but it is clearly neither Black nor White.

Migrants' Racial Schemas in a Single Context

Table 4 shows the predominant racial schemas used by the migrant groups to racially identify the photographs, compared with the schemas used by non-migrants, and divided by the respondents' level of education. The same pattern emerges when respondents' are divided by occupational status, which is closely tied to education. Again, there were no clear differences in racial schema use by respondents' gender, age, or color. There were also no differences in schema use by the length of time migrants had lived in the United States or the age at which they arrived. While this result may seem surprising, the pattern reflects the fact that it is not simply the time spent in a new country that leads migrants to adopt Americanized concepts of race, but their degree of structural assimilation within the society.

Scholars have long suggested that Puerto Ricans and Dominicans, whom they viewed as maintaining a continuum model of race in their home countries, would come to adopt an Americanized view of race, divided into White and Black. With the photos, we see this pattern only among Dominicans with higher education, although we learned in Chapter 2 that their limited continuum schema does not fully represent the continuum model in the literature. More generally, racial acculturation can be understood as the adoption of U.S. racial schemas. We see this pattern among some Puerto Ricans with higher education as well; this group is evenly split between those who use a U.S. schema and those who use a nationality schema to assess the photos. To the extent that racial acculturation is occurring, as measured by how they classify the race of

Table 4. Non-migrant and migrant respondents' predominant racial schemas on photographs, by nationality and level of education

	Puerto Ricans		Dominicans	
	Lower education	Higher education	Lower education	Higher education
Non-migrants	Nationality racial schema	Nationality racial schema	Nationality racial schema	Continuum racial schema
Migrants	Nationality racial schema	U.S. racial schema and nationality racial schema	Nationality racial schema	U.S. racial schema

NOTE: Higher education includes those with a bachelor's degree or higher; for Dominican non-migrants it includes those with some years in a bachelor's program (see Chapter 2, note 4).

unknown others in the photographs, it seems to be primarily a phenomenon of college-educated migrants.

Nationality and Culture: Migrants with Lower Education

Migrants with lower education levels, both Puerto Ricans and Dominicans, primarily adopt a nationality schema to classify the photographs, much like their counterparts in their home societies. For example, Alberto is a Puerto Rican migrant in his 70s who has lived in New York for nearly 50 years. He left high school after the eleventh grade and worked as a school custodian until he retired. Alberto used a basic nationality schema on the photos, identifying them as Puerto Rican, Dominican, Cuban, Venezuelan, American, Mexican, Colombian, Honduran, and Salvadoran. Alberto's responses were typical, especially of Puerto Ricans, who tended to use only nationality labels to identify people's race. Dominicans with lower education more often adopted a pan-ethnic nationality schema, using Latino or Hispanic as racial labels along with nationality terms. Maura, a Dominican prison official in her 50s with a high school education, illustrates this pattern. She classified the race of the people in the photos as Dominican, Puerto Rican, Latino, Colombian, American, Cuban, Peruvian or Salvadoran, and one person as Latino mixed with American. Notably, Maura identified both someone with very European features (photo 8) and someone with very African features (photo 6) as American, showing that a nationality schema does not differentiate between those who may be seen as White Americans and Black Americans.

A small subset of migrants with lower education levels distinguish between White and Black Americans by using a hybrid of a nationality schema and a U.S. schema. They typically assign nationalities to people they believe to be Latino and classify non-Latinos as White or Black. Rogelio, a Dominican migrant in his 20s who drives an armored truck, uses such a hybrid schema when he identifies the photos as Dominican, Puerto Rican, Salvadoran, Black, White, and Ecuadoran, specifying that those he labeled as Black (photo 6) or White (photos 8–11 and 17) are not Hispanic. This hybrid schema reflects a recognition of the social distinctions between White and Black Americans, while still giving prominence to nationality in classifying the race of Latinos.

Most of the migrants with lower education, like their counterparts in their countries of origin, adopt a cultural definition of race, one that is more associated with what American scholars think of as ethnicity. They associate race with roots, traditions, and territory—or the place where they were born. Adelaida, a Puerto Rican woman in her 70s who is a retired school aide with a high school education, explained that race means, "Well, where you were born . . . your parents, your country, where you were raised." Enrique, a 21-year-old Dominican student pursuing an associate's degree, agreed that "race is like the catalogue of people, the different cultures. . . . [R]ace is your culture, your roots, where you're from, your background." According to these respondents, race does not have to do with appearance, but only with the culture and country one is "from."

Migrants bring these concepts of race from their home countries, but they are also influenced by how they are seen by others in the United States. Yesenia, a retired garment factory worker in her 80s with a seventh-grade education, begins to assert a cultural definition of race, but ends up emphasizing the boundaries that Americans construct around racial groups.

> Q: For you, what is the meaning of race? What is it based on?

> Race is the culture. The person's culture. And also, for example, wherever the person is raised.

> Q: And people that are born in the U.S., like . . . your grandchildren, are they Americans because they were born here?

> No. They say they're Puerto Ricans, and they let Americans know that they are Puerto Rican. Because when they make the distinction, you're Puerto Rican or you're Cuban, they don't tell you that you're American even if you were born here. The only thing you have is that they put you down that you were born here on the passport. Apart from that Puerto Ricans don't have that distinction as being Americans. We have always been labeled. (Puerto Rican migrant, retired factory worker)

Yesenia and her grandchildren are proud of being Puerto Rican, but they also recognize how they are labeled by others. Although migrants with lower education use the same nationality schema as their counterparts in their home countries, nationality labels have a special resonance for migrants. They represent both how they differentiate themselves from other Latinos and how they believe Americans classify them.

U.S. Race and Biology: Migrants with Higher Education

Migrant respondents with higher education and middle-class occupations were much more likely than their co-ethnics with less education to adopt a U.S. schema in classifying the photos. And practically everyone who did so employed a Hispanicized U.S. schema. Only one migrant respondent—Raquel, quoted in the introduction of the book—classified the photos as only White and Black. A more common response was that of Manolo, a Dominican engineer with a master's degree. He classified the photographs as Hispanic, Black, and White or Anglo-Saxon. He later specified that the people he identified as Black or White he considered not to be Hispanic.

Many migrants with higher education also adopt a biological definition of race, like their counterparts in the sending societies. They see it as based on physical and biological characteristics rather than cultural ones. Hugo explains:

> What happens is that I see culture as one's ethnicity. Race, I see it more as skin color, in my opinion. Not as skin color necessarily or exclusively, but it could also be the features, the height, the physique including all the details. Well, because it's of the people that make up your past, you know, your grandparents and your parents, so you become what you are. But where you are from, your culture, is where all of these things come from that don't necessarily have anything to do with race. (Puerto Rican migrant, IT manager)

College-educated respondents like Hugo typically distinguish between race and ethnicity, adopting the same definitions as most American scholars. This also extends to their understanding of the Hispanic/Latino category. Many have learned that Hispanic is not a race, a view confirmed by the U.S. census classifications and other forms of federal data collection. A Dominican lawyer, Filomena, claims, "Many Hispanics, when you ask their race, think you're asking if they're Latino. Or Hispanic. But for me race is *blanco*, *negro*, or the combination, and the origin would be Hispanic or Latino." Yet even those who assert that Hispanic is not a race frequently use it as one when identifying the photographs, as part of a Hispanicized U.S. schema. Although they do not define it as a race, they recognize that this is how most other people classify them. Filomena continues, "It's difficult because I always say 'Hispanic' when they ask me 'what are you?' . . . I don't say 'I'm *blanco*' or 'I'm *negro*' or whatever. So, no, in reality, I don't know if the races would be Hispanic, but for me it's like an ethnic group instead of race." She feels that "Hispanic" is an easier label because most Americans would not understand terms like *mulato*, which is how she identifies herself and many other Dominicans. Respondents who adopt a definition of race and ethnicity that is more consistent with that of American scholars and the census classifications could employ the binary U.S. racial schema, which is most consistent with it. Yet their daily experience tells them that this is not how they are really classified by others. Even if they do not define Hispanic as a race, they use the term in a way that helps it to be treated as one.

A small number of Dominican migrants with higher education use a continuum racial schema on the photos. Like their counterparts in the Dominican Republic, these respondents use a limited number of terms; for example, Adrián, a journalist with a college degree, identifies the photos as *blanco, negro, mulato, mestizo,* and *mezclado* (mixed). And like the highly educated Dominican non-migrants, Adrián also recalls the lessons he was taught in school in the Dominican Republic about the names for the specific mixes of races. Explaining the difference between *mulato* and *mestizo,* he says:

> In the Dominican Republic, the history books make a clear distinction. *Mestizo* is a person that descends from an *indigeno* [Indigenous] and a *blanco.* And *mulato* is a person descending from a *blanco* and a *negro....* And in reality I don't think there are any pure *mestizos* left in the Dominican Republic ... because from the *Taínos* all we have is memories. (Dominican migrant, journalist)

Adrián's concept closely resembles the explanation in the social science textbook described in Chapter 2. This small group of educated Dominicans that uses a continuum schema to classify the photos is aware of U.S. racial schemas—they have added them to their portfolios. But they assert that these U.S. schemas simply do not reflect the race of Latinos, because Latino is not a race—yet most Dominicans are neither White nor Black. As a result, they resist racial acculturation and continue to use the schema that they claim they used back in the Dominican Republic.

Assimilation and Race

The extent to which migrants learn the different variants of U.S. racial schemas depends considerably on their structural location in U.S. society. All migrants learn, even from casual interactions, how they are racialized by Americans—by their ethnicity or their panethnicity. This view, that Americans classify them as Puerto Ricans, Dominicans, or Latinos, is consistent with the nationality racial schema that many used in their home societies.

But migrants who become integrated into mainstream structures in American society also learn something else—they learn about the binary U.S. racial schema and the definitions of race and ethnicity that claim that Latino is not a race. An understanding of the binary U.S. schema does not simply seep in over time in the United States. The contradictions between this schema and those that would classify Latin Americans by their ethnicity or panethnicity are conveyed not through *cultural assimilation* to an American way of life but through *structural assimilation.* Sociologist Milton Gordon drew a crucial distinction between these processes. Cultural assimilation, or acculturation, involves a change in cultural patterns and practices. It can include taking on the language, dress, and daily activities of the dominant group, as well as embracing their ideas, attitudes, and values. However, this can occur without structural assimilation—the adoption of primary relationships with the dominant group by entering into their clubs, cliques, and institutions. According to Gordon:

> [M]any of the memories, sentiments, and attitudes of the receiving group are common property; the inclusive ones in America—such as patriotism, Christianity, respect for private property, and veneration for legendary heroes—are vested in the total society, and they are readily accessible to all. On the other hand, the matter of sharing experience and incorporation in a common life is limited, first, by a willingness on the part of the receiving group, and second by a desire on the part of the new arrivals to foster social participation.[9]

Those who integrate into the social institutions of a society access its social networks and develop sustained relationships with members of the dominant group. It is through those relationships and institutions that migrants learn the binary U.S. schema.

If we view acculturation as the awareness of different strategies of action and the tendency to use some more than others, then what structural assimilation brings is fluency in the values and practices of the dominant culture. But those who learn how to navigate mainstream society—an important tool for their success within it—may nevertheless choose not to enact some of its strategies of action. Puerto Rican and Dominican migrants who have made their way into the educational and work institutions of the core society often choose to maintain the family values, religious practices, customs, and traditions of their society of origin, seeing it as an advantage to navigate between the strategies of action of the home society and the host society, rather than routinely adopting one set over another. Likewise, many structurally integrated migrants learn a binary U.S. schema but do not use it because it conflicts so strongly with the racial schemas they experience in their daily lives and the symbolic boundaries that become salient for them. Effectively, these migrants, who incorporate but do not use the binary U.S. schema, experience the brunt of the confusion over the racial classification of Latinos in the United States.

It is primarily middle-class respondents with college degrees who experience structural assimilation into the dominant social groups and institutions. Working-class respondents with lower levels of education typically do not; many have limited English abilities, and their meaningful interactions are mainly within their ethnic group or with other Latinos, while interactions with non-Latinos remain cursory. They interact casually with Americans in stores, restaurants, or on the subway, but these exchanges are not sufficient to change their conception of race. As Robert Park and Ernest Burgess noted:

> Assimilation naturally takes place most rapidly where contacts are primary, that is, where they are most intimate and intense, as in the area of touch relationship, in the family circle and in intimate congenial groups. Secondary contacts facilitate accommodations, but do not greatly promote assimilation. The contacts here are external and too remote.[10]

Casual contact exposes migrants to an understanding of how they believe they are classified racially by Americans, but not to a deeper understanding of how Americans define and conceptualize race. Because working-class migrants' interactions remain primarily within a Latino community, nationality remains the most salient social boundary in their lives, reinforcing their use of the nationality racial schema.

Racialization without Structural Assimilation

The lives of most migrant respondents with lower education were mostly bounded by the Spanish-speaking community of New York. The vast majority of the friends they listed in their social networks were Latinos, and a substantial portion of respondents listed only Latino friends. These patterns were true even for migrants who had been in the United States for several decades. Yesenia's experience represents that of many early migrant respondents. Now in her 80s, she moved to New York in the late 1940s to earn better wages so that her husband could afford an operation. She has lived in Spanish Harlem—el barrio—for 55 years, in a building that is populated primarily by Puerto Ricans. Even the artwork in the lobby incorporates Puerto Rican flags and symbols. Yesenia explained that she has never been confronted by American perceptions of race because she has not had the opportunity for such interaction. Language and cultural differences create a barrier to her venturing into areas dominated by Americans.

> I have always been among Puerto Ricans. . . . I don't interact with the American society. Only my people. . . . Here [in el barrio] I feel fine because the majority are Hispanics and in the stores they welcome you. . . . I think Americans all have their society and if you go and don't know their language . . . it closes people's doors. If you don't know the language, [you just] sit there. Why go to

a society to sit and not have anyone to talk to? And Americans, if you're not introduced or a friend, they won't talk to you. You could go to any of their places and they won't come and talk to you because they don't know you. We're not like that. (Puerto Rican migrant, retired factory worker)

Many early migrants came to the United States to earn a better living and improve opportunities for their children. Their own structural incorporation was not necessarily a goal. Meaningful social interactions are therefore restricted to their own ethnic group or to other Latinos, and spending decades in the country does not lead to adopting U.S. racial schemas.

Many of these migrants view New York as providing a remarkably diverse social environment and the opportunity to meet and interact with people from a variety of nationalities. But in their eyes, that diversity consists of other Latino groups. For example, Odalys, a Dominican migrant with a high school degree, has tried to learn English but finds it very difficult. The busy main street of her Bronx neighborhood leading to the subway has several stores with Spanish signs and moving vans promoting shipping to the Dominican Republic. Odalys also uses a nationality racial schema in classifying the photos. Her social network is almost entirely composed of Latinos, primarily Dominicans and a few Puerto Ricans and Guatemalans. After she described her network, I asked if she has much contact with other groups, but she could only conceptualize this question as referring to other Latinos:

Q: Do you interact much with people from other groups?

Yes. I like to.

Q: With which groups?

Everything that's different attracts me. I always want to know what they eat, how they cook things. Since I like to cook a lot, I like to know a lot about the foods. How for example Cubans like black beans, Guatemalans also like black beans, we like the red. (Dominican migrant, unemployed factory worker)

The world in which Odalys lives is delimited by her language abilities. In New York she has access to many diverse ethnic groups with whom she can communicate. But in this all-Latino social circle, the importance of nationality is reinforced; it is being Dominican or Guatemalan that distinguishes one friend from another.

This is not to say that working-class migrants have no contact with non-Latinos. They attend school together, live in the same neighborhoods, and often share workplaces. But for many of these respondents, their interactions with non-Latinos are casual and less intimate. They are the "secondary contacts" that Park and Burgess described. Even Gloria, a retired assistant teacher who described herself as speaking English "pretty well," explained that while she had Jewish and African American coworkers, her most substantive interactions at work were with the other Puerto Ricans.

Q: What were the ethnic groups of your coworkers?

Well, Puerto Ricans.

Q: The great majority?

Yes, [of] our little group [that has] lunch. Because always at work, each individual looks for her own group. The Jewish were with the Jewish. *Morenas* with the *Morenas*. The Hispanics were with the Hispanics, in Lisa's [class] room, where we always met for lunch.

Q: But were there teachers of each group in that school?

Yes, yes, yes, yes. We got along well with every[one]. If there was a little party we would get along, share and everything. But at lunchtime we used to get together—Lisa, Margarita, our group of Hispanics. One is always looking [for] one's kind. (Puerto Rican migrant, retired assistant teacher)

Gloria immediately thinks of her coworkers as the core group of Hispanics she socialized with, because of the social divisions among the Jewish, Black, and Hispanic teachers. Many working-class respondents similarly explained that their primary relationships were with co-ethnics and other Latinos, even those who had been in the country the longest.

The fleeting and casual interactions that these migrants have with non-Latino Americans are sufficient to convey to them a sense of how they are racialized in daily life, but they are rarely sufficient to communicate a more concrete understanding of how Americans define race and ethnicity. These migrants tend not to learn the binary U.S. schema, but instead see themselves labeled as a cultural group, defined by their nationality or by a panethnic category like Latino. This view of how they are racialized by Americans—as Puerto Ricans, Dominicans, or Latinos—often suits them just fine, because it is consistent with the concepts of race that most of them brought to the United States.

The context of racialization has changed since the early days when the major waves of Puerto Rican and Dominican migrants first arrived in the United

States. The "Great Migration" of Puerto Ricans to the mainland U.S. began in the mid-1940s, while the first major wave of Dominicans arrived in the 1960s.[11] In those early days, many Puerto Ricans and Dominicans were shocked to find upon arrival that they were viewed as Black. Several of my respondents recalled these experiences when they first arrived in New York. Celia, now in her 60s, was sent to New York to live with her older sister in 1955. Her medium-brown skin and thick, straight hair give her an Indigenous appearance and led relatives back home to call her *trigueña*. But her experiences in New York opened her eyes to how different race was in her new home.

> I discovered so much about racism when I came to this country. . . . When I came to school, attended school, because I was very dark-skinned, and I was Indian-like, you know? I was very dark. And then my sister had to go to school because they had put for my ethnicity, they put Black. And then my sister went and she said, "She is a Lat—" At that time we didn't use the word "Latino." We said Puerto Rican.

> *Q: . . . Did they change your race on the form?*

> Yeah, they changed it. They changed it. . . . I don't think they gave her a hard time. But yet, it was a problem. It was a problem. (Puerto Rican migrant, school counselor)

The problem, Celia claimed, was one of respect. Being classified as Black was, to her and her sister, a sign of disrespect that merited correcting.

It was not only White Americans who viewed Puerto Ricans as Black; Black Americans did as well. Antonio arrived in New York with his family in 1947 on the *Marine Tiger*, the boat that transported hundreds of Puerto Ricans to New York before airplane migration became common. Settling in *el barrio*, he became aware of racial divisions through the territorial demarcations that divided his neighborhood landscape.

> *Q: Do you remember how it was that you became aware of the differences in how people thought about race in the U.S.?*

> Yeah, . . . because East Harlem was divided into two portions: the portion east of 3rd Avenue, and the portion west of 3rd Avenue. East of 3rd Avenue was where all the Italians lived, and there was a tremendous amount of fights between the kids. And the demilitarized zone was 3rd Avenue because it had an "el," an elevated train. I had to go to the elevated train to go downtown or whatever so that was a place that it was safe to go. But you wouldn't go past

[east of that] and the Italians couldn't go west of that. I was very young when I first became aware of that because we were told "Don't go east of 3rd Avenue or your life is in danger." . . . And then west of that was Central Harlem where all the Blacks were living and we mixed with Blacks, and a lot of my friends as I was growing up were a combination of Black and Puerto Ricans. . . .

And I remember all the African Americans having very definite ideas of races that I couldn't understand where they would hold such ideas. To them there was Black and there was White. And I always thought to myself, "I'm neither one, I'm a mix of those two races," and they couldn't understand why anybody could say that. "You're Black, what are you talking about? If you're mixed, you're Black." I said, "No, I'm mixed. I'm not Black." . . . My grandmother was a White woman and I remember going to her house and loving her. And then I would go to my father's mother's side and they were all from Luiza Aldea and they were really Black. . . . So to me there was never anything that one was better than the other. I loved them dearly, and I refused to give either one up, which is what I think I was being asked by a lot of my Black friends, and that always bothered me. (Puerto Rican migrant, artist)

In those days, White Americans used the one-drop rule to classify Puerto Ricans as Black and to restrict them with Black Americans to the west side of Third Avenue. But many Blacks also internalized that rule. To them, Puerto Ricans' assertion that they were anything else was simply denial.

Dominican respondents who were among the early migration waves were also sometimes seen as Black. Ida, a part-time social worker with dark skin and moderately African features, arrived in 1963. People often thought she was a Black American and would speak to her in English, assuming she understood. In those days New Yorkers were simply unfamiliar with Dominicans, she claimed, who tend to be darker on average than Puerto Ricans.

The early migrants arrived at a time when Americans did not know what to make of their race and tended to fit them into preexisting classifications. But much has changed since those days, led in no small part by the tremendous growth of the Puerto Rican and Dominican populations. Table 5 shows the size of the Puerto Rican, Dominican, and entire Latino population of New York City from 1960 to 2000. The Puerto Rican population grew from 612,574 in 1960 to almost 900,000 in 1990, before declining for the first time in the 2000 census. Between 1960 and 2000, the Dominican population grew by more than 3000% to become the second-largest Latino population in the city. Moreover, the entire Latino population of New York City has surged from less than 10% in

1960 to 27% in 2000. It has also become increasingly diverse; Dominicans and Puerto Ricans together made up only 55.3% of the Latino population of the city in 2000, compared with 82.6% in 1960. In this context, where more than one in four New Yorkers is Latino, native-born Americans are more familiar with these populations, and the communities themselves have more power to determine how they will be classified.

Most migrants feel that times have changed since the days when Puerto Ricans and Dominicans were seen as Black. Celia, who had been classified as Black on her school form, responded forcefully when asked if something like that could happen today.

> Oh, no. Are you serious? No! No, no, no. With the bilingual [programs], especially in schools now, I work in a school, and I said, "My, God! I remember back in the days when I was in school that it was completely different." Completely different. Nowadays everybody speaks Spanish, everybody. (Puerto Rican migrant, school counselor)

Celia teaches at a school in East Harlem, in the center of *el barrio*. In her school, Latinos are the majority, and there is no question that staff and administrators speak Spanish and are fully sensitive to their cultural backgrounds.

More recent migrants to New York enter an established Latino community. Raimundo, a young man with brown skin, came to New York from the Dominican Republic in 1991 and settled in the Dominican community of Washington

Table 5. Puerto Ricans, Dominicans, and Latinos in New York City, 1960–2000

	1960	1970	1980	1990	2000
Puerto Ricans	612,574	811,843	860,552	896,763	789,172[a]
% of NY Latino population	80.9	67.5	61.2	50.3	36.5
% of total NY population	7.9	10.3	12.2	12.2	9.9
Dominicans	13,293	66,914	125,380	332,713	406,806[a]
% of NY Latino population	1.7	5.6	8.9	18.7	18.8
% of total NY population	0.02	0.09	1.8	4.5	5.1
NY Latino population	757,231	1,202,281	1,406,024	1,783,511	2,160,554[a]
% of total NY population	9.7	15.2	19.9	24.4	27.0
Total NY population	7,781,984[b]	7,894,862[b]	7,071,639[b]	7,322,564[c]	8,008,278[c]

Selected data from Gabriel Haslip-Viera, "The Evolution of the Latino Community in New York City: Early Nineteenth Century to the Present," in *Latinos in New York: Communities in Transition*, ed. Gabriel Haslip-Viera and Sherrie L. Baver (Notre Dame: University of Notre Dame Press, 1996), Table 3, pp. 14–15.

[a] New York City Department of City Planning, NYC 2000 Results from the 2000 Census: Demographic/Household Characteristics & Asian and Hispanic Subgroups, NYC DCP #02-07, 2002), Table 13, p. 26.

[b] Campbell Gibson, "Population of the 100 Largest Cities and Other Urban Places in the United States: 1790 to 1990" (U.S. Bureau of the Census, Population Division, Working Paper No. 27, 1998), Tables 19–22.

[c] New York City Department of City Planning (2002), Table 1, p. 2.

Heights. He claims that Americans think his race is "Dominican" and contrasts his experience of relatively easy integration with that of the first waves of Dominican migrants.

> When you come here, in the year I came, there were already a lot of Hispanics. In the beginning, in the '60s, the '70s, it was different when they came here. They'd look at them in another way. . . . They looked at them, for example, they thought Dominicans were *Morenos*, that they were Haitians, in those times. A Dominican was Black, *negro* color. But no, . . . not now. . . . Those problems have already passed a lot. The Hispanic community has developed a lot. (Dominican migrant, casual laborer)

Not all recent migrants settle in an ethnic enclave, a factor that has aided Raimundo's incorporation. But Raimundo's lack of problems in navigating a new racial classification system represents the experiences of most recent arrivals with dark or medium skin—those most likely to be seen as Black. Among these migrants, those who had been in the United States for the shortest amounts of time (3 to 13 years) described considerably less conflict with American racial classifications upon arrival than those who had lived there for 20 years or more.

The overwhelming majority of migrant respondents believe that today Americans classify them racially as Latinos or by their nationality.[12] Skin color does play a role in how migrant respondents believe they are racially classified; those with dark skin were more likely to say that Americans saw their race as Black, but this view was only held by a minority of those with dark skin. Of the migrants with light skin (and in fact, of all migrants), only one respondent believed that Americans saw his race as White. The more common view is expressed by Bolivar, a retired Puerto Rican who worked as a taxi driver and factory worker: "They say that we're of Hispanic race; . . . they don't care about the color. . . . They don't say that you're White or even if you're *prieto* [Black]. [If] you speak Spanish, you're the Hispanic race."

Even if migrant respondents believe that Americans generally classify them by their nationality or as Latinos, migrants are still sometimes confused for Blacks, especially migrants with dark skin. Racial ascription is a complex process based on various kinds of cues, but it typically begins with physical appearance. Many Americans are not able to distinguish Latinos from Black (or White) Americans on the basis of appearance alone. However, respondents emphasize that they are not *classified* as Black but *confused* for Black, and usually only temporarily until they say something in Spanish.[13] Even speaking English with an accent causes their reclassification as Latino. Others note that Americans realize they are Latino when they learn their name. That such information prompts a reevaluation implies that even Americans recognize their first impression as a mistake.

Of course, not all interactions lead to such basic exchanges as a few words or a name. Discrimination and prejudice may rely on appearance alone. Latinos' experiences may also be quite different outside New York City. New Yorkers have had time and opportunity to become familiar with Latino populations. Even those with little personal interaction are aware of these communities and attuned to Spanish language as an indicator of group membership. The concentration of Spanish speakers within the city reduces the need for Latinos to learn English; thus migrants to other regions may lose the markers of their immigrant origins more rapidly. Alfonso, a Dominican mortgage broker with medium-dark skin and European features, claims that many Americans see him as Black, but the experiences that he describes to support that claim occurred outside of New York City, in less diverse areas such as upstate New York and Westchester County.

Within New York City, it is not simply the visible presence of Latinos but their own efforts that have contributed to this changing context of racialization. This is a change which Latinos' own racial conceptualization has helped bring into being. Many respondents arrived with a nationality racial schema and viewed their race as Puerto Rican or Dominican even before they were classified that way by Americans. By using a nationality racial schema in the United States, they have added this concept to the racial repertoire of their new society. Migrant respondents believe that a Latino classification is close to their cultural concept of what race means and does not challenge the nationality schema that many of them use.

Latinos have also mobilized politically, influencing how they are classified in the United States. As the Latino community of New York has fought for greater political power and representation, Latinos have asserted their strength and their interest in being treated as a distinctive group in the New York political landscape.[14] Sometimes those efforts result in attempts to distinguish their group from Black Americans, whether out of group pride or anti-Black sentiments that exist in many Latin American countries. Adelaida arrived from Puerto Rico in 1948. Claiming that Puerto Ricans today should be classified as Latinos on the census race question, she recalled an earlier questionnaire that grouped Puerto Ricans with Blacks and how the Latino community fought against it.

> Some years ago . . . they put a question [in] questionnaires like that. It came [out that] we were considered as Blacks, and we fought that. We fought. . . .

They always put us with the Blacks, the Hispanic race. For us, here, around the 50's, . . . everything was with the Blacks. . . . Since the Black race was poor, they treated us, I believe . . . like humiliating us, treating us like . . . the *prietos*. . . . So when politicians started there [they said,] "We are Hispanics, we are Latinos, we are Puerto Ricans. But we aren't either Whites or Blacks." We were identified as we wanted them to identify us. (Puerto Rican migrant, retired school aide)

Through collective action, as well as the more subtle influence of their daily presence, Latinos have managed to influence how mainstream America views them.

Latino migrants influence native-born Americans, leading them to add a new racial schema to their portfolios. While less-educated migrants do not adopt drastically different racial schemas in the United States, even those who use a nationality racial schema in the U.S. believe they *are* using an Americanized concept of race, because they think this is how Americans classify them. Migrant respondents who do not experience structural assimilation find the U.S. racial classifications fairly unproblematic, because what they experience in their cursory interactions with Americans is not that different from what predominated back home.

Structural Assimilation and Learning Racial Schemas

While all respondents learn from their casual interactions that Americans classify them as Latinos or by their nationality, those who experience structural assimilation by entering into the social circles, clubs, and institutions of the dominant group also learn about competing racial schemas in the United States. By attending college, developing friendships with non-Latinos, and entering into mainstream workplaces, migrants with higher education develop primary relationships with White and Black Americans who teach them about the binary U.S. schema, the one-drop rule, and what they see as the "official" view that Latino is not a race.

Institutions of higher education perform an important function in how these migrants come to understand race in the United States. They play a formal role, through their lessons and curricula, in educating students about the nature of race, much like the educational institutions in the sending societies do. But they also serve an informal, social role. Attending a U.S. college literally opens the door to new worlds for these migrants. It brings them into meaningful contact with new ethnic and racial groups—often for the first time. Respondents commonly described the transition from a very insular ethnic community to a diverse college campus, especially Dominican respondents who often arrived when they were in their teens and settled in densely populated Latino communities. Hernando, who was surrounded by other Dominicans in high school, chose to attend college in upstate New York to have more exposure to people of different backgrounds—his first in-depth experience with aspects of White culture.

> When I was in high school . . . I was always surrounded by Hispanics. And so that's why I decided to go to [my college upstate], in order to be around Whites, Chinese, *Morenos*, etc. So I learned a lot from them. I lived on the university's campus. . . . The food was very different. . . . The cafeteria—oh, my God, nothing was Hispanic. I never ate rice over there, or beans. It was always turkey burgers. . . . Sometimes we went to Olive Garden or Macaroni Grill. And so there I started to see a different world. I also saw that many of the Whites . . . like if they needed help I could help them, but when I needed it they came in a way, "Oh, I don't have time for you," like straightforward. . . . But I had time for you!. . . . With the Latinos, it's very different. There's more affection. If you need anything, if I have it I try to help you. (Dominican migrant, business administrator)

Leaving New York City for college gave Hernando his first meaningful contact with the dominant American culture. He learned about new cultural forms: new foods and new kinds of music. He also learned about different cultural values and ways of behaving, not all of it welcome. Nonetheless, Hernando says, now that he has broadened his horizons, he has trouble going back to that "isolated, segregated" community where "it's only a Latino world."

Part of what migrants often learn at college is an understanding of race from a historical American perspective. This is precisely what Raquel learned from her college sociology class, an experience that completely transformed her understanding of race and who she was. Before that class, she used a continuum racial schema. In college, she learned about the binary U.S. schema, and its view that Latino is not a race:

> There was a confusion—at least for [me] . . . about what race is, what ethnicity is, what nationality is. So, for me, it was an experience like an epiphany, one day when I found out that there are only three races . . . and you have to decide which you belong to. So not only by the color of the skin, but there are a lot of other factors. . . . There would be your ancestry—you need to look at your grandparents, your great-grandparents. . . . So I don't have any other

option than choosing Black because I'm not White or Asian. So I must be whatever is left. . . .

Those are the races that exist. The other stuff is ethnicity because being Hispanic or Latino doesn't fall under "race." That isn't a race. . . . I remember having a conversation with my mom [after that] and my mom said, "No! This can't be! . . . I couldn't be Black. How could I say that? Impossible!" But it's that people get confused with race, ethnicity, nationality and what it really involves to be of a race. . . . (Dominican migrant, assistant principal)

In this college class, and through her subsequent conversation with her teacher, Raquel came to add a new racial schema to her portfolio. Because she learned that Latino is considered an ethnicity and not a race, she came to use a binary U.S. schema on the photographs and in classifying the people in her social network, as well as herself.

Like Raquel, many respondents learn explicitly how race is defined in the United States through their coursework, which can be confusing for those who believe they are classified racially by Americans as Hispanic. Carla, a Dominican lawyer, also said she learned that Hispanic is an ethnic category and not a race from discussions in college classes, explaining "obviously when you're at a university you're building terms, categories, right?" This creates conflicts for her because she feels that Hispanic is what people usually want to know, and is even an option on many forms. Even though migrants like Carla recognize that the binary U.S. schema conflicts with their everyday experiences, they still believe it represents a more official American view of race because this is what they learned in their college coursework.

Substantive social interactions with non-Latinos at college or in the workplace also teach migrants about racial schemas in America. During my fieldwork, I frequently spoke with Dominicans and Puerto Ricans, often from the second generation as well as the first, who explained that their interactions in college were the main influence in their understanding of racial classifications. While in New York, I was introduced to Sandra, a Dominican woman who had come to New York as a young child and thus did not meet the study criteria. But Sandra's experiences were very similar to those of my respondents. Sandra had grown up in Washington Heights and had always identified as Dominican. The public school system there was mainly Latino, perhaps 90 percent, she estimated. When Dominicans came to New York, she said, "They only put themselves under an ethnicity umbrella," by identifying as Dominican. Sandra did not know the difference between race and ethnicity until she got to college, she claimed; she always thought that Hispanic was a race. But she learned this distinction very quickly, in her first semester at college. In a friend's room, she got into a discussion with another student, a Haitian American who was born in the United States. "He kept saying to me, 'What are you? You don't know what you are. You're Black.'

"No, we're Hispanic."

"But what race are you?"

"We're Hispanic."

"But what *race* are you?"

"Hispanic."

"Hispanic isn't a race."

"This sat in the back of my brain," she said. Over time, she mulled it over and thought more and more about the student's comment. She began to pay attention to everything around her, how people were described and classified, and she realized that he was right. Hispanic was not a race, she discovered, because White and Black were races and she saw both of those among Hispanics. This realization made her uncomfortable as she recognized that she did not know what her race was. At that time, she felt that saying she was Black would have been like denying she was Hispanic. Other students put the question to her in dichotomous terms. "Are you White or Black?" they would ask. She decided that the best way to respond was by refusing to accept the premise. "Yes and yes," she would reply. Today, if someone asks what her race is, Sandra says, "Everything." "But," she would say to the person, "if what you want to know is where I'm from, I'm from the Dominican Republic." Like many of my respondents, Sandra recognizes the multiple layers of meaning in the question "What are you?" This recognition brings with it the burden of having to resolve the conflict in these different ways of classifying Hispanics.

Migrants with a college degree are particularly likely to adopt a biological definition of race, and to claim that Latino is not a race. Such views are common among those with higher education in their home countries as well, but migrant respondents who attend U.S. colleges also come to understand American concepts of race and ethnicity. During the interviews, I asked respondents how a child with one White American parent and one Black American parent would be classified in the United States. Migrants with a college degree were more likely to say that the child would be seen as Black or African American.[15]

Miguel, a Puerto Rican community liaison, explained, "I think that here there's a concept that if a person has even some percentage of blood of the Black class, legally they consider them Black, even if he looks completely White. . . . That's the custom here, and legally it's that way." College life and the mainstream workplaces that these migrants later enter provide substantive interaction with non-Latinos and begin the process of structural assimilation, which teaches them about the binary U.S. schema.

Policing the Boundaries of Whiteness

At the same time that college-educated migrants learn that Americans do not "officially" define Latino as a race, they also learn through their social interactions that Latinos, even those of European appearance, are not considered White by American standards. They experience a form of boundary maintenance around the most privileged racial category, such that many are excluded from the privileges of Whiteness that they experienced in their societies of origin. Hernando, who has dark skin, explained that being White means something different in the United States than in the Dominican Republic:

> Over there, we classify Whites [as those who are] lighter. But when we talk about Whites here, it could be the ones from here, Europeans like you or any other person. . . . If you're Italian, Irish, all of them, we call them White.
>
> Q: And if someone is Dominican with white skin?
>
> If we recognize that he's Hispanic, we can say, "Oh, this person is Dominican, let's not call him White." If he's Hispanic, we're not going to say, "You're White." . . . We categorize you based on where you come from. . . . When the Hispanics are here, it's the nationality [that matters], even if you look *rubia* [blond]. But if it's another race, we categorize them as White, Black. (Dominican migrant, business administrator)

Although migrants with higher education adopt a biological definition of race that is based primarily on skin color and appearance, they perceive an additional cultural layer that is not specified in such a definition. Only non-Latinos are allowed to be White, regardless of the physical and biological criteria.

Many light-skinned respondents arrived in the United States thinking of themselves as White. As they were corrected by those around them, their racialization brought an unpleasant shock. Among my respondents, it was largely those who were considered White back home who had the most difficulty with their American racialization, and they often described this as the most troubling of their migration experiences. Perhaps in contrast to years past, the racialization experience now creates greater conflict for those at the lighter end of the spectrum than those at the darker end. A Latino classification gives those who are darker a way to avoid being classified as Black, but those who were previously viewed as White experience a loss in status.

Carla learned that she is no longer seen as White through her interactions at college. She shared this experience early in the interview, before any explicit questions about race, in response to a general question about the most surprising aspect of U.S. life for her.

> The main change I noticed was that I—in my country, I'm very light in color. That is, very, very light among Dominicans. I even think that my personal identification card . . . said White. And actually I considered myself White before, until I came here. And later when I arrived here I realized that no, that I'm not White and that actually I realized what discrimination was, that is, being treated differently.

> Q: And how did you realize that you . . . aren't White?

> That happened one day when we were at the university, my friend and me. My friend is also Dominican and she is *negra*. We were studying at the university until very, very late and we wanted to go home. The university's campus is not very safe for women so what they told us was to call the security office and ask them to accompany us to our home. . . . So I called and they asked me how we looked so they can know, so I told them that we were two women and that one was Black and the other one White. And my friend who had lived in the U.S. for some time laughed and she told me, "Do you think that you're White?" And I—Oh, my God—I remember, it was a very important moment for me. I was a little embarrassed for considering myself White and it was like [a] realization, you know?

> Q: . . . And your friend was Dominican? . . . Did you have similar experiences with Americans?

> Yes, . . . I realized, when I went to the stores, that I was being treated differently than how they treated White people. And that hurt me a little bit. And . . . that experience creates a rage . . . yes, a rage inside you. (Dominican migrant, lawyer)

Miguel related a similar experience. A highly educated Puerto Rican whose light skin and European features would lead many to take him for a White non-

Latino, Miguel learned from coworkers that he, like other Puerto Ricans, is not considered White in the United States:

> It is a little disconcerting for us, people who were born in other places and were raised in other places, when we arrive here, and usually in our countries we think that there are people of Caucasian, Black, Asian race. And it's the biggest surprise when you come to New York and see that you don't qualify in any category that you thought you belong to. And you see there a change and you think for the first time that you are facing discrimination and crime because they don't consider you as you thought you were.

Q: Are you saying that they don't consider you White?

> [Yes.] I think it's that there's always a perception that Hispanics are another thing different than Caucasian. . . . I first realized [it] when I was . . . working as a teacher in a program in Brooklyn and in the summer we had assistants, students, and most of them were Black. And one day one of the girls told me, "Ah, you're the Puerto Rican that thinks he's White." And I was so surprised because until that moment I didn't think that there were any differences between [them], and then I learned that each thing is seen different. (Puerto Rican migrant, community liaison for public corporation)

Both Miguel and Carla describe their experience as "discrimination." In their eyes, discrimination consists of being treated differently (i.e., inferior) because of who you are, or who you are perceived to be. These were disturbing experiences for them, as the first time each was treated as a minority and excluded from a privileged social position they had held before.

American society has always guarded the privilege of Whiteness more zealously than any other social category.[16] Miscegenation laws and the principle of hypodescent were constructed to protect the privilege of those deemed racially "pure" enough to be White. New immigrant groups initially denied this status have been reclassified as White over time,[17] but entry to the legions of Whiteness is closely regulated, Blackness not at all. Marisela, a Dominican with brown skin, observed this double standard when I asked if Dominicans are ever confused for Americans, "For *moreno* Dominicans, Americans may confuse them on the streets. If it's a *blanco* [Dominican], they don't confuse them."

The everyday interactions, corrections, and reminders that light-skinned migrants experience are a form of boundary work, the means of policing the borders of Whiteness. Both Miguel and Carla describe being "corrected" not by a White American, but by another minority. Those outside the White category can explain the rules of the game more directly, but White Americans have their own forms of signaling. Carla notes how she was treated differently by sales clerks in stores. Miguel relates that once when trying to rent an apartment, the landlady told him as soon as he mentioned his name, "I don't rent to Hispanics."

In more subtle cases of boundary work, American coworkers or associates may use indirect slights or tokenism—treating an individual as a token representative of her minority group—to achieve the same effect. These subtle signals are easy to overlook or explain away. Angela, another light-skinned Dominican, considered herself White back home. Her family had been financially comfortable, and her color gave her a certain amount of status there. Coming to the United States was a hard experience, compounded by her loss of social status. For months, she slept on her aunt's couch, and she was frustrated to learn that she was treated as a minority. She nonetheless worked her way into college prep programs and to a prestigious liberal arts school and business school. She described the more overt forms of discrimination she experienced, but after the interview, her husband, John, reminded her of a few more subtle instances:

> John: With your boss, you were always like a World Vision child. Whenever he described your story, he acted as if she had a distended belly. And anytime she was meeting with other investors with her boss, who was the CEO, it was as if he had claimed her from the streets, you know, and had rescued her. He always acted as if she should owe everything to him. . . .
>
> Angela: You're exaggerating a little but—yeah. But I don't think that was because I was Dominican.
>
> John: Yeah, it was totally because you're from the Dominican Republic.
>
> Angela: . . . I don't know where [my boss] got this idea. Because I told him my story: I came here and I don't come from like a rich family, I mean I was very middle class. But I came here and I had to be on a sofa. . . . I didn't come like "Let me go to [an elite college]." You know, because I couldn't do that. Somehow, he just thought that I was a World Vision child. He said that I had a large belly, bare feet. I mean, I had a lot more advantage growing up there and going to a private school and all that than a kid here in Harlem even if he's American. (Dominican migrant, investment banker, and her husband)

Angela shrugs off her boss's condescending behavior and his use of inaccurate stereotypes. But in constantly repeating this exaggerated story to investors, her boss is subtly reinforcing Angela's status as an outsider, as someone who is "not quite one of us," despite her White appearance.

These experiences are about class as much as race. Those who have the most difficulty reconciling themselves to their U.S. classification are light-skinned migrants with higher social status. Light-skinned migrants with lower status may not expect privileged treatment because of their class location. For instance, Octavio, a light-skinned Puerto Rican parking garage attendant with a high school education, said that Americans sometimes think he is White until they hear him speak Spanish or hear his accent. But he enjoys these interactions, explaining, "When they confuse me with a White American, it makes me feel a little good because they're telling me that I'm American." Octavio does not expect to hold a privileged status, and he sees the instances where he can as a treat. Professional migrants with light skin, on the other hand, are the least accustomed to experiencing social stigma.

Although middle-class migrants perceive Americans as constructing symbolic boundaries to define them as non-White, we know that many Puerto Ricans and Dominicans do classify themselves as White on the census. In 2000, 47.2% of Puerto Ricans and 22.7% of Dominicans self-identified as White alone, and those of higher socioeconomic status are generally more likely to mark "White" than those of lesser status.[18] How can we reconcile this fact with the descriptions here of middle-class migrants expressing how they believe race is understood in the United States? Classifying oneself on the census created internal conflict for many middle-class respondents. They described having considerable difficulty determining what to do.[19] Hugo expressed this reaction. He used a Hispanicized U.S. schema on the photos, and a U.S./nationality hybrid on his social network—in both cases classifying Latinos by their nationality or panethnicity—and asserted throughout the interview that he is not classified as White in the United States. In open-ended terms, he identified his own race as *mestizo*. When I asked him to complete the race and Hispanic origin questions from the 2000 Census, he asserted:

> You're setting me up! . . . Because, yes, I am Puerto Rican, but I don't consider myself White. Obviously, the options that the questionnaire gives don't have anything like mixed, don't have anything like *trigueño*, which is what I consider myself. And the options that are given to me make me fill out what's closer to what I consider myself. (Puerto Rican migrant, IT manager)

Hugo eventually checked "White," despite insisting that he does not identify as White. But with his medium-light skin, he sees himself as closer to White than to Black. He saw this as the closest option available, since he recognizes that the census question does not treat Puerto Rican or Latino as a race.[20] Checking the box does not necessarily imply identification, or that this is how a person is viewed by others.[21]

Although some have argued that when Latinos check "White" or "Black" on the census race question they are accepting American racial classifications,[22] for many of my respondents, the two-question structure on the census confounds the issue because they see these questions as inseparable. Checking "Latino" on the Hispanic origin question, they claim, modifies a "White" or "Black" response on the race question. They do not see themselves as White or Black by American standards, nor do they believe they are viewed this way by others. A White Latino or Black Latino, in their minds, is racially different from a White or Black American. The fact that half of all Latinos check "White" on the census race question can therefore mislead those who believe the White category is expanding to include them; very few of them check "White" when "Latino" is listed as an option on a race question.[23] This is another reason why it is more valuable to examine racial schemas than racial self-identification on surveys; taking survey race responses at face value is likely to overestimate the number who, in checking "White," really view themselves as White in the United States.

The binary and Hispanicized U.S. schemas conflict around the treatment of Latinos, and middle-class migrants get caught in the middle of this contradiction. Significantly, although most have internalized a binary U.S. schema, very few of them use it on the photos. Even though they believe this schema has the imprimatur of the United States, it simply does not match the reality of what they experience. Most of these migrants opt for a Hispanicized U.S. schema on the photos, even though they see it as problematic, because it more closely resembles their daily experience. In the battle between the binary and the Hispanicized U.S. schemas, the latter, in their minds, wins out in terms of their racial reality in the United States.

Use of a Continuum Racial Schema

With the exception of the small number of highly educated Dominican migrants who use a continuum racial schema on the photographs, very few migrant respondents used the continuum terms on their own during the interview. Yet when asked about these terms and shown the list of items in Table 3 (in Chapter 1), most respondents recognized them and said they use them. Some respondents, like many in the sending societies, claimed that these terms were not about race, but only about color. Referring to the list of terms, César explained:

> The first thing that you see is the physical [appearance] . . . like, someone is more *trigueño* or *blanco* or *cano*. . . . I would say that these are more categories that Puerto Rican society has given based simply on skin color. . . . It's more skin color because it's understood that the race is Puerto Rican. . . . We are all Hispanics, Puerto Ricans, so that's why you classify by color.
>
> Q: *If we were in Puerto Rico now, and you had never lived here, would you still say that your race is Puerto Rican?*
>
> Yes, if they ask me what race I am, I always say Puerto Rican. All my life. If they ask what color I am, I say *blanco*. (Puerto Rican migrant, film producer)

Rafaela agreed, claiming that in the Dominican Republic there is only one race, Dominican. Pointing to the list of continuum terms, she said, "I saw that more as color. . . . I didn't think [of that] in terms of race, but only as the color of the skin. . . . I see race [as] more like culture and language." Because many migrants bring a cultural definition of race with them to the United States, the intermediate terms associated with the continuum schema do not fit their understanding of race.

Others, much like non-migrants, explained that they did not use these categories on the photos because they associate this taxonomy with casual social interchange among Latinos, not the type of classifications they made of the photos, or even something that would be appropriate in a formal setting like an interview. Before seeing the list of terms, Hugo revealed his awareness of different racial schemas that are used for different purposes, insisting that the continuum terms are a colloquial form of speech.

> Q: *People from each country have their own ideas about race and what race each person is. I would like you to think now about the words or terms that are used in Puerto Rico to describe people's race. Could you mention the categories you can remember?*
>
> Slang or the correct terms in Spanish?
>
> Q: *Is there a difference?*
>
> Yeah. Oh, yeah (laughing). . . . Slang in Puerto Rico, I'm talking about certain words that are only used in Puerto Rico. If you ask a Colombian, the Colombian won't know. In Puerto Rico, they talk about being *jabao*. *Jabao* is the person

that has White skin but has Black features . . . *negro, blanco, jabao* in slang. They also talk about, in Puerto Rico, being *trigueño. Trigueño* is mixed. . . . [But] *jabao* is slang. It's used on the street but it's not studied or in books. But you can ask any Puerto Rican what a *jabao* is and they'll be able to tell you. . . . This is colloquial. . . . You would not use this in surveys for doctoral theses (laughing). (Puerto Rican migrant, IT manager)

Hugo, like others, laughed throughout this conversation. It seemed funny to many respondents that I would even be asking about such informal slang expressions, illustrating that different schemas are triggered and used in different contexts, and bringing up a certain schema in an inappropriate context can seem like a social breach.

With the photos, my asking respondents to "classify" the race of each person triggers a different type of schema than what many think of as "descriptions" and "color." Migrant respondents do not think of the continuum terms as classifications. In the United States, classifications are what are imposed on them by Americans, evoking a different context for the application of labels than what migrants see themselves doing when they use the continuum terms. Juanita, a young Dominican who sells cell phones, explained:

Dominicans who live here, use [those terms]. Including [me], I have a friend that I call *negra*, and I call her in that way for affection. So we use that a lot, calling us by color. But we don't do it in the way they do it here, to make decisions or to fit you in a place that sometimes isn't [the right place]. And also in the way to treat people, making them feel that they are of this type. (Dominican migrant, salesperson)

Juanita sees the act of classifying as putting people in boxes where they may not see themselves fitting, such as on the census race question, and interacting with them on that basis. In her mind, the casual use of color terms and endearing nicknames do not have the same implications for how people are grouped and treated.

My presence in the interview also made the use of a continuum racial schema less appropriate. Most respondents insisted they use these terms only with other Latinos, and sometimes only other people of their own nationality, or people they know. This is both because they do not expect non-Latinos to understand the terms, and because they fear offending someone from a different cultural background. Respondents have learned that there is greater sensitivity to using explicit racial language in the United States than in their home cultures, and they are never sure how someone there is likely to react. Sylvaria expressed this caution in using the terms, and a sensitivity to even being asked about them.

> I never tend to put a stereotype to anybody. I treat them the same way. I mean, I never say to anyone, when we talk sometimes "*tu eres trigueña*," you are *trigueñita*, or whatever they say, we say. Or *negro* . . . We have more respect [than] to say that because we don't know if the person is offended. Or the person has a complex about it and somebody was humiliating them before. If we know the person, we could say it, or maybe in back of the person you would say it, but not in front of the person. . . . Because that could cause some tragedies or whatever. We're careful with that. (Puerto Rican migrant, community college counselor)

Like many respondents, Sylvaria initially insisted that she does not stereotype or treat people differently by using this colloquial language. They worry that some may see them as racist for even employing such expressions. Sylvaria's concern is to avoid offending, which leads her to use the terms privately, or with people she knows, but not in front of someone whose reaction she cannot anticipate. Antonio explained that this is one reason why my respondents may not use the continuum terms during the interviews, "I know that people use them. Sometimes people don't use them in public, outside of the Puerto Rican [group] . . . since race has become such a sensitive thing, people tend to be private about those things and I don't know if that is the reason why they [your respondents] may not have used them." In addition to the formality of the interview, and the use of words like "classify" and "race," respondents may be discouraged from using a continuum schema on the photos by an uncertainty about how a non-Latino will react to such language. As Antonio suggests, there may be one set of answers about people's races that is more commonly used in front of Americans, and another set that Puerto Ricans and Dominicans use among themselves.

For migrant respondents who spend much of their social or work life away from their ethnic community, the continuum terms have faded into the background of their racial schema portfolios. They are still familiar with the taxonomy and can define what most of the terms mean, but they do not use or hear them often. Antonio, who has been in New York for more than 50 years and lives in the gentrifying Chelsea neighborhood, was one of the few respondents who asked me to conduct the interview in English. He explained that he does not use the continuum terms much anymore. "Not that much now because

I've sort of separated, since my parents died, and my brothers and sisters, some of them are in Puerto Rico, I'm basically more alone here in New York, and all of my friends are English-speaking and even the Puerto Ricans that I know here are English-speaking. A lot of those terms are out of my vocabulary." Because respondents use this language primarily within their own ethnic group, those who spend less time among co-ethnics have shifted their language use accordingly. Those who have socially integrated with non-Latinos provide an example of how a schema within one's portfolio can fade from lack of use, but not fully disappear.

Symbolic Boundaries and Racial Schemas

The symbolic boundaries that are most meaningful to respondents influence the racial schemas that they adopt. It is for this reason that less-educated migrant respondents are more likely to use a nationality schema. Because more of their primary social relationships are with other Latinos, it is nationality and not Latino panethnicity that is important in differentiating one person from another in their social world. College-educated migrants have more opportunity to develop relationships with White and Black Americans, and those interactions reinforce the importance of the symbolic boundary between Latinos and non-Latinos. Panethnic identities become most prominent in that context, even for individuals who maintain that Latino is not a race. Thus, when Hugo identified every photo as Hispanic, African American, or White American, he was reflecting the distinctions that are important in his world with his American coworkers and friends. Migrants who work and study in the mainstream society are daily reminded of their status as Latinos by those who are not. Indicating the importance of this category, many middle-class Dominicans use panethnic labels on their social networks, identifying people whose nationalities they undoubtedly know only as Latino or Hispanic.

While strong class differences cut across nationalities in the types of schemas used, nationality differences reveal themselves in the variants of those schemas chosen, reflecting different kinds of symbolic boundaries established by Puerto Ricans and Dominicans. Puerto Rican respondents reveal a greater tendency to use only nationality terms in a variety of contexts, while Dominicans more often choose panethnic terms. Even college-educated Puerto Ricans who use a Hispanicized U.S. schema on the photos often use a U.S./nationality hybrid on their social networks, listing the nationalities of their Latino friends even as they distinguish Whites and Blacks. Among respondents with lower education, Puerto Ricans more often use a basic nationality schema on the photos, while Dominicans are somewhat more likely to use a panethnic nationality schema. The tendency is particularly clear in respondents' identification of their own race. Both in their responses to the U.S. census question and in their open-ended racial identifications, Puerto Rican respondents were more likely to identify their race just as Puerto Rican, while more than half of Dominican respondents identified their race as Latino or Hispanic.[24]

Puerto Rican respondents' tendency to emphasize nationalities, especially their own, derives from their political status and unique position among Latinos as U.S. citizens by birth. As such, Puerto Rican respondents take pride in emphasizing their national identity and distinguishing themselves from other Latinos.[25] Arsenio, a light-skinned Puerto Rican, is a recovering drug addict who supports himself through disability payments. Although he professes shame for his drug abuse and past criminal activities, his national identity is a source of self-esteem. He proudly asserted his racial identity as Puerto Rican and explained, "The Puerto Rican here, sometimes we think that we're better than others, that we have a higher social status, we're defined as majority and middle class. That's the definition in this country among Hispanics. Maybe Americans don't classify us like that, [but] we classify ourselves like that." While many Puerto Ricans have mixed feelings about their island's political status, migrants in the mainland U.S. recognize the advantage their position bestows upon them relative to other Latino migrants.

Being Puerto Rican provides instant immunity from the stereotype of Latinos as illegal immigrants. When Paulina hunts for an apartment or for a job, she brings her passport along to show that she is different from other Latinos—she is a U.S. citizen.

> When I, for example, was looking for a job, one of the recommendations that my sister gave me was go out with your passport, and I [said,] "What for? I'm a U.S. citizen, I don't need to." And she told me, "Go out with your passport," and the truth is that there was a time that I used it. Because I felt that in that moment I was placed in doubt and then it was like, I took out my passport and then the conversation turns in a completely different direction, "Oh, yes, well—!" And I thought, "Look at this! If I weren't a U.S. citizen they'd be looking at me badly." (Puerto Rican migrant, research coordinator)

Such an advantage can create tensions with members of other Latino groups, who may be jealous of Puerto Ricans' ability to freely enter the United States and find work. For example, Raimundo, a Dominican casual laborer, felt that Dominicans are in a worse situation because if they are arrested, they can be deported, even if they are in the country legally. But an American citizen, like a Puerto Rican, "he serves his sentence and he stays here. . . . They aren't going to deport him anywhere, but they deport us." This gives Puerto Ricans a strong incentive to assert their Puerto Ricanness and focus on these nationality differences within the Latino community.

Because of their unique status among Latinos, Puerto Rican respondents expressed less enthusiasm for the idea of uniting politically under a panethnic banner. They may recognize that certain benefits come from aligning their interests, but few Puerto Rican respondents spoke enthusiastically of the need for Latino unity. Dominicans, by contrast, while also proud of their nationality, expressed a stronger sense of panethnic identification and a desire for the political power that Latin American groups can gain by joining forces. Maura, a Dominican migrant in her 50s, identified as Latina, and maintained that all Latinos need to unite around this identity.

> I'm Latina. . . . It doesn't matter where you come from, if you're Latino, . . . you have to carry it up high. Being Latino is very important in this country. The Latino vote is very important and if we don't vote as Latinos we're doing very badly. I can't say just because I'm a citizen that I'm American. No, I'm not American—I'm a Latina. (Dominican migrant, prison official)

Maura associates a unified Latino identity with power, and perhaps status and respect that she would not otherwise have in the United States. This is why she, like other Dominicans, emphasizes and uses panethnic categories more often.

Encouraging panethnic solidarity is one way for Dominicans to confront feelings of hostility they experience from other Latinos. Some Dominicans feel that other groups, particularly Puerto Ricans, look down on them. Prejudices are imported from the countries of origin; the Dominican minority in Puerto Rico is stigmatized both racially and for the perception that Dominicans are illegal immigrants. It is not uncommon for Dominicans to enter Puerto Rico illegally, sailing the 75 miles that separates the islands on makeshift rafts in search of better opportunities or passage to the mainland United States. Dominicans in Puerto Rico are concentrated in poor neighborhoods, have high rates of poverty, and suffer considerable discrimination.[26] Other tensions between Puerto Ricans and Dominicans develop in New York, as territorial issues arise from the influx of Dominicans into a traditionally Puerto Rican locale.

Puerto Ricans' political status leads them to emphasize national labels more than panethnic ones, because they draw a symbolic boundary around nationality to distinguish themselves from other Latino groups who lack such political and civic advantages. Such boundary work affects the different variants of a nationality schema—encouraging their use of a basic rather than a panethnic nationality schema—more than the type of schema. Class differences play a stronger role in influencing the types of schemas, suggesting that while nationality is important, class is a more powerful structure in organizing migrants' lives.

Conclusion

Chiqui Vicioso's famous quote—"Until I came to New York, I didn't know I was Black"—captured the experience of many Puerto Rican and Dominican migrants to New York in the mid-20th century. Upon arriving in the mainland U.S., these migrants encountered a new system of racial classification that emphasized the polarity between Black and White. Those with darker phenotypes had to cope with a new racial classification, one that was highly stigmatized in their societies of origin and in their new home. Scholars have focused on this contrast between continuous and dichotomous racial systems, and the potential problems for Puerto Rican and Dominican migrants who find themselves reclassified as Black in the United States.[27] Yet the dissonance of reconciling the racial labels from their home society and their new host society has largely diminished for the darker-skinned Puerto Ricans and Dominicans I interviewed. With a growing Latino population, a Hispanicized U.S. schema is effectively replacing the binary U.S. schema in popular usage, creating a changing context of reception in New York. While skin color and appearance still affect how migrants are initially seen, signals such as language, accent, dress, and name trigger a racial classification as Latino or a member of a specific Latino group.

Migrant respondents learn from their casual interactions, American mass media and popular culture, and even some government sources that they are classified in the United States as Latino or as a Latino nationality. These categories conform to the cultural definition of race that many Dominicans and Puerto Ricans bring with them from their home country. When claiming that Dominicans and Puerto Ricans have largely failed to adopt an "Americanized" view of race because they check "Some Other Race" rather than "White" or "Black" on the census, scholars operate with a conception of "Americanized" race that differs from migrants' experiences of it. The scholarly view focuses on the binary U.S. schema represented in the census, and the view that Latino is an ethnicity, not a race. Yet when migrants write in "Latino" or their nationality on the census—as when they adopt racial schemas that classify people in national and panethnic terms—they believe they *are* adopting an American view of race.

They are using the classifications that they experience every day in a city where they believe they are not seen by Americans as either White or Black.

Migrants in New York have a Hispanicized U.S. schema available to them in part because they helped bring it into being. Their growing presence, their own use of the nationality schema and cultural definitions of race, and the boundary work conducted both by them and by White and Black Americans to distinguish their groups from one another, have helped to give Latino nationality and panethnic labels a racial status. Some have argued that U.S. racial stratification has become "Latin Americanized," with more of a tri-racial ordering of groups now than a bi-racial hierarchy between Black and White.[28] Yet it is not only the number of categories that has changed; even American conceptions of what race means have become Latin Americanized. Americans, too, seem to think of races in terms of cultural groups rather than groups distinguished by socially designated biological characteristics. The idea that Latinos are a distinct race, cross-cutting appearance to include those who look European and African as well as those who look mixed, is influenced by the cultural definition of race that Latin American migrants bring with them to the United States. Racial acculturation works as a two-way street, a melting pot, rather than immigrants' simply conforming to the dominant American culture. Latino migrants contribute a new racial schema—the Hispanicized U.S. schema—to the U.S. racial repertoire, without necessarily adopting it themselves.

4 Transnational Diffusion

AN IMPORTANT CHARACTERISTIC OF PUERTO RICAN AND DOMINICAN MIGRATION—and of migration by many Latin American and other immigrant groups—is the active transnational connections that link the sending and receiving societies.[1] Migrants frequently communicate with family and friends who remain in the home country, send gifts and money, return to visit, or spend periods of time living in each society.[2] Some are even involved in the political activities of their home society from abroad, run transnational businesses, or participate in cultural activities and exchanges that connect the two societies.[3] With so many Puerto Ricans and Dominicans living in the mainland U.S. yet straddling borders in these ways, the migrant experience and the host society that colors it are an everyday presence in the lives of those who stay behind.[4]

Immigration research often focuses on how migration affects the ethnic and racial identities of migrants and their children, as well as the classification system of the society that receives them.[5] We expect individual migrants to be changed by living in a new society and for that new society to be changed by their presence. Yet there is considerably less focus on the way mass migration also influences the racial concepts and classifications of the non-migrants left behind.[6] The focus on the receiving society rests on the traditional view of migration as a one-way process, neatly divided into "before" and "after" a single act of relocation. Yet for many migrant groups—including Dominicans and Puerto Ricans—migration is not a single act, but an ongoing, transnational way of life. Therefore the experiences of the migrants slowly influence the culture of their home society, including its concepts of race and ethnicity.

In this chapter, I examine how concepts of race and ethnicity are shaped transnationally and, drawing upon scholarship on cultural diffusion,[7] explore how processes of mass migration and globalization can diffuse racial categories and schemas. Focusing on concepts of panethnicity, U.S. racial schemas, and Americanized notions of Whiteness and Blackness, I show how concepts of race and ethnicity that are formed in the mainland U.S. are sent back to migrants' societies of origin and layer additional racial schemas onto those that non-migrants already maintain. These rarely replace their existing concepts; when non-migrants add such remitted ethnic and racial constructs to their racial schema portfolios, they use them in specific situations, often where environmental cues trigger an awareness of the United States or how they are seen outside their society. Cultural diffusion across borders is thus another way that individuals come to maintain and use multiple racial schemas simultaneously.

This transnational diffusion occurs through specific mechanisms. One such mechanism is migrants' *social remittances*—interpersonal exchanges that communicate the ideas, practices, and identities they learn in the host society back to people in the society of origin. Sociologist Peggy Levitt found that Dominican immigrants in Boston adopted more liberal ideas about women's roles from their involvement in the workplace and the public sphere. They communicated these ideas to women in their home community, who began to embrace new gender identities.[8] Similar individual-level exchanges communicate concepts of race and ethnicity. Diffusion also occurs at the macro level, through a globalized mass media. Mass migration promotes the development of international business ties and media infrastructure, creating media markets that span national boundaries. As news, television programs, and films created for one national audience are broadcast to others, the categories and concepts conveyed within them also spread.

But neither the diffusion of new racial schemas to the sending society nor their addition to non-migrants' portfolios means that non-migrants will regularly adopt these new schemas. For widespread cultural change to occur in a nation's racial constructs, those schemas have to be relevant for individuals' daily lives, typically because the symbolic boundaries that are embedded within them have become meaningful for non-migrants as well as the migrant population. Symbolic boundaries that differentiate migrants from their host society population can become salient for non-migrants as they, too, come to draw boundaries between their own group and this foreign population. Transnational communications, globalization, and political and institutional connections can bring that foreign population increasingly into the national imagination. If the symbolic boundaries become strong enough that non-migrants regularly de-fine themselves relative to that foreign population, then racial schemas reflect-ing them will become used often enough to effect a noticeable cultural shift in concepts of race or ethnicity. I argue that this is occurring around non-migrant Puerto Ricans' adoption of Latino panethnicity and their use of racial schemas that include a Latino category.

Examining differences between Puerto Ricans and Dominicans in their adoption and use of new racial schemas reveals the role played by Puerto Rico's political status in fostering cultural diffusion. Foreign colonial powers have always served as a reference group in the formation of racial and ethnic boundaries by the societies they dominate, and Puerto Rico's relationship to the United States is no different. Yet while the construction of a *Puerto Rican* racial category, embraced by so many non-migrant respondents, may stem in part from this political affiliation, the political relationship does not necessitate adoption of a *panethnic* category. Given the origins of Latino panethnicity in the shared experience of marginalization in the United States, this is a concept that has diffused from the U.S. diaspora rather than one created by the fact of Puerto Rico's political affiliation. That affiliation plays an indirect rather than a direct role in fostering the adoption of panethnicity, and to a lesser extent U.S. racial schemas, in Puerto Rico. As a result of its political status, Puerto Rico is more economically developed, receives more American media, and has greater institutional ties to the United States than does the Dominican Republic, all of which support the diffusion of American racial concepts. Thus, while Puerto Rico's political status places it at the far end of a continuum of development and globalization, these patterns have relevance for many other immigrant-sending nations.

Latino Panethnicity in the Sending Societies

Latino panethnicity—the extension of ethnic boundaries to incorporate many Latin American groups that previously considered themselves distinct ethnici-ties—is associated with the ethnic experience in the United States. The pan-ethnic label Hispanic began to be widely used in the early 1970s as an official designation by U.S. state agencies to identify people of Latin American and Spanish descent living in the United States.[9] When different Latin American groups arrive, the Hispanic category is ascribed upon them by Americans who fail to recognize their diverse origins and histories.[10] At first, they accommodate this ascription, assuming the label because their host society organizes itself around such classifications, but without necessarily accepting it. However, such panethnic categories also serve as a basis for political mobilization, allowing diverse people to recognize their shared grievances and fight for a common agenda. As diverse ethnic groups mobilize around their common structural conditions, they create cultural solidarity that leads many to identify with those panethnic labels as well.[11]

In their home countries, however, these groups are the majority society, leading many to believe that Latino and Hispanic classifications are irrelevant to their lives in their home societies. Scholars state that "Latino panethnicity is something created in the United States"[12] and "is largely a phenomenon of American urban life."[13] Latin American historian Miguel Tinker Salas states, "Rarely do Mexicans, Venezuelans, Puerto Ricans or Peruvians, within their own countries refer to themselves as Hispanic or Latino."[14]

Yet my non-migrant respondents—particularly in Puerto Rico—regularly used and embraced a Latino classification. This was not merely an expression of *latinidad* or pan–Latin Americanism that developed independently in the region;[15] non-migrants used labels and reference categories that come from the United States. The use of a panethnic category cuts across the racial schemas I have identified; it appears in both the Hispanicized U.S. schema and the panethnic nationality schema. In fact, the vast majority of Puerto Rican non-migrant respondents and a sizable minority of the Dominican non-migrant respondents used a panethnic category while classifying the photos, even though they used different racial schemas while doing so.[16] And in describing how they came to adopt these categories, respondents revealed the influence of American mass media and the migrant communities abroad.

In Puerto Rico, the use of Latino panethnic terminology is widespread. For example, a local business near my San Juan residence called itself "Latino Dry Cleaners." One of my Puerto Rican research assistants suggested that I omit interview questions about whether people use terms like "Hispanic" or "Latino"; the terms are so widespread, she said, that people would think the questions were silly. Yet the interviews proved valuable in revealing how Puerto Rican non-migrant respondents understand the Latino category.

Many respondents who used a cultural definition of race viewed the category Latino as representing the cultural traditions and values that connect the people of Latin America, including those who have migrated elsewhere. It encompasses language, food, traditions, and music. Despite internal differences within the region, respondents also see shared cultural elements, especially in comparison to groups outside Latin America. Leandro is a 45-year-old supervisor at a large factory. He used a panethnic nationality schema on the photos and classified everyone in his social network as "Hispanic." He feels a strong cultural bond with other Latin Americans, including those living in the United States. As he has learned more about different Latino groups, their common identification as Latinos and shared tastes, he has come to see himself and all Puerto Ricans as part of a broader panethnic group.

> For me, as a child, race . . . wasn't Hispanic or Latino race, it was Puerto Rican
> race. So I expanded my education and I was able to understand that we are
> all Hispanic and Latino. . . . For example, I can know that Panamanians think
> a lot like us, that Mexicans see us as their equals . . . in the sense of being
> Hispanic, of race, of being Latin American. I can tell you that I can go to Texas,
> for example, and I sit at a table to eat with some Mexicans, with some Cubans,
> with some Panamanians and we can eat the same thing. We don't have differ-
> ences in . . . tastes because we are raised more or less in the same way. (Puerto
> Rican non-migrant, factory supervisor)

Leandro's sense of cultural unification with non–Puerto Rican Latinos closely resembles descriptions of panethnicity expressed by Latinos in the United States. Significantly, Leandro developed this conception at the age of 16 or 17, before he had ever traveled outside Puerto Rico or known any Mexicans, Panamanians, or Cubans. He broadened the boundaries of his group iden-tification without having personal interactions with other Latino groups to support the shift.

Other Puerto Ricans who privilege a biological definition of race associate what it means to be Latino with physical characteristics such as racial mixture. Pablo, who used a panethnic nationality schema to identify the photos as La-tino, American, and Puerto Rican, explained why he would classify someone as Latino.[17] In doing so, he drew on a racialized construct.

> I can classify her as Latina because I see mixes. She can have something that's at-
> tributed to the White race, she can have something that's attributed to the Black
> race, but she has everything mixed together represented in one single thing. I
> can't leave it in limbo, so how can I classify it? Well, it's within what happened
> to us here. It's within the Latino. (Puerto Rican non-migrant, billing clerk)

Pablo described a similar concept in classifying his own race on the U.S. Census question, saying, "I had to [write "Latino"] down here, because I'm not White or Black . . . I'm Latino . . . because the Latinos among all of Latin America have different mixes." Instead of describing these racial mixtures as particular nationalities, as many others do, he associates them with the racial mixture that all Latin Americans share. Thus, non-migrant respondents differ in how they define the Latino category; much as they do with nationality, some adopt a biological definition, while others adopt a cultural definition.

In the Dominican Republic, considerably fewer respondents use panethnic terms to identify others, although almost all recognize such terms when asked. Most say the terms are rarely used in the Dominican Republic, and apply primarily to those living in the United States, typically used by Americans. Rodolfo's view is typical of Dominican respondents from all backgrounds:

> When you go to a different country you're already Latino . . . because here in my country I'm Dominican. . . . We're Dominicans.
>
> Q: Okay. So here, people don't say, "We are Latinos."
>
> No. I've never heard it here. Only when you go to another country, [do they say] "the Latinos". . . . But I've never heard a Dominican say "I'm Latino" in the Dominican [Republic]. Only "I'm Dominican." (Dominican non-migrant, part-time social work assistant)

Dominicans recognize the term, but it does not have salience for them in their own society.

The few Dominicans who did use Latino labels in classifying others or embraced those identities themselves were often those with the strongest personal connections to migrants in the United States. For instance, Pilar, who identifies herself as Latina, is married to a Dominican migrant who splits his time between New York and Santo Domingo. Herberto, a retired government accountant, used panethnic categories in classifying the photos; he speaks with his sister in Florida every week and has visited her there many times. Although such Dominicans are in the minority, those who adopt panethnic terms typically attribute these terms to the influence of their close relatives abroad.

Among *migrant* respondents in New York, more Dominicans than Puerto Ricans use panethnic categories and identify their own race as Latino rather than as their nationality. Among *non-migrant* respondents, these patterns are reversed; more Puerto Ricans than Dominicans use a panethnic nationality schema than a basic nationality one, and embrace a panethnic identity. In the U.S. context, while Puerto Ricans emphasize their unique privileges as citizens, Dominicans gain status from being part of a larger panethnic group. But in the sending society, few Dominican non-migrants use or identify with a panethnic label. Many strongly embrace their national, Dominican identity, and while they recognize what it means to be Latino, this panethnic label has little resonance for them. Manuel, who earns money from odd jobs fixing electronic equipment in Santo Domingo, said of the Latino label, "It has a meaning, but it's not, you don't carry that so deep inside, as a person with that pride. You don't carry it like that, not as you would say your nationality."

Mechanisms of Diffusion

How are panethnic categories that developed in the United States extended to non-migrants? Interviews and ethnographic observations reveal two important mechanisms. Messages are transmitted at the macro level through the mass media, particularly a growing transnational media that broadcasts the same programming to Latinos in the United States and to Latin American markets. At the micro level, messages are spread through communication between individuals in the home and host societies.

Scholars argue that the mass media have effectively shaped and reshaped national and transnational identities.[18] Concepts of race and ethnicity are communicated through television and radio programming, music, and the press. Media outlets may also act as "panethnic entrepreneurs"—organizations with a vested interest in fostering panethnicity that do so through their products.[19] Here, I focus on television media and show how multinational Spanish-language television networks act as panethnic entrepreneurs, spreading panethnicity across borders.

Anthropologist Arlene Dávila argues that Spanish-language television and marketing shape concepts of Latino identity in the United States by creating a homogenized panethnic culture that overlooks internal differences among Latinos.[20] National media define and promote a single concept of *latinidad*, emphasizing what are seen as cultural commonalities among Latino nationalities. Material is presented in a generic Spanish with national references expunged, and newscasters lose their accents to hide their national origins. Networks such as Telemundo and Univisión—literally, "One Vision"—deliberately promote a model of panethnicity to Latinos across the United States to broaden their markets by eliminating the need for culturally specific material.

The same programs that promote a homogenized concept of Latino panethnicity in the mainland U.S. also broadcast in Puerto Rico and the Dominican Republic (and many other Latin American countries). In Puerto Rico, Telemundo and Univisión are the dominant networks on terrestrial (i.e., non-cable) television, reaching the vast majority of the population.[21] Puerto Rico's broadcast media infrastructure is relatively well developed as a result of its close ties with the United States. For many years, the island has had nearly universal television penetration (in 2000, 98 percent of households had a television).[22] In January 2006, nine of the top ten programs in Puerto Rico were on Telemundo and Univisión.[23]

The Dominican Republic's telecommunications industry developed relatively late. Largely controlled by Trujillo until his death, new national channels began to emerge in the 1970s.[24] As late as 1991 only 53.3 percent of Dominican households had a television. As out-migration expanded in the late 1990s and migrants remitted significant amounts of money back to the country, this situation quickly changed. By 1997 the percentage of households with a television rose to 83.0 percent.[25] However, Telemundo and Univisión are available only on cable, which is accessed by a small minority. Only some of those networks' programs are transmitted on local channels.

Importing television programming is nothing new in these countries; transnational media corporations and local stations have long imported programs, such as *telenovelas* (soap operas) and other popular shows from Mexico, Venezuela, or other producer nations. Similarly, a media emphasis on the migrant diaspora and on Latin American populations elsewhere is a common feature of local media.[26] But in terms of cultural influence, non-migrants feel the United States has the strongest impact. Geraldo, a Dominican political campaigner, bemoaned the invasive cultural influence that he saw North American television and music playing for Dominican youth. When I asked whether he saw this influence as stronger than that from other Latin American countries, he replied, "Of course, the U.S. is the empire. Most people want to be like them. Nobody wants to be Puerto Rican or Haitian or Cuban." Furthermore, with multinational media corporations expanding their reach in Spanish-speaking markets in both Latin America and the United States, programs are increasingly created to appeal simultaneously to an audience of both migrants and non-migrants. This is achieved by promoting the same expansive definition of Latino panethnicity beyond U.S. borders.

In non-migrants' discussions of how they learn what "Latino" means, Puerto Rican respondents frequently referred to the media, particularly popular television shows that target multinational audiences, such as *Despierta America, Primer Impacto, Laura, Sabado Gigante, El Show de Cristina,* and *El Gordo y la Flaca*—all of which appear on Univisión and Telemundo. The variety shows depict various Latino groups, promoting what producers describe as shared cultural elements. News programs regularly feature segments on different Latin American nations, as well as Latinos in the United States. Earlier, Leandro described his sense of connection to Latinos throughout the world, a sense he developed at a young age, before he had traveled outside Puerto Rico. Explaining how this happened, he placed a heavy emphasis on the mass media:

> Okay, I can tell you: through media of communication, through reading, through the press. . . . I like to watch international news in Spanish that review[s] the happenings in the Latin American countries and through that you learn about everything.

> *Q: And all of these sources—the press, television, the news—are about Latin American countries. They're not about the U.S.?*

> I see a lot about the U.S. through cable and I make comparisons. . . . Right now they talk a lot about the Hispanic race . . . immigrants, the problem of legal documentation in the U.S., about hard times these people go through when they get to the U.S. without documentation. . . . And you start identifying with that mass of Hispanics that are Spanish-speaking that look like you physically. . . . For example, I never go to sleep without watching *Primer Impacto.* Why? . . . Because they review everything that happens with Latin Americans in the U.S. Not what's going on in Mexico or what's happening in Panama. No, what happens in the U.S. with Hispanics. (Puerto Rican non-migrant, factory supervisor)

Many respondents in Puerto Rico explained that they began to see Latinos as a race because of these television programs that promote a sense of familiarity among all Latin Americans.

Many Puerto Rican non-migrants learned about other Latino groups from these shows and came to see themselves as part of a Latino group. Roberto was one of my research assistants and also a non-migrant who would have been eligible for the study. He described how these television programs familiarize him with other Latinos:

> We're creating, all of the Latinos are creating, like the same culture even if we don't live in the same country.

> *And why does this happen? Many people here don't travel outside the country. How does that happen?*

> I consider that [it's] television . . . it's like a continuous voyage of people. You turn on the television and Don Francisco can take you in *Sábado Gigante* . . . to Chile, Guatemala. Therefore, I know that in Mexico there are pyramids, and I've never been to Mexico. . . . And I know many cultures and many foods that are

eaten in different countries and I've never visited them, but I've visited through the television. And the television is the connection of Latin America, that "look, you're Latino just like me."

> *Despierta America* is on . . . Univisión from Puerto Rico, and it's a program that's made in Miami. . . . There are two Mexicans, one Puerto Rican, one Honduran. . . . It's a program that presents the life of Latinos in New York. And every time there's a reporter and she's in a place . . . she says, "Here we are with the Latina community from Long Island," or. . . " the Latina community from Florida". . . . And they present people who are like us, who speak Spanish, who are in the U.S., they're the Latina community. Therefore [Puerto Ricans] say, "Well, if they're the Latino community, then I'm Latino." (Puerto Rican non-migrant, research assistant)

The global focus on Latino communities unifies these groups. However, Roberto noted, it also reinforces boundaries between them and everyone else. "All the messages that are coming, all our programs, present us as the Latino race. Every time there are Billboard Awards, there's the *Latino* Billboard Awards. There's the category of *Latino* rap music, category of *Latino* pop music. . . . And 'that's yours. Mine is pop music, yours is *Latino* pop music'" [emphasis his]. By heightening their awareness of group boundaries, foreign producers create new reference categories that shape Puerto Ricans' classifications, even in their own country.

Multinational programming was mentioned less often by Dominicans. Those who did mention similar programs typically did so in the context of explaining how they hear the term "Latino." Often Dominicans took away from these programs a sense of racial classification in the United States, but few felt the programs affected identities or classifications in their country. Pilar described how she hears the word "Latino."

> I hear it a lot on the television, in the press. . . . Every time they talk about race, they talk about the Latino race. . . . On the news shows they almost always [say] Black, Latino, White. . . . They show a lot of programs from the U.S.: from Univisión and all that. . . . I like the news, *Primer Impacto.* . . . You find out about things that happen there. (Dominican non-migrant, domestic worker)

Such media coverage often conveys the sense that panethnic labels are ascribed by Americans to differentiate Latinos from the rest of society. Marcela, a part-time office worker in her 20s, said she learned about panethnic labels from American television programs where the police are chasing a thief and identify him as a "Latino male suspect." From this, she concluded that Dominicans are seen as Latinos by Americans. The media bring panethnic labels into Dominican non-migrants' consciousness, but these labels simply do not resonate for them.

Panethnic identities are also communicated at the individual level, through social remittances from those in the sending societies. Because so many migrants maintain transnational lifestyles, most non-migrant respondents have friends or relatives in the United States and keep in frequent contact. Puerto Rican and Dominican respondents have similar amounts of contact with their U.S. ties by phone or e-mail. But the groups differ with respect to visits to the United States. Facing no entry restrictions, every Puerto Rican respondent except one had visited the mainland. Several non-migrant Puerto Ricans respondents said they typically visit a few times a year, and have visited between 50–100 times. By contrast, most Dominican respondents had never visited the mainland U.S., and for those who had, the number of visits was much lower, typically three trips or fewer.

For the communication of concepts of race and ethnicity, in-person contact and firsthand experience have a more powerful impact than word-of-mouth transmission or contact by telephone or writing. Respondents with the most frequent face-to-face contact with their U.S. ties typically use panethnic classifications more and express the strongest panethnic identification. Through their observations during these visits and their communication with friends while there, they learn firsthand that their group is classified in the United States as Latino, and many migrants come to self-identify this way. Because of their citizenship status, Puerto Rican non-migrants have more firsthand experience in the United States than Dominicans non-migrants do.

Isandro, the Puerto Rican income tax auditor profiled at the beginning of the book, attributed his own Latino identity to what he has learned from his vast network of between 50 and 100 relatives on the mainland: his family told him that Latinos are a separate group, a race in the middle, because they are not White or Black.

> Q: And do you think that the Americans . . . accept you as being a race in the middle?

> I think so, yes. Because they're even considering them even for matters of politics, for the votes. So, it's like they take them into consideration as a special group, or a group apart. . . . Over there, you're either one thing or another. . . . White, Black, or Latino. . . . Even if you're White [and] you speak Spanish

or whatever, they don't tell you that you're White. They say that you're Latino.
(Puerto Rican non-migrant, tax auditor)

Through his many visits to the United States, Isandro has observed the similarities of different Latino groups firsthand because his migrant networks
broadened his contact with other Latin Americans. He has become close to his
Mexican stepmother, his Colombian sister-in-law, and their extended families,
reinforcing his Latino identity as well as his sense that they are all seen as the
same race by Americans.

U.S. visits also provide firsthand experience of the discrimination that Latinos face there. The only time Rubén, a Puerto Rican college student, experienced discrimination was during his one visit to the mainland. On a trip to
Chicago, his band entered a music store to buy instruments. A White American
salesperson refused to sell to them, and Rubén claimed it was because they were
Puerto Ricans. Even without sustained group interactions from living in the
United States, visits help non-migrants learn about the marginalized treatment
that Latinos can experience.

Additional information about U.S. life comes from return migrants. Most
non-migrant respondents have friends or relatives who lived in the United
States for a time but returned to their country of origin, so they regularly interact with people who have experienced U.S. society firsthand. Nearly all Puerto
Rican respondents described return migrants as friends; with earlier mass migration streams, return migrants' observations about U.S. classifications have
spread within Puerto Rican society. Discussing why so many Puerto Rican non-
migrants identify as Latinos, Roberto attributed it in part to widespread return
migration and communication with migrants.

> What happens is that since Puerto Rico had already experienced a cultural
> shock in the '50s, with all the people who had emigrated to the U.S., and by
> those people coming to Puerto Rico, they brought, perhaps in the '60s, this
> classification, saying that "in the U.S. . . . we aren't Blacks or Whites. Over
> there, they treat us in a different way. You know, we don't live in the White
> neighborhood or in the Black neighborhood, we live in our own neighbor-
> hood, of the Latinos, of the Puerto Ricans or of the Dominicans, or of any
> Latino. . . . Over there we're Latinos." . . . And it's like it's continued to be said.
> It's continued to be passed from generation to generation, and when I was
> born, we already knew that we were Latinos in the U.S. or in the whole world.
> (Puerto Rican non-migrant, research assistant)

During their years in the mainland U.S., migrants become accustomed to being viewed as Latinos, and many embrace a panethnic identity. On their return to Puerto Rico, they use this classification when talking with people who have never lived outside the island, and thus reinforce the use of the category in the island's taxonomy.

Dominican non-migrants also hear from their connections abroad and from return migrants how Dominicans are treated in the United States, and they frequently hear the term "Latino." Friends and neighbors tell stories about their own migrant ties, and stories about the diaspora circulate and become part of the cultural landscape. Word-of-mouth information abounds as people even chat about Dominicans abroad with strangers in public places. I frequently overheard conversations on street corners and buses that involved the migrant diaspora. In Santo Domingo, a cheap form of transportation is the *carros pú-blicos*, cars that drive up and down the major avenues allowing as many people as possible to crowd in for a few pesos apiece. During this imposed intimacy, passengers chat amiably with the strangers wedged next to them. Even in this forum, I heard stories about Dominicans' lives in the United States and how they are treated, permitting a flow of information about the migrant experience that may be several degrees removed from a personal transnational connection. Yet non-migrants are less likely to adopt new concepts or identities from these casual exchanges than through personal interaction with known sources.[27] Such mediated experiences do not have the same impact as the closer, firsthand connections and personal observations that more Puerto Ricans describe.[28]

Resonance with Symbolic Boundaries

Whether or not imported categories of race and ethnicity are adopted in new places depends upon how much they resonate or conflict with meaningful symbolic boundaries within those societies. Transnational migration and globalization have made awareness of U.S. society a feature of daily life in the Dominican Republic as well, but in Puerto Rico, Americans have become a ubiquitous racial and ethnic reference category. Puerto Rico's long-standing political association with the United States has institutionalized such relative comparisons. Not only do Americans conduct boundary work to differentiate themselves from Latinos; Puerto Ricans also construct symbolic boundaries to differentiate themselves from Americans. This heightens Puerto Rican non-migrants' consciousness of racial classifications—and how they themselves are classified—beyond their own society.

Benjamín, a Puerto Rican respondent in his 70s, conveyed a sense of Puerto Rico's dependence on the United States and how the U.S. is a frame of reference for non-migrants.

Q: How did you start to see Latinos as a race?

Well, I don't know. For me it's always been a race. What happens here is . . . we don't pay it too much mind because we depend on the U.S. The U.S. gives us everything here.

Q: Have you heard that people in the U.S. talk about or see the Latinos as a race?

Well, because in the U.S. . . . . they try to put Latinos apart, you know. They want to keep their race apart. . . . And what happens? My brother suffered a lot in the United States. You can't imagine what he suffered because of segregation. (Puerto Rican non-migrant, retired factory worker)

Much of what Benjamín has learned about racial classifications in the United States has come from social remittances from his brother, who suffered severe discrimination in pre–civil rights America because of his dark skin. Yet because of Puerto Rico's dependence on the United States, the boundaries that separate migrants like Benjamín's brother from Americans are felt in Puerto Rico too.

Americans are constructed as the cultural "other" as well as the racial one. The same cultural distinctions that cause Puerto Ricans to differentiate themselves from Americans can also reinforce a positive pan-Latino identification. Pablo explained.

When you have the opportunity, when you integrate yourself to the U.S., . . . you notice that you don't have any cultural similarity with those people. Outside of the dollars and the Burger Kings and the McDonald's. . . . But in essence, you get into the culture and their way of eating is different, their way of thinking is different, their way of going about is different, totally, although we have a hundred-year relationship with them. You hop to any country in Latin America, where you've never gone in your life, and you find something that has to do with you, with your way of thinking, with your way of relating, with your way of eating, something with the music. . . . You fall in there and starting with the language, even if they have different things, you can begin to familiarize with things and you feel that those people have things in common with you, even if they've never had a relationship with your country. (Puerto Rican non-migrant, billing clerk)

Just as migrants' experiences with panethnicity in the United States may begin with ascription by others and develop into a cultural identification, non-migrants also become aware of Latino panethnicity as a boundary constructed by Americans, yet they reconstruct and embrace its meaning as they engage in boundary work of their own.

Curious as to how my presence, as an American, influenced respondents' use of panethnic categories, I discussed this theme at length with my research assistants. Roberto provided a native Puerto Rican's take on why non-migrants use Latino panethnic categories even in Puerto Rico, where almost everyone else is also Latino. He suggested that, like racialized nationality labels, the panethnic categories are not used as much by our respondents when they are conversing with other Puerto Ricans in San Juan. But the interview, and my presence, evoked the symbolic boundaries that respondents draw with the United States, and their awareness of their own position in a global classification system, one that references America's cultural influence worldwide.

I think that the Puerto Rican says he's Latino because when he sees himself—worldly, on the outside—he doesn't have any other category. When a Puerto Rican travels to the U.S., he's not White, like the White Americans, the Anglo-Saxons. Nor is he Black, like the Black North Americans. Another category of people comes in, that the Americans themselves classified them as Latinos. . . . Therefore, a Puerto Rican in the U.S. considers himself Latino, before the world.

And in Puerto Rico, even though he knows he's Latino, he . . . doesn't commonly call himself Latino. Here, he does classify himself as White, Black, *trigueñito*, *blanquito*, *cano*, but he only classifies himself in that way when he's with people like him, when he's with Puerto Ricans, when he's with Latinos. But when he exposes himself to a different reality than the one that's there in Puerto Rico, when he begins to live in the U.S. or in another part of the world, he already comes with his Latino race. Because it's like the only category that he's allowed to be in the U.S.

. . . . The Latinos almost have two classifications and it's very difficult because of that. It's because if you're Black, you say, "I'm Black" and that's it. And if you're White, "I'm White" and that's it. But if you're Latino, . . . if they ask you, "What are you?" because it's not only the race that I'm going to be here in Puerto Rico, it's the race that I'm going to be if I travel, the race that if I'm in Japan, I say, "I'm Latino," if I'm in the U.S. I say, "I'm Latino," that's like your race. But we also have another race within the Latino. (Puerto Rican non-migrant, research assistant)

What Roberto expressed is Puerto Ricans' dual consciousness of their race at home and abroad. Another way to describe this is as multiple racial schemas—one that operates in their own society and refers to internal racial distinctions that they draw within their population, and another that operates on a broader scale, referring to racialized differences between world populations. Roberto described this global racial schema as how Puerto Rican non-migrants see themselves "before the world." The symbolic boundaries embedded within that schema are triggered by the fact of a research project by an American, under the auspices of an American university, which is why Roberto and my other research assistants received similar responses when they led the interviews. But these global racial schemas, which include panethnic categories, are also triggered often enough in the lives of Puerto Rican non-migrants that the categories are salient to them.

The United States has also had ongoing political and economic involvement in the Dominican Republic throughout the late 19th and 20th centuries.[29] And there is widespread awareness about the U.S. Dominican community and how it is treated by its host society. Yet the United States has not become the automatic reference category for constructing racial and ethnic boundaries; Haiti still holds that position in the Dominican imaginary.[30] Most Dominican non-migrant respondents have also internalized an understanding of U.S. racial schemas that includes a Latino panethnic category. But they do not regularly use these schemas; rather than using "Latino" as a regular term, they use it only when they deliberately refer to those populations. Alicia stated:

> The Latino race? No. It's not a common term. . . . Latino is not used . . . unless we are among a group of foreigners, like North Americans, Germans, French, Chinese, Italians, and that she's there and someone says she's Latina. . . . [In the Dominican Republic, it's used] only in certain contexts, for example, . . . to differentiate the Latino—the one that has dark hair, ordinary features—from others that are not [Latinos], that are fine, profiled nose, thin mouth, light eyes. So the one that seems like this is Latino. Like Jennifer Lopez, like that. That she seems Latina because she has the mouth like a Latina, the buns. . . .
>
> Q: So where do you hear this word?
>
> On television, in the entertainment news. Among the jet set of Latino origin, [they say, for example,] "she was born here but grew up over there, she's of Latino origin." . . . [In] U.S., European movies. . . . In North American pro-

grams. . . . The North Americans use that term a lot. Yes, the gringos say that.
(Dominican non-migrant, teacher)

Alicia sees the term "Latino" used primarily to reinforce racialized boundaries between Latin Americans and foreign populations, but reveals that this symbolic boundary is only rarely used in the Dominican Republic. Although Dominicans are aware of how they are racialized by foreigners, especially "gringos," this cognitive awareness is rarely triggered in their daily lives.

Puerto Rican non-migrants do not restrict their frame of reference to Puerto Rican society. Their concepts of race are formed in distinction to a society that greatly influences their lives from afar. While local conceptions of racial categories used in Puerto Rico are seldom replaced by this Americanized view, many adopt a secondary understanding of their racial classification—how they are viewed beyond their national borders—or their race on an international stage that is dominated by the United States. These non-migrants develop dual understandings of what race means in the contexts of their own society and "before the world."

Using U.S. Racial Schemas

Although the main pattern among Puerto Rican non-migrants was to use a nationality racial schema to classify the photographs, a smaller group of respondents adopted a U.S. racial schema. Most of these respondents used a Hispanicized U.S. schema. Matilde, for instance, a Puerto Rican secretary in her 60s, classified the photos as Latino, Black, and White, determining who was Latino by using Americans as her reference group. She explained that she identifies someone as Latino "because he's not *blanco-blanco.* . . . They're not *jinchos*, like we say about Americans." Several other Puerto Rican non-migrants used a hybrid of the U.S. schema and the nationality schema in classifying the photos, combining categories like Latino, Black, and White with a variety of nationalities. While less common among Dominicans, a few respondents in Santo Domingo adopted a Hispanicized U.S. or hybrid U.S./nationality schema for the photos as well. For some people, an American concept of race has seeped into their consciousness, even if they use other schemas to classify the people in their social networks.

Estrella, a Puerto Rican secretary in her late 40s with medium skin and mixed features, was initially uncertain how to classify the photos, and seemed torn between two competing schemas. She began by using a continuum schema

including the term *trigueño*, but then switched to a binary U.S. schema partway
through as she recalled hearing that *trigueño* is not considered a race.

Q: *Can you tell me how would classify the race of these people?* . . .

The race. Okay, *trigueño* (1). (2) [laughs] This is like Caucasian. My God, this
one (3) [is] *negra* [unsure]? (4) *Blanco.* (5) *Blanca.* (6) *Negro.* (7) Is Caucasian
too. (8), (9) Is like Caucasian too, to me. (10) *Blanca.* (11) *Blanca.* (12) To me
her race is *negra.* (13) To me this is Caucasian. . . . (14) *Blanca.* (15) It's that I
don't want to say trigueño because it's not—or you can't say *trigueño*?

Q: *Why?*

You can?

Q: *You can use the categories you would normally use.*

(15) To me is *negro.* (16) *Blanca.* (17) *Blanca.* (18) *Negro.* (19) *Blanca.* And
(20) *negro* too.

Q: . . . *And why didn't you want to use the word* trigueño?

Oh, because that's not like a classification, right? Or can you—is that accepted?
. . . Because there are people who say it's *blanco* or *negro.*

Q: *Who says that?*

I've heard it. . . . You know, that the person is *blanco* or is *negro.* . . .

Q: *Here in Puerto Rico they say that?*

. . . I've heard it here . . . in some places. But people always say that they're
trigueño. . . . I don't know if it's that I'm confused, maybe. (Puerto Rican non-
migrant, secretary)

Here, Estrella revealed that she has multiple schemas in her racial schema portfolio and is not sure which one to use. The continuum schema with its *trigueño*
category, as she said, is commonly used and seemed more natural to her. Because
I had gotten to know her a little before we conducted this interview, she may
have felt comfortable enough with me to start out using the terms she would
use with other Puerto Ricans. But she was also conscious of what counted as an
"official" racial classification. While she could not recall where she had heard it,
she had heard in Puerto Rico that only White and Black should be used as races.

This understanding that people she would consider *trigueño*, or mixed, should really be classified as Black is redolent of an American influence.

Although only two Puerto Rican non-migrants used a binary U.S. schema on the photos, several did so for their social networks, describing all their listed social ties as either White or Black.[31] Because it can be considered impolite to refer to someone as *negro*, especially if you do not know their sensitivity to race, some respondents who have internalized a binary U.S. schema may feel more comfortable applying it to people they know and whom they feel would not be offended by the characterization.

The non-migrant respondents who used a U.S. racial schema for the photos or their social network were usually people who have a great deal of contact with the United States or have close relatives living there. Estrella, for instance, is very close to her daughter who lives in New York, and calls and visits frequently. Matilde, who spends most of her free time traveling, estimates that she has been to the mainland U.S. more than 50 times. While almost everyone in San Juan and Santo Domingo, it would seem, knows someone who lives or has lived in the United States, and hears regularly about life there from neighbors, the news, and the entertainment media, the respondents who adopted its racial schema were the ones who had the closest firsthand contact and personal connections. Greater familiarity with a new concept of race, for instance gained through the media, can help to make it retrievable—available to the audience to access[32]—but people are more likely to adopt ideas that they receive from close ties than those from the media or other impersonal sources.[33] Interpersonal communication with U.S. contacts and the frequency of such interactions therefore play an important role in diffusing Americanized concepts of race and ethnicity to people back in the sending societies.

A Latent Binary U.S. Schema

Although relatively few non-migrant respondents adopted a binary U.S. schema to classify the photos or their social networks, many nonetheless reveal that they have internalized it as part of their racial schema portfolio but simply do not summon it often. Its presence is reflected in a dual understanding of what Whiteness and Blackness mean both in their own societies and in the United States, or in a larger global framework. While some respondents simply view this schema as how Americans would classify their race in the mainland U.S., others feel the influence of these Americanized notions in their own societies as well. They may rarely use a binary U.S. schema in their own society, but certain contexts evoke a sense of how their race is viewed in a broader system of racial classification beyond their own society.

In the binary U.S. schema, because the one-drop rule included people with any amount of Black ancestry, "Black" became a broad, phenotypically diverse category, incorporating people of different skin tones, appearances, and fractions of Black ancestry. By contrast, "White" was associated with racial "purity," the narrow group of those deemed to be "untainted" by Black ancestry. In the continuum schema, Blackness is restricted to those with the least amount of racial mixture; those with mixed Black ancestry became *mulato*, *moreno*, or *indio*. There, Blackness conveys racial "purity," while the criteria for Whiteness are more relaxed. One Puerto Rican woman summarized this with an old platitude: "In the U.S., if you're not White, you're Black. In Puerto Rico, if you're not Black, you're White." That people with fairly light skin or mixed features can qualify as White allows a broader segment to claim the race, as shown by the fact that 80 percent of Puerto Rico's population identified as White on the 2000 Census.[34]

Many non-migrant respondents have cognitively internalized both of these racial schemas, even if they do not use both regularly. Some have learned about the different racial classifications and hierarchies in the United States, and recognize how these categories are defined differently there. Manuel, for example, explained his view of how Whiteness differs in the two places:

> It doesn't mean the same, because White here, we call White those that are lighter than the *mulato*, not the ones that are like you over there. Because over there they are really White, as they say "*blanco-blanco*," like a sheet of paper. But not here.

> Q: Can a person here be darker than paper and be White?

> Exactly, because our predominant color is *mulato*. So, if there's a person lighter than the color *mulato*, they could be called a White person.

> Q: But that same person, if he goes to the U.S. he's not going to be White?

> He wouldn't be White, because he's going to mix with a group that is lighter, much lighter than him. (Dominican non-migrant, electronic handyman)

Manuel compared his own, broad sense of Whiteness to the more restrictive definition in the United States. The very use of the expression *blanco-blanco* suggests a different understanding of Whiteness there than what he normally employs. Similarly, Elisa, a Puerto Rican college student, explained the different concepts of Blackness: "Here, . . . you could have a dark color but it doesn't mean you're Black. . . . I understand that a person is Black [if] their complete race, their blood, their father and mother and him are Blacks. If not, they aren't Black, they're dark-skinned, *trigueño*. . . . But over there [in the U.S.], they would say that the *trigueños* are Blacks." Elisa and Manuel both used the nationality schema when classifying other people, but they have also internalized the Americanized notions of race associated with the binary U.S. schema.

Some believe that these foreign classifications apply to them even in their own societies. They are attentive to American and global influences on their society and sometimes place themselves within an international frame of reference that is shaped by Americanized concepts. This dual consciousness led several non-migrant respondents to refer to themselves as *mulato*, *indio*, or *trigueño* at home, but *negro* on a broader scale. Agustín described this as the difference between race "in the macro sense," where a larger, international stage is evoked, and race "in the micro sense" of how it is understood in the local Dominican context. Agustín has fairly dark skin and a mixture of African and European facial features. Early in the interview, when asked to describe his racial identity in his own words, he responded "Black." However, much later in the interview, he explained that this was not how he would normally describe his race.

Q: *Have you always said that your race is Black?*

Well, I say Black now, but I would never [normally] say Black. I once said *indio*, because that's the idea that we've formed in this environment. And then I said *mulato*. But now in the general sense, in the macro sense of race, I'm a Black person. If I'm going to put it on a document of mine . . . like in a passport, a *cédula* [identification card], driver's license and those things. . . . I won't say Black, I say *mulato*. . . . In the everyday sense I say that I'm *mulato*. . . . Now if you talk to me in the macro sense of race, I'm Black. I'm more Black than White.

Q: *And why didn't you say* indio *or* mulato *in this interview?*

Because that is a general sense, to you. Because I'm talking in a macro sense of race. I'm talking about race, in the larger sense of the word, "race." And it's more Black than White.

Q: *But in a social situation with other Dominicans you would say . . . ?*

Mulato. (Dominican non-migrant, small-business owner)

In his everyday life in Santo Domingo, Agustín sees his race as *mulato*. He claims that terms like *mulato* and *indio* fall within a larger Black category because they are closer to Black than to White, conveying an implicit use of a racial dichotomy. For him, a macro sense of race references categories that exist beyond his own society.

Later, to get a native Dominican's perspective on Agustín's distinction, I discussed it with my research assistant Ramona, who was present at his interview. A Dominican non-migrant in her 40s, Ramona would also have qualified as a respondent for the study. She gave her opinion of the different "senses" of race:

> The macro sense of race is the general sense. The feeling of how the U.S. wants to box us.

> *Q: But when you say general, "general" means the U.S.?*

> To us, the U.S. is our reference point. It's our, the pattern to follow. [Agustín] understands that the macro sense is how the U.S. wants to box us, classify us. Why? Because the Dominican colony in the U.S. is rapidly growing and it's becoming something important for them and also for us. So because of that, it's macro because it's important there in the U.S. and it's important here in the Dominican Republic, because of the money that they send, because they affect North American society. . . . The macro race idea is, to us, that at this moment the U.S. wants to box us. Put us in a place. . . . They want to put us in the place of the Latinos. And among the Latinos, the Dominicans. . . . And to them we are Black Latinos because of our color. So that's how people see it. And [Agustín] . . . sees it that way, and that's why he says that in the macro sense "I'm Black," but in the other sense, here, arguing with any person here in the Dominican Republic, he feels *mulato* and defines himself as *mulato* in the Dominican Republic. Because in the Dominican Republic he's not Black, he's *mulato*. . . . That's the micro sense of race. (Dominican non-migrant, research assistant)

Both Ramona and Agustín distinguish between their race at home and abroad. While the limited continuum racial schema captures how they think of race in the Dominican Republic, they are also affected by an awareness of how they are classified racially beyond their society, and specifically in the United States.

Gustavo, who has dark skin and mostly African features, also alluded to having different, simultaneous understandings of his race when he explained that he is both Black and *indio* at the same time.

> Culturally, I'm *indio* but in reality I'm Black. . . . In our history, for example Trujillo, we say he invented a color and it was *indio*. I'm *indio* colored. [Ramona]

is *indio* colored. But in reality I'm Black if we go with what's essential. . . . Now even though I don't have many characteristics of the Blacks because we are a mix which could be what we call the *mulato*. In reality, that's what I am, a *mulato*. (Dominican non-migrant, teacher and school principal)

In one moment, Gustavo says he is Black in reality and in another he says he is *mulato* in reality. But this is not a contradiction; it's an indication that he recognizes multiple racial classifications on different levels. When he says he is Black, Gustavo is rejecting the cultural belief that Dominicans are *indio* because he views this as a fabrication of Trujillo to deny the nation's African heritage. While Gustavo rejects an *indio* classification, he recognizes that by the cultural standards of his country, this is what he is considered. In part, he and Agustín are both expressing their comfort with having African ancestry. While they may not assert their Blackness to other Dominicans, they are situating the categories *mulato* and *indio* within a broader concept of Blackness, as defined outside their society.

I was particularly interested in whether these respondents identified their race as Black because they thought this was the response that I, as an American, wanted to hear. Did this macro identity have any real meaning in the lives of non-migrants? In our discussion, Ramona expressed her view that Agustín and other respondents who identify as Black really do feel Black, but that they have two ways of understanding their identity—one that they use at home on an everyday basis and one that is informed by a consciousness of how Dominicans are seen globally.

Q: Do you think that [Agustín] identifies himself as Black in this macro sense, or that was just what he thought I wanted to hear?

He knows that you are doing an investigation without any orientation, he understands that. But he identifies himself in two ways, because for us, we know, culturally we're unfortunately already depending on the U.S., whether we like it or not. Also economically, and now, all of that affects society.

Q: . . . But in his normal life, in what other situations other than this interview do you think he would answer that his race, in the macro sense, is Black?

I think that very little, because it's not common here for people to ask other people "What is your race," because we're all Dominicans. . . . We don't have to give explanations to other people because we all know who we are. . . . We all have the same culture, the same language.

Q: . . . So if it had only been you in the room, you would have only seen the micro part? . . . They wouldn't have answered with this part of their identity.

No, because they're identifying me as a Dominican, and maybe our conversation would be different. . . . It wouldn't have come up. . . . Because I'm talking with you like this, but I wouldn't talk with a Dominican this way, because it's not our culture. We wouldn't be talking about [their race].

Ramona believed that these respondents would not identify as Black in their daily lives, in part because people rarely discuss how they identify racially. Asking Dominicans or Puerto Ricans about their race or color can be met with reluctance or unease. Asking his respondents what race they considered themselves, anthropologist Jorge Duany found responses ranging from "embarrassment and amazement to ambivalence and silence";[35] some simply shrugged, pointed to their skin, or did not answer. In this sense, being a foreigner can be an advantage. I rarely experienced such reactions, as respondents sought to teach me about their society. While my presence and the interview scenario caused respondents to tap into racial schemas that did not come up often, it also gave them a chance to express a concept that is clearly within their racial schema portfolios but that is not commonly triggered by co-ethnics.

Marcela, a Dominican in her early 20s with bronze skin and mixed features, was more explicit about where her sense of fitting within a broad concept of Blackness comes from: globalization. Although she described her race as *mulata*, she checked "Black" on the U.S. Census race question. She discussed her thought process in completing the question:

There is no *mulato* [option]. Okay. [It's] very decisive, you're either White or Black. So a *mulato* would be Black.

Q: . . . Why did you mark Black?

Because there is nothing else.

Q: But why not White?

I don't know, I maybe marked it because of the globalization that whoever is not White is Black. (Dominican non-migrant, part-time office worker)

Marcela was referencing the U.S. side of the truism "In the U.S., if you're not White, you're Black." She believes this concept has come from globalization—the communication of an American classification standard across national borders. Unlike Agustín and Gustavo, Marcela does not consider herself Black. But she recognizes how she is racialized in this global context. Discussing the list of continuum terms, she described them as "something vulgar . . . to not admit the negritude of the Dominican people, to not admit that in other places we are Blacks." Marcela recognizes that it is *in other places* that Dominicans are considered Blacks, not in their own society. Her knowledge of this alternative standard influenced her response as she completed a survey question associated with that U.S. context.

Several Puerto Rican respondents who used alternate schemas when classifying the photos also conveyed an additional sense of a binary U.S. schema, or a Black-White racial binary, at some point in the interview. Rubén, who has dark skin, used a Hispanicized U.S. schema on the photos, but he later switched to using only the terms "White" and "Black." When I showed him the list of continuum terms in Table 3 (in Chapter 1), he voluntarily drew a line below *piel canela* and explained, "All of these classifications, from *negro* to *piel canela* . . . these people can be put together in one race which is the *negro*, in reality. The same thing from *blanco con raja* to *blanco*, you can also put them all together and just make them one simple *blanco*." Benjamín, who used a panethnic nationality schema on the photos, did the same with the list, but drew his line below *jabao*, claiming that everyone from *jabao* up was Black and everyone else was White. He said, "Here a person that is *blanco, blanco, blanco*, very *blanco* but has bad hair, they're *negro*. Here, we consider him *negro*, no matter how *blanco* he is." This conception resembles the one-drop rule, and reveals that he sees even those intermediate classifications associated with the Hispanic Caribbean as reducible to Black and White.

The non-migrant respondents who learned about a binary U.S. schema did so primarily through their transnational contact with friends and relatives abroad. Most respondents explained that they first came to understand the different classification system through their ties to U.S. migrants, who often remit this knowledge through a sense of bewilderment at Americans' treatment of race. Elisa, the Puerto Rican college student, explained, "I've not lived in the U.S. but my relatives that live there or people that I know that live there, well, they say that . . . even if you are *blanquito* here, you're Black over there."

The mass media were a less influential source of information about the binary U.S. schema. Fewer contemporary U.S. media focus on this aspect of American race than on the expression of Latino panethnicity. One way that Martina, a young Dominican secretary, became aware of how multiracial individuals are classified was by following news media on American celebrities. She says, "I've seen cases, artists that are mixed, that they or their family . . . descend from African people and are married with Americans, and I've heard that the classification that they give to [the children] is Afro Americans." But respondents were affected most by the experiences and communications of people they know. A conversation Martina had with an American missionary made a much deeper impact on her. She explained that once, when the missionary visited her house, "we were talking about how over there you're either *blanco* or you're *negro*, but we didn't talk that much about race, we just talked briefly about it. We were talking about the way of life over there and all of that." During that conversation, Martina, who has light skin, European facial features, and coarse but straight black hair, said she asked the missionary what her race would be in the United States. "I said I must be *negra* over there and he said no, that over there I could pass as *blanca*. . . . I don't know why. . . . Over there if you're either *blanco* or *negro*, I thought I would be *negra*." Martina does not use this schema to classify others, but she has internalized a latent understanding of these U.S. classifications.

As Martina's example shows, social remittance of racial concepts comes not just from migrant co-ethnics but from interactions with Americans in the sending societies as well. Both countries receive visitors such as tourists, business travelers, and exchange students, and those who interact substantively with such visitors can learn how race works in other societies. Gustavo not only runs a Dominican school, he also teaches Spanish to foreign students at a language school in the summers. He learned about the U.S. classification of people with mixed Black and White heritage through an American student who came to Santo Domingo to study.

> Something else that I found weird from there—when they see girls that to us are White, they're African American [in the U.S.] because of the kind of hair they have or because they're daughters of African parents and one American, then they are African American. . . . For example, a girl that was one of our students, her father was from Africa and he got married with an American and they would call her African American. There she's African American. . . . I found that really strange. . . . [I thought,] "But how is that possible? Here you're White." She didn't consider herself White. (Dominican non-migrant, teacher and school principal)

This experience influenced Gustavo's understanding of how he is seen beyond his own country's borders and contributed to his dual consciousness of a broader, American notion of Blackness together with a narrower, Dominican notion of *negro* as racially "pure."

An important influence on cultural diffusion is the extent to which new ideas or concepts are institutionalized.[36] Local institutions support the validity of new ideas, making them the subject of common reference. In particular, state institutions that incorporate those concepts lend them power, especially when they become part of the knowledge required for employment or resources—such as completing a race question on a form or a job application. Puerto Rico's Commonwealth status provides Puerto Rican non-migrants with regular exposure to American institutions, which reinforces the racial schemas they learn about from their migrant contacts.

The binary U.S. schema is institutionalized in the OMB's federal standards for data collection, which affect federal data collection in Puerto Rico as well. The U.S. Census had not included a race question in Puerto Rico since 1940 until the 2000 Census, when the same race and Hispanic origin questions used in the rest of the United States were included on Puerto Rico's census.[37] At the time of my fieldwork, respondents had completed the 2000 Census only a few years earlier, and it had received considerable publicity and media attention. While Puerto Ricans complete the census at most once a decade, other agencies adopt the same standards, which means that Puerto Ricans now encounter these classifications more regularly in their interactions with institutions. Eva referred to the census categories in describing her uncertainty about what "counts" as a race.

> The problem is that I don't know if the color, the *marrón* [brown] skin tones, qualifies as race. . . . Because when I fill out an application I don't see an option that says "*marrón.* I'm *marrón.*" You never see it. What you always see is *blanco* and *negro*, Indian, Afro [American]. All of those things. But you never see an intermediate [category]. . . . Here [the forms] say *blanco, negro. Blanco, negro.* (Puerto Rican non-migrant, journalist)

Other respondents, too, remembered seeing only White and Black race categories on job applications and forms. While many respondents dislike these question formats and believe other options are needed to represent race in Puerto Rico, the very fact that such questions are asked in a range of institutional settings reinforces an understanding of U.S. racial schemas, and a view of what counts as racial categories.

Many Puerto Ricans interact with the U.S. military,[38] which can serve as a socializing influence with regard to concepts of race. Several Puerto Rican non-migrants mentioned learning about race in the United States while serving in the army or from a relative who had served. Leandro served in the U.S. military in Puerto Rico, where he encountered the federal U.S. racial classifications. Despite his light skin, which leads many Puerto Ricans to see him as White, Leandro recognized that he had to adopt a different standard when interacting with the military infrastructure. He explained:

> When I went to fill out my military service papers. There, we weren't . . . *trigueño, piel canela*. There we were White or Black. And I said "Black" right away. I didn't have to think twice. The [Puerto Rican] guy that was with me said, "Why are you putting Black? You're White." I said, "No, I'm Puerto Rican. Ask to see what group I fall in." Obviously in the Black one. As far as I understand, I don't know how true it is, but in the U.S. they classify you for the military service as White or Black. It doesn't matter what color you are. (Puerto Rican non-migrant, factory supervisor)

Leandro had a conception of U.S. racial classifications before he enlisted, which the military reinforced. For others, the military communicates these racial standards for the first time. Daniel, also a Puerto Rican with light skin, served in the Army Reserves and explained that it taught him how Americans classify race:

> What happens is that in the U.S., . . . you yourself can be White but if you're of Hispanic race, then you're not White. . . . According to the census [you] aren't.

Q: And how did you learn this?

> Oh, because of the Army. Once they told the White people to get up, and I stood up, and they all started laughing. And that's when . . . I realized it was different. I stood up, because I didn't know that it was because of blood, I thought it was the color. So I stood up and then when everyone started laughing, then I realized it was different. (Puerto Rican non-migrant, medical technician)

During this training exercise, supposedly to start a dialogue about racism, Daniel learned that Americans define Whiteness differently than he did. Institutions like the armed forces both communicate and lend support to a U.S. classification system.

Dominican non-migrants receive little institutionalized support for a binary U.S. schema. Dominican government agencies include intermediate categories such as *indio* and *mulato* on their census questions and identification cards.[39] Furthermore, being a mixed-race people is central to Dominican nation-building efforts to distinguish Dominicans from Haitians and the Haitian minority living within its borders. Given that Dominicans receive little support, and often contradictory messages, from government institutions, it is not surprising that more Puerto Rican non-migrant respondents than Dominicans internalized a binary U.S. racial schema.

Yet for many Puerto Rican respondents, and for some Dominicans, an Americanized conception of Whiteness and Blackness—represented by the binary U.S. schema—is added to their racial schema portfolios. It often remains latent, but can be triggered by situations that evoke the United States and its global influence. That Puerto Ricans and Dominicans who have never lived abroad recognize these external meanings of Whiteness and Blackness reveals the influence of U.S. culture on Latin American racial awareness. The internalization of the binary U.S. schema by non-migrants, even when infrequently used, suggests that at the same time that American conceptions of race are seen as becoming Latin Americanized,[40] Latin American conceptions of race are also becoming more Americanized.

Conclusion

In mass migration processes today, the physical act of migration is not a prerequisite for living one's life with the simultaneous influence of two distinct social contexts.[41] People who remain in migrant-sending societies not only learn about the physical environment and daily activities of their migrant ties, but they also learn about the host society's systems of classifying race and ethnicity, including their own. This can also affect the symbolic boundaries that they draw, as racialized boundaries between the sending and receiving societies can become salient for non-migrants as well. Migration processes, then, transform concepts of race not only for those who migrate and the host society that receives them, but also for those who stay behind.

Latino panethnicity and the Black-White dichotomy associated with the binary U.S. schema are clearly influenced by the cultural diffusion of concepts from the United States. It is also possible that non-migrants' use of a nationality racial schema is influenced in part by migrants' experiences there. In Chapter 3, we saw that many migrant respondents believed that Americans classify them racially by their nationality or their panethnicity. The ethnically diverse context of the receiving society reinforces the salience of such national labels, perhaps encouraging more migrants to identify themselves and others by nationality and communicate these patterns to friends and family in their home societies. While there is historical evidence of Puerto Ricans' and Dominicans' using nationality labels in racial terms even in the 18th and 19th centuries, such labels are also reinforced by migration experiences. Since I examine only one point in time, it is difficult to say how much non-migrants' use of the nationality schemas reflects the home countries' traditional ways of classifying race and how much their use of these schemas is shaped by cultural diffusion. Panethnic categories and a Black-White dichotomy are easier to trace to U.S. influences; historical and longitudinal research can explore how much the widespread use of nationality racial schemas is attributable to influences inside or outside these societies.

It is not surprising that Puerto Rico, given a political affiliation with the United States that is often described as modern-day colonialism,[42] should reveal the greater impact of U.S. concepts of race and ethnicity than the Dominican Republic does. Those political ties make the United States a much stronger presence in the daily life of Puerto Ricans, and position Americans as a ubiquitous reference category in the construction of their own group boundaries. As an indirect influence, that political relationship makes U.S. schemas more widespread and retrievable for Puerto Ricans than for Dominicans—through stronger institutional penetration, greater media influences, and the greater ease and freedom of travel that Puerto Ricans experience.

Yet it is noteworthy that some Dominican respondents, even though a minority, do adopt Americanized racial schemas and categories. Even in sending societies where symbolic boundaries are weaker at the macro level, they can become relevant at the micro level for individuals with close connections to migrants. Transnational influences and globalization can lead non-migrants to internalize a dual understanding of their race at home and abroad. Those with close transnational ties and frequent contact become aware of that foreign context more regularly. Thus, while Puerto Rico is in many ways a unique case because of its political status, all migrant-sending societies fall somewhere along a continuum of transnational connections and media penetration from the receiving society; the stronger and more frequent those connections, the more they are supported by local institutions, and the more they create meaningful frames of reference for individuals who stay behind, the more likely that concepts of race and ethnicity will diffuse transnationally, be added to non-migrants' racial schema portfolios, and be used by them in various situations.

The transnational diffusion of racial schemas from the receiving society back to the sending society means that later migrants are likely to move having already incorporated new receiving-society schemas. We saw that more-recent migrants were less surprised about how they were classified in the United States, because they arrived already knowing about a Latino community and where it fit within an American racial hierarchy. It is partly due to the communication of U.S. racial classifications from migrants to those back home that newcomers less often experience the shock of racial reclassification upon arrival, suggesting that future generations will have a smoother integration process than those who preceded them.

The socially shared cognitive organization that makes up a schema of racial classification can be diffused just like other forms of culture. As non-migrants choose between the new schemas they have internalized and old ones previously held, they perform numerous individual-level, often subconscious actions of retrieving particular ways of dividing up the world and the behavior that follows from those divisions. These choices are not random, but are structured by particular situational cues—perhaps a reference to the diaspora, an interaction with an American, or filling out a form shaped by American categories and interests—that trigger frames based on those symbolic boundaries. Non-migrants' more and more frequent use of diffused racial schemas, in more and more contexts—like the adoption of Latino panethnic categories in Puerto Rico—is one type of cultural change brought about by migration.

5   Multiple Forms of Racial Stratification

THIS CHAPTER TURNS FROM HOW INDIVIDUALS CONCEPTUALIZE RACE to the way that race and color stratify their lives.[1] A central argument of this book is that people maintain—and switch back and forth between—multiple cognitive constructs of race, sometimes consciously and deliberately, but often not. This would seem to imply a certain amount of individual agency when it comes to racial classifications. Yet how race affects people's lives is rarely a matter of their own choosing. While they have a certain element of choice in the racial schemas they use, and together with others can influence larger cultural change in concepts of race over time, such choices rarely allow them to escape existing racial inequalities. There are real consequences to how people are seen by others and which racial schemas those in power use to organize, order, and rank them into a racial hierarchy.

I draw on my respondents' experiences with racism and discrimination to describe their encounters with racial hierarchies, and I focus on the way that multiple forms of stratification, related to different racial schemas, simultaneously affect people's lives. In the Hispanic Caribbean, a nationality racial schema shapes the treatment of local immigrant and minority populations, such as Haitians in the Dominican Republic and Dominicans in Puerto Rico. Yet for the Puerto Rican and Dominican majorities, color—or a continuum schema—is the more important form of social stratification. Gender and class also shape how people experience racial discrimination; the Hispanic Caribbean color hierarchy has different meaning for men and women, and is intricately entwined with social class. In the United States, migrants experience discrimination on the basis of their Latino panethnicity, again in different ways for men and women. But they also are stratified by color, especially as they climb higher up the socioeconomic ladder.

The way that these distinct aspects of race affect Dominicans' and Puerto Ricans' lives suggests that the dominant groups who hold most of the power in a society also use multiple schemas in viewing others, creating intersecting planes of racial inequality. Thus, even as societies experience cultural change in their concepts of race, racial stratification remains firmly in place.

Racial Hierarchies in the Home Countries

The Puerto Rican and Dominican non-migrants I interviewed frequently used a nationality racial schema; many asserted that their race was "Puerto Rican" or "Dominican." This schema would seem to have little function as a system of drawing boundaries between races in the sending societies, where most people are Puerto Rican or Dominican, respectively. But in fact it represents the nationality-based hierarchies that separate the majority population from local minorities, particularly the Dominican minority in Puerto Rico and the Haitian minority in the Dominican Republic. In both cases, an understanding of race as nationality organizes society, with the lowest status reserved for members of these stigmatized nationality groups.

Haitian immigrants and their descendants are particularly stigmatized in the Dominican Republic. The long history of conflict between the two nations, as well as Dominican leaders' efforts to foment a racialized fear of the Haitian people, has been well described.[2] Many Haitians are undocumented, and are extremely vulnerable economically and socially. Haitians tend to perform the worst jobs, with few legal protections, and are subject to frequent raids and deportations. During my fieldwork in Santo Domingo, several people told me it was common practice for Dominicans to hire illegal Haitians for construction work, promising a lump payment after the job, only to call the police to deport them before completion of the job. Police often pluck dark-skinned individuals off the streets and drive them across the Haitian border, not infrequently picking up dark-skinned Dominicans by mistake.

I constantly observed people making negative comments about Haitians, or treating them in subtle or not-so-subtle ways as social pariahs. In the *carros públicos*, the "Haitian problem" was a frequent topic of conversation among the passengers crowded in together: that Haitians are invading the country, that they are dirty, or that they sleep and defecate in the streets. One quiet Sunday evening, I was the only passenger in a *carro público*. The drivers are usually eager to take on more passengers and tap their horn inquiringly at anyone waiting on the curb. As we came to the corner of Nuñez de Caceres, a Haitian man signaled for the car to stop. The driver, without pulling over to the curb, yelled at him roughly, "Quick! Quick!" to make him get in. The driver wanted to make the green light, but I had never seen a driver treat a potential customer so brusquely, especially on such a slow night. The Haitian man started to ask a question, but rather than answer, the driver stepped on the gas and drove off, leaving the man behind. He said to me, exasperated, "These Haitians never have the money to pay!" On another occasion, a middle-aged Dominican woman offered what she thought was sage advice to a visitor learning to navigate around Santo Domingo: "If you get on a bus, don't ever sit next to a Haitian because he'll stink. These Haitians all smell bad!"

Many Dominicans perceive Haiti, and particularly the Haitian population living in the Dominican Republic, as a source of political, economic, and cultural threat. Like undocumented immigrants in many countries, Haitians are regarded as an economic threat to Dominican jobs and resources. The work Haitians get is often work that Dominicans are unwilling to do, but Haitians are seen as having higher designs on Dominican privileges. Inés, a beauty salon owner, explained: "We have a problem with Haitians, because we see Haitians and we don't even want to see them . . . because they want . . . to own us, or what's ours." Many Dominicans have not overcome their political distrust of Haiti stemming from the nation's early origins. Haiti conquered Dominican territory in 1822, while it was still part of the Spanish Empire, and the Dominican Republic emerged as an independent state by expelling the Haitians in 1844. Dominicans still fear that Haiti is plotting to forcibly unify the island again. Ramona remarked that in the Haitian constitution it says that the island of Hispaniola "is one and is not divisible," explaining "that is why we are so afraid of them." Haiti's ability to conquer the Dominican Republic is surely tempered by its own recurrent political-economic crises, but Dominicans' fear has been instilled by opportunistic leaders and even children's stories and sayings that treat Haitians like a bogeyman or a monster under the bed.[3] The sense of political threat is further amplified by fears of a Haitian immigrant takeover from within. Such fears are reflected in the political decision to withhold citizenship rights from the children of undocumented Haitians born in the Dominican Republic.[4]

Haitians are most frequently described as a cultural threat, bringing their own culture, religion, and language and being unwilling to assimilate. Because the essence of *dominicanidad* is associated with Hispanic heritage and Catholic roots—or precisely what distinguishes Dominicans from Haitians[5]—these cultural differences can be seized upon to justify hostility to Haitians on a number of fronts. Federico expresses this sense of cultural threat:

> Remember that our independence is not from the U.S., or from Europe . . . it's from Haiti. They had us for 22 years, which generates [in] us a . . . I myself am not capable of giving a Haitian employment.

Q: Because of this history?

> In part because of that, and in part because I believe that the Haitians should be in their country. . . . And us in ours. . . . Because we are . . . different. And here comes the question that culturally, . . . there are roots that are different. Those people have the African [roots] that they came from. We are not Africans, at least not completely, we aren't. We have evolved. (Dominican nonmigrant, small business owner)

Federico views Haitians as not only different but culturally inferior and less "evolved." Such attitudes affect social inequality along lines of nationality, as Federico exemplifies by admitting that his views prevent him from hiring a Haitian.

In Puerto Rico, hostility toward the Dominican minority is less ubiquitous. But Dominicans are nonetheless a stigmatized group there, also seen as largely undocumented and a threat to Puerto Rican jobs.[6] As I was looking for a place to stay in Puerto Rico, several people advised me against certain neighborhoods because there were a lot of Dominicans living there, and they therefore believed that those areas would be plagued by crime and drugs. One young Puerto Rican man from a wealthy family who had attended an Ivy League college told me that he had not realized how much racism there was in Puerto Rico until he came back after his first year at college and heard his grandfather say, "I'm not going to hire this guy because he's Dominican." Before that time, he acknowledged, such views had been so commonplace that he did not even think of such situations as racist. Many respondents, when I asked if there was any racism in Puerto Rico, first mentioned racism toward Dominicans before considering racism toward other Puerto Ricans, revealing the use of a nationality schema that associates being Dominican with race.

Like Haitians in the Dominican Republic, Dominicans in Puerto Rico are a stigmatized and marginalized minority, showing how a nationality racial schema shapes social stratification. At the same time, both groups are associated with Blackness. In the Dominican Republic, the word *negro* is frequently reserved for Haitians, with many respondents claiming they would not consider a Dominican *negro*, regardless of his appearance, because all Dominicans are racially mixed. This is why, Federico explained, a *carro público* driver gets in trouble if he calls another driver "*negro*" in a traffic dispute because "*negro* is associated with the Haitian" and is therefore a more extreme insult. Many Puerto Ricans associate Blackness with Dominicans. After describing the negative views toward Dominicans, Daniel admitted that this could be related to color "because Dominicans are *negros*" and "if they don't seem to be Dominicans, then it's not a problem." In other words, lighter-skinned Dominicans in Puerto Rico do not necessarily receive the same negative treatment. Marginalization based on nationality is intertwined with group-wide images based on color and appearance.[7] Although racial stratification occurs along a nationality racial schema within both sending societies, it intersects with a continuum racial schema in the public imagination and, most likely, in the minds of those with the power to restrict opportunities and privileges.

Within the majority population, however—the Puerto Ricans and Dominicans in their own countries—neither a nationality racial schema nor a U.S. racial schema serves as a source of racial stratification because the entire population falls in the same location in these classification systems. Rather, a continuum racial schema forms the primary basis for racial hierarchy among the majority group, associating individuals with status positions on the basis of racialized appearance—what respondents refer to as color. From the countries' earliest days as colonial societies, European ancestry and lighter appearance have always been associated with the highest social status and privilege, as in most Latin American societies.[8] Light skin and European appearance is still associated with higher incomes and status in Puerto Rico and the Dominican Republic.[9] In Puerto Rico, people who identified themselves as White on the 2000 Census received significantly higher wage returns for their education than did those who identified as Black.[10] In the Dominican Republic, *blancos* are perceived by the general public to have the highest social status, and status ratings decline with progressively darker descriptions of appearance.[11] In both countries, as in much of Latin America, light skin is culturally valued, making those who are dark less desirable as employees, marriage partners, and patrons in upscale establishments.[12]

Many non-migrant respondents, especially in the Dominican Republic, denied that there was any discrimination on the basis of color and seemed resistant to the idea that they had personally suffered any discrimination.[13] Yet when probed about specific experiences they might have had—for example, receiving worse service than other customers in a store or restaurant, being followed or watched by security guards more than other people were, being treated unfairly in their search for an apartment, a job, or a promotion, or being stopped by the police—respondents with dark skin recalled such experiences more than those with light skin.[14] Rosaria, who has dark skin and African features, believes that racism in Puerto Rico is subtle and eventually recalled an experience of being a target herself.

Q: *Do you think that people here are treated differently based on their race or their color?*

At least here in Puerto Rico, it's not so openly. If there is, it's like more hidden. . . . It's like in the TV commercials. The majority of the TV commercials, they're all *blanquitos*, blonds. . . .

Q: *Do you think that the opportunities for economic success are different for someone with dark skin as for someone with light skin?*

It's said that the one with darker skin has to struggle more than the one with lighter skin. For instance, [in] the banks, there's more people who are lighter, *blanco*, than people who are *negro*. And in places like that you have to struggle more and make a bigger effort. . . .

Q: *Have you ever suspected that someone has treated you unfairly due to the color of your skin or because of your race, even if you're not sure?*

. . . No. . . .

Q: *When you are in a store, have you been watched more by the security guards than other customers?*

That, yes (laughs). That, yes. For instance, the supermarket over there, the one that is behind here, the man, why is he following me so much? If every day he sees my face, he thinks that I'm going to steal something from here? . . . [The] people who are darker than others, more *negro*, well, they pursue them more. (Puerto Rican non-migrant, temporary clerical worker)

In both countries, I frequently observed similar instances of darker-skinned people being served last or treated with less respect. On one occasion in a cafeteria in a fashionable part of San Juan, I was chatting with the very European-looking proprietor by the cash register, when several customers finished more or less simultaneously and came to pay their bills. Some of the customers seemed to be American tourists, while others looked like Puerto Rican regulars. In each case, the proprietor took their money and handed them back their change. At the end of the line, a middle-aged man with darker skin and mixed features was waiting. With this customer, the proprietor threw the change forcefully down on the counter—first the coins, and then the bills—rather than putting it in the man's hand. The gesture was not subtle, and there was no mistaking the difference in his treatment of this customer compared with that of those who preceded him—nor was there any doubt that the proprietor wanted the customer to notice it, too.

Because color is closely associated with social class, it is common to attribute perceived mistreatment to one's class location rather than color. For example, Teresita, who has light brown skin and moderately African features, after describing an experience similar to Rosaria's, explained that it was due to her class rather than color, although in describing her experience, she subtly made color an issue:

Q: *Have you ever suspected that you've been treated unfairly due to the color of your skin or because of your race, even if you're not sure?*

No, I don't know. If I've thought that they've treated me badly, [it's] because of my social class. . . . When you're poor, you suffer many things. . . . I consider that a lack of respect and I'm treated badly because I'm from the lowest social class, and well, not by my color, but by my social class, due to the economic question.

Q: *At any time, because of your color—or because of your social class—have you had an experience of being treated worse or of receiving worse service in a store or a restaurant than other customers?*

Well, yes. I think that when you go to stores where I know I'm never going to buy anything, I can give you an example, a store called Nous, it's French. For clothes. For example, if I go to Nous, but a *blanquita* goes, they're not going to serve me, they're not even going to notice me, they're not going to offer me anything, but they are to her. (Puerto Rican non-migrant, college student)

The word *blanquita* refers to someone who is wealthy and light-skinned, two traits that often go together. As Teresita suggested that the salespeople will offer better service to someone who is well dressed in the hopes of making a sale, she also noted that this person is often White. Teresita's comments reveal the association of Whiteness with high social status in people's minds, a connection undoubtedly made by salespeople and servers as well as by customers. People may focus on class markers, but arguing that one has a stronger causal force than another in a particular instance is difficult to unpack when they are so closely intertwined.

Several respondents noticed similar slights targeted at their darker-skinned friends, and they believed that such treatment was based on color, despite their knowledge of their friends' class background. Alicia, a light-skinned Dominican woman, described how subtle status markers are used to differentiate *blancos* from *negros*, giving the example of the treatment she receives compared with that directed toward her darker friend, Lena.

> Q: *Do you think that people here are treated differently according to their race?*
>
> Yes, I believe so. . . . That is, what costs me one [amount], a person of *negro* race of the same sex as me, it costs them three times [as much]. . . . You go to a restaurant for example and to me the waiter, it's likely he'll ask me, "What do you want, *señora?*" [with a polite tone]. I have seen it, I see it every day. But to the person, for example, my friend, [Lena], they say, "*Y tú?* What do you want?" [with a harsh tone]. You see? There is a very large difference in the treatment. . . ." *Y tú?* What do you want" [versus] "*Usted,* what do you want?" . . . Or, look, you go to the supermarket to buy cheese, and there's a line. [The clerk would say,] "Tell me, *señora,* what would you like?" . . . Even if you go to buy a cheap cheese and the *morenita* [darker woman] goes to buy a more expensive cheese. But I am sure that the clerk pretends he hasn't seen her and leaves her for last. (Dominican non-migrant, teacher)

Using the informal *tú* is a sign of condescension. Alicia sees this disrespectful voice taken with her darker friend, while she and others of light skin tone receive the more respectful formal address of "*señora*" and "*usted.*"

In both countries, high-end establishments and nightclubs were known to refuse entry to darker patrons. In these cases, the racial exclusion is covert, with reasons other than color used to justify the acts. Carmela, a light-skinned Puerto Rican in her 20s, described an experience where a club cited its dress code to try to exclude her dark-skinned friend but not her.

> I've seen it at discos. For example, this disco has this dress code, that you have to go [dressed] very formal. And it can be that a *blanco,* or someone with *blanco* skin, doesn't go dressed so formally, but the *negro,* if he wants to get in, has to go very well dressed. Because what they can do is use the dress code [as an] excuse to deny you entrance. And I have lived that with friends of mine. I have a friend, the same one who visited me, we were going to celebrate something and my brother was already at the place and some friends and I

went with him. I went in sandals and some mid-leg pants and I had something else that they didn't allow in the place, but I don't remember what it was. And he had some jeans and a shirt, not a T-shirt, a buttoned shirt, and they didn't want to let him in. He didn't have sandals. He didn't have the other things that they didn't allow. He simply had jeans. When we managed to get in, after talking, because we wanted to see the people inside, there were people wearing polo shirts, with *blanco* skin, with polos and jeans. And they were allowed to enter. (Puerto Rican non-migrant, customer service representative)

As Carmela noted, ostensibly color-blind criteria such as a dress code are used to pick and choose customers who are racially desirable.

The value attached to lighter skin not only affects subtle treatment and interactions but can influence career opportunities as well. Respondents in both countries mentioned job advertisements for service positions asking for candidates with a "good presence," a code word for light skin. Mónica, a Dominican woman of medium skin tone and mixed features, claimed:

They say here that being *blanco* is a profession . . . because if you're *blanco* doors open up. If you're *blanco* they hire you even if you don't know [anything]. . . . Even if you don't have an education, because you're *blanco*, because it looks good and that sells. They use it a lot for sales, beautiful people. . . . Let's say a person that sells door to door, people would open the door much easier to [a] *blanco* than to a *negro* because you can confuse the *negro* with a thief. Even if the *blanquito* is a thief, you think that he's not going to steal. (Dominican non-migrant, accountant)

Mónica's belief that darker people may be seen as thieves but lighter people are not reveals a system of valuation tied to the categories of a continuum schema. Inés, who has a European appearance, can attest that Whiteness literally does open doors. On one occasion where both she and some darker-skinned women were waiting to pick up documents at the Spanish embassy, she said, "They let me go through a door and didn't ask me anything and when these *morenitas* went they stopped them and didn't let them through. . . . They always give the preference to the most *blanquito*." In Puerto Rico, too, respondents with light skin like Daniel feel that they are helped by their color. He said, "I think I have received preferences because of my [color]. It's like because of prejudging me, they see me as the profile of a clean-cut [person]. They prejudge me favorably. I believe maybe a *negro* person would have fewer advantages." Although he sees the treatment as subtle, noting "it wasn't like 'You're White, you're in,'" nevertheless he perceives an advantage over others and has never experienced treatment he believes is discriminatory.

In both countries, the higher status associated with light skin creates an obsession with lightness, ranging from the prevalence of skin-whitening creams to a cultural emphasis on *mejorando la raza*—improving the race, by choosing a lighter-skinned marriage partner who will contribute to producing lighter children.[15] Rodolfo explained:

> If a *negro* gets married to a *negro*, it's not very common. One wants to look to somehow refine the color. . . . I mean, if I marry with, for example, a *blanca*, I try that my kids . . . turn out *lavaito* [washed], meaning different.
>
> *Q: And when you say refining . . . to refine the race, does that mean that it's something good to have that mix?*
>
> Yes, it's good. . . . Because, for example, if I marry a *negra*, what am I going to give? *Negro*. If I were to marry a *blanca*, what will come out? *Blanco*. . . . They come out . . . cleaner, meaning lighter. The color is prettier. (Dominican nonmigrant, part-time social work assistant)

Stories abound in both countries of people who had violated this edict by marrying someone dark, and who caused social catastrophe and condemnation by their families. Ramona's mother planned an elaborate ruse to gain her parents' approval, having a *negro* friend pose as her fiancé so that her parents would be relatively relieved when she presented her true fiancé, who was *mulato*. Pilar, a dark-skinned Dominican with hazel eyes, shared that her mother was disinherited for marrying her father, and that her own husband's family, which is White, has rejected her as well. Of course, while these stories reveal underlying cultural values, they also show that people continue to marry across racial lines despite their families' objections.[16]

Because having light skin matters for people's lives and their life chances, another expression of the cultural obsession with lightness lies in the extreme concern over the appearance of new babies. Because many are unsure how much African heritage their family has, how dark or light a new child will look is a source of great curiosity. One woman I spoke with who was not originally from Puerto Rico but had lived there for many years told me how surprised she was by the meticulous consideration Puerto Ricans gave to figuring out what a child's color would be. She told me about a computer technician who worked in her office, a woman she described as "*negra-india*," who would discuss the racial appearance of her new babies in minute detail with the other workers—whether they were Black under the soles of their feet, whether they were White on the inner sides of their hands. They were collectively trying to figure out what color the children would be considered and how they would look when they grew up. The Dominican newspaper *Hoy* has advertised a Web site that promises to assuage these concerns: make-my-baby.com, which asks readers to "combine two pics [of] you and your significant other to see what your kid will look like!"[17]

The role that skin color plays in people's lives is very gendered. As with other childrearing issues, concern for the racial appearance of new babies falls within the female domain. Skin-whitening creams are targeted to women, not to men. In the traditional marriage trade-off of male economic stability for female beauty, lightness is more important for women—a form of social capital, providing them with a means to social mobility through marriage.[18] Yet concerns about "improving the race" and not marrying someone darker fall on both women and men. Both men and women jokingly describe the pressure to marry lighter and the teasing that ensues if someone bucks the trend. For women, a darker man's social class or earning potential could offset the disappointment of a lighter woman's family, but is unlikely to fully dispel it. One woman whose light-skinned daughter was engaged to marry a college-educated man with medium-dark skin defensively justified the decision. As I started to ask if her daughter's fiancé was Puerto Rican, she interrupted me, assuming I was going to ask about his color, exclaiming, "He's *trigueño*, but he's a very good type of person." Later, the fiancé told me that some of her family members had made racist comments about him. Men are not as actively invested as women in trying to improve their skin color to make themselves more desirable mates, yet color is one aspect of what makes a good match for both men and women.

The national obsession with skin color reflects its very real social consequences. For most Dominican and Puerto Rican non-migrants, color—or what I have described as a continuum racial schema—is the primary form of racial stratification affecting their lives. This reality diminishes the importance of debating whether to call it color or race. This schema is clearly the basis of a social hierarchy that distributes rewards and privileges on the basis of socially designated physical characteristics, which is what many consider to be the very definition of race.

Racial Hierarchies in the Host Society

When Puerto Ricans and Dominicans migrate to the mainland U.S., they are positioned into new racial hierarchies based on classifications used by the dominant society. There, the Hispanicized U.S. racial schema demarcates their structural position as Latinos. Yet at the same time, their social locations are influenced by Americans' own (sometimes subconscious) attention to color, much as in their sending societies. In migrants' daily lives, their Latino panethnicity and their color intricately intertwine to shape their position in America's racial pecking order.

Skin color has always been a stratifying element in the United States, particularly in the African American community.[19] Those with lighter skin formed the African American elite, and their exclusive clubs and organizations have been reputed to use the brown-paper-bag test—holding up a bag to check if an individual was lighter than it—as a condition for membership.[20] In the late 20th century, skin tone still had net effects on educational attainment, occupation, and income among African Americans.[21] The value given to lighter skin is particularly gendered here. Black women are accorded more status for lightness than Black men, a practice with roots in the slave era, when lighter women, often the targets of slave owners' sexual attention, were given higher-status positions as house slaves and spared the worst forms of manual labor.[22] Even today, skin color affects Black women's self-esteem more than Black men's, and is more closely tied to conceptions of female beauty and mate selection.[23] A lexicon of terms describing different skin colors—much like that found in the Hispanic Caribbean—has long been used within the African American community.[24]

Skin color, of course, is not the same as racial classification in the United States. It does not form the basis for social classifications, and during times of segregation the same rules and restrictions applied to Blacks with even the lightest skin. But when we move away from thinking of a society as having only one concept of race to recognizing that multiple racial schemas can be in play simultaneously, we can view phenotype as an additional form of racialized organization and sorting. While the binary U.S. racial schema, which designated most Americans as either Black or White, was obviously more determinant of their life chances, a cognitive schema that sorted people based on color played a secondary role in organizing society.

Among Latinos in the United States, both Latino origin and color influence where people fall in the racial hierarchy. Even after the immigrant generation, native-born Latinos fall well behind non-Latino Whites, and are generally close to but typically slightly ahead of non-Latino Blacks, on a range of socioeconomic outcomes including educational attainment, labor force participation and employment, occupational status, personal earnings, health insurance coverage, home ownership, and home loan approval.[25] Within the broader Latino grouping, there are also nationality differences, with Dominicans and Puerto Ricans having some of the highest poverty rates among all Latino groups.[26] At the same time, significant inequalities exist between light and dark Latinos within the same ethnic group that cannot be explained by differences in human capital or resources. Lighter and more European-looking Latinos generally do better than their darker counterparts in earnings, educational attainment, occupational status, housing, self-esteem, and mental health.[27] Migrants' daily experiences with racism and discrimination, and their placement within the U.S. racial hierarchy, reflect all of the ways that they are viewed and classified by others.

The examples of Tomás and Paulina illustrate how Latino status and phenotype are intertwined in migrants' experiences with discrimination. Tomás is a 27-year-old Puerto Rican actor with the trendy dress and swagger of a hip New Yorker. He left Puerto Rico with his family and arrived in New York as a young teen. His medium-brown skin, tightly curled hair, wide nose, and thin lips give him what he describes as a "multiethnic" look. In everything from his daily chores to his career choices, Tomás has repeatedly confronted racial bias and discrimination. In restaurants, waiters often ignore him while catering to other clients; the service is sometimes so bad that he has to complain to the manager. When security guards follow him around a shop, he has learned to make a game of it, picking up an item and walking around the store, ducking down different aisles, and hiding to force the guards to keep up. He is particularly concerned about police brutality, and for good reason. The police are a steady presence in his Bronx neighborhood, and they are often suspicious of people matching his profile. He described one especially memorable incident, as police responded to a gunfire report:

> Somebody had taken a shot somewhere in the neighborhood. I was going home, but a cop went up the stairs running and they passed us. Then we hear them coming back down, we make way for them because they're coming at full speed. They pull their guns out at us and they're like "Freeze! Put your hands against the wall, drop your bags. . . . " I was like "What the fuck?" They had a shotgun to my face and they searched our bags. Then they were like, "Okay, you can go." That kind of stuff happens and it shakes you up. I can't trust these people for help. From the way they look at me, why am I going to call them for help?

There was a time when Tomás wanted to be a cop. Some of his wariness about the police stems from that experience.

> I wanted to be a police officer here in New York about 10 years ago. I was 19, [and] I did pursue that. Predominantly, the police force here is White, 80%.

It's really tough to get in. . . . When the selection started I passed the written test with flying colors, a 98; it was awesome. I thought I was going to be in, but there's some investigation that goes on. There was nothing against me that was bad, never been arrested or anything like that. They investigate your whole family and your background. They assign you to an investigator. He's your guy; he's the one that knows your IDs, references, school records. The guy was an incredible asshole. He was always trying to deter me from being a police officer: "You should try hospital police." . . . Hospital police are predominantly Black or Latino. They carry no guns and [the] pay [is] lousier. It's way less. Every time I would see this guy, I saw him periodically, he would say things like that. He was trying to discourage me. . . . Then I went to the psychological exam and I failed it. I was like, "Whoa!" The answers were pure and simple. I had nothing I was hiding so I appealed it because it didn't sound right. The process for appealing was to get your own psychologist and have them test you and submit the paperwork to the NYPD.

Q: And you had to pay for it?

Oh yeah, out of my pocket. They screw you no matter what. My friends who were cops told me not to waste my money. Once they disqualify you from the psychological test, most likely they're not going to take you. I went and I took it, . . . [the psychologist] sent the papers and told me, "I don't see why they failed you." It took work [to appeal], but of course I was turned down. About five years later I didn't want to be a cop anymore, but I got this paperwork in the mail about the psychological exam saying that the person who conducted the exam made an error of judgment. They asked me if I wanted to continue and try it again. By this time I was so disillusioned that I didn't want to bother with that crap, so I ripped it up. So I was like, this is the way things are in this situation in this particular job. . . . [They] don't want to be around people of color. One guy actually said, "I arrest people of color because I don't want to hang out with them when I have a drink."

· · ·

Paulina left Puerto Rico to attend college in Pennsylvania, and now, at age 24, she lives in Washington Heights and works as a research coordinator. She has light skin and mostly European features. Her long, straight brown hair was pulled into a hasty ponytail and she looked comfortable as she curled up on a plush Starbucks armchair in Old Navy pajama bottoms. Paulina describes few experiences with discrimination, yet she is alert to its dangers. And while it has not affected her opportunities much to date, she is not immune from feeling its sting. She feels certain that when her current job became available at her workplace, her boss was hesitant to promote her because she is Puerto Rican:

> I started at this work in another position, and later . . . [the person] who was working as the coordinator left. . . . I'm not trying to flatter myself, but I was the ideal person because I knew the program, I was there since the beginning of the program, and I knew it from top to bottom. And well, my preparation, everything, everything was perfect for the job. . . . And they thought about [the promotion] and they thought about it again and again. And I know that it had to be for the fact that I was not American, because one of the people that was influencing the principal investigator of the project a lot was a woman who, when I talk with [her], I feel like she looks at me differently, and that she treats me differently, so I said [to myself] that must be the reason. Then, my own boss, the current one, she sometimes looks at me, [like I'm] inferior. She knows that I'm very smart . . . but I know that deep in her thoughts, she has doubts. And that bothers me. It bothers me.

Eventually, Paulina was given the promotion, but she worries that being Puerto Rican will limit her future opportunities in her office.

Yet Paulina reports few problems with discrimination in other areas of her life. She has never had negative experiences with the police, and is rarely disturbed by her treatment in shops or restaurants. In fact, the only time she is watched by security guards or receives substandard service is when she is accompanied by a Puerto Rican friend who is very dark:

> Q: *When you're in a store, do you think that the security guards watch you more than other people?*

> No, not at me. Not at me, but for example, . . . [my friend,] he's Puerto Rican, he's *negro* and . . . sometimes we go out together and it's "Quick, look how they're looking at us!" "Look how that waitress is not coming." . . . He keeps looking, and those are things that I don't pay attention to, but he does, he does.

Latino ethnicity and skin color together influence the opportunities and racial experiences of migrants like Tomás and Paulina. Both of them have had negative experiences that they believe stem from being Latino, but color also plays a role. Tomás has to confront the "double minority status"[28] of being dark and Puerto Rican; so, too, does Paulina's friend. Paulina is able to ignore those types of concerns until her friend points them out to her. She observes barriers of her own, but the racism she faces is much less persistent and she is frequently able to overcome it. In Tomás's daily life, it is largely irrelevant whether he is being discriminated against because he is Puerto Rican or because of his darker appearance. The two are so intertwined that even those discriminating against him may not know which influences them more. But the relative influence of these factors becomes clear by comparing the experiences of those with the same ethnicity and different phenotypes. Among the migrant respondents overall, those with darker phenotypes describe the most experiences with discrimination, a pattern that is particularly pronounced for workplace discrimination, the type that arguably matters most for their socioeconomic position.[29] This observation is consistent with what larger studies have found for Latinos in the United States.

Migrants' experiences with discrimination are also strongly gendered. Male respondents reported more experiences than women of every type of discrimination except in finding housing. In particular, experiences of harassment by the police were almost exclusively the province of men.[30] They described being stopped repeatedly and questioned or searched, being stopped for speeding but then pushed or cursed at by police. Salvador, a Puerto Rican restaurant worker with dark skin, described several confrontations when the police stopped and searched him in what he described as cases of mistaken identity. And Bartolomé, a Dominican engineer with medium skin, was repeatedly harassed by police when in the company of a White college friend in the Bronx or upper Manhattan, on the assumption that a White guy and a Latino guy together are looking for drugs. In dealing with the police, the conflation of being male, Latino, and dark-skinned is a triple threat.

Migrants also import gendered patterns of behavior from their home countries. Women's social lives are often more closely tied to the home. Many middle-aged women respondents, in particular, have limited social engagement outside of home, work, and church. By contrast, men have a greater public presence, and are more likely to be seen spending time in shops and public places around the neighborhood, a fact not fully unrelated to their greater harassment by the police. Octavio, a Puerto Rican parking garage attendant, revealed this gendered pattern one night after my research assistant and I finished interviewing him at his apartment on the Lower East Side. He announced in front of his wife that he needed to walk us safely to the subway. We protested that we did not need an escort, but he whispered to us, out of her earshot, that he just wanted to get out of the house and his wife did not like him hanging around outside. While male respondents with dark or medium skin were frequently stopped by police because they fit a racial profile, women of similar skin tone never reported being targeted, harassed, or stopped unfairly. The gendered pattern of police harassment is a fundamental part of race in the United States.

Migrants' class status also influences experiences of discrimination, as well as perceptions of its basis. Both Tomás and Paulina have college degrees, and like other middle-class migrants, they perceive that both their color and their *latinidad* influence how they are treated in different situations. Working-class migrants more frequently assert that discrimination does not exist and that they have had no experience of it. Many of them steadfastly believe that America provides equal opportunities to all who seek them. Yet those who do perceive structural barriers to their opportunities believe that such barriers affect all Latinos equally; they believe their skin color makes no difference in Latinos' interactions with American society because they are all classified as Latino. Those who recognize that, even among Latinos, the color of your skin influences what doors are opened or closed typically learn this lesson as they enter the professional world.

In her study of African Americans' belief in the American opportunity structure, political scientist Jennifer Hochschild observes a similar paradox of class divisions.[31] As the circumstances of elite Blacks improve, they lose their belief in the American Dream, even as they are effectively achieving it; yet poor Blacks—those with the most reason to doubt the opportunity structure—remain convinced that anyone can "make it" in America. Hochschild attributes this paradox to the difficult journey of climbing the socioeconomic ladder. Wealthier Blacks confront the structural constraints that stand in their way even as they achieve a measure of success, while poorer Blacks have less opportunity to learn those hard lessons firsthand. This explanation also applies to Puerto Rican and Dominican migrants' belief in the existence of color discrimination. Middle-class respondents have confronted it directly in the professional world—or in the case of those with light skin, they observe it and guiltily recognize that they benefit from it. Working-class migrants less often confront barriers based on color in their occupational settings.

A Dominican hotel cleaner, Margarita, insists that when Latinos are treated badly in the United States, it is "not because of skin color. I think it's more because of customs." Americans classify her race from her Spanish language, her Dominican dress and habits, she claims. And when the doorman refuses to let her enter the upscale building where she works part-time as a home aide, these are the things he notices, she claims, not whether she looks light or dark. Working-class migrants believe Americans classify them racially by their nationality or their Latino panethnicity; it follows for them that Americans also discriminate against them on the same basis. Marisela, a brown-skinned Dominican, insists that Latinos' skin color does not matter to Americans: "If you're Hispanic, you're Hispanic. You'll always be Hispanic for the Whites."[32]

The fact that even light-skinned Latinos experience unfair treatment convinces working-class migrants that Americans do not discriminate by appearance. Bolivar, for example, a retired Puerto Rican factory worker and taxi driver, has light skin and European features. He is often mistaken for Russian, the dominant White community in his Brooklyn neighborhood. Yet he believes that the African American manager of his housing project discriminated against him because he is Latino. He was badly injured during a fire in the building. He returned from his hospital stay to find that an African American neighbor had been approved to move into a new unit and receive reimbursement for her damaged property from the Red Cross. When the manager came to his apartment, she claimed there was no damage and would not approve him to move. Shortly afterward, his ceiling collapsed, destroying much of his remaining property. Bolivar feels certain that the manager was helping her own kind while ignoring the rights of her Latino tenants. When he found out that she had similarly rejected a Dominican neighbor's request to change units, he saw her actions as a pattern of discrimination against Latinos. Such experiences confirm his belief that all Latinos, regardless of color, are treated the same.

Working-class migrant respondents' lives are also more bounded by their ethnic connections. Their social interactions and workplace locations are less likely to produce experiences of color discrimination. Josefa, a Dominican home aide in her 50s with medium-dark skin and mixed features, claims she has never experienced any discrimination, but her life and routines are strictly relegated to environments where she feels comfortable. She has not received worse service than other clients in a shop or restaurant, but noted, "I haven't been in that many restaurants. . . . I don't go out that often." On the rare occasions when she does eat out, it is usually at a Dominican restaurant, where she has no problems. She shops mainly at Latino stores where she is known. She has never had problems finding a place to live, as she moved directly into her brother's house when she arrived in the country from the Dominican Republic. As a young woman, Josefa primarily worked in factories. Factory jobs had bad working conditions, but neither being Latino nor her phenotype was likely to hurt her chances there. She noted, "Before, you went to a factory to look for a job and you got it. And if you didn't like it you would go to another factory and there wasn't any discrimination." Josefa feels that her skin color plays little role in her life chances, but that is because of the particular life she inhabits. She said:

> [Color matters] here in the important jobs. Because in the mediocre jobs no, it doesn't matter. . . . If you go to a factory here, they won't tell you "no" because of your color because what they need is hard-working people. But if you go for a job in the government I know that they will put up more barriers for you to get it. (Dominican migrant, home aide)

Certainly ethnicity plays a role in finding and succeeding even in factory jobs. Migrants tend to find jobs through members of their ethnic group and often rely on ethnic-owned workplaces when they face barriers in the mainstream economy.[33] But in working-class jobs, Josefa and others emphasized, color simply does not matter.

Compared to their working-class co-ethnics, middle-class migrants report many more instances of discrimination in general, and considerably more workplace discrimination in particular.[34] But they also describe more problems in service establishments, such as receiving worse service than other clients or being watched more by security guards. This situation stems partly from the fact that they frequent more-exclusive establishments than working-class migrants do. Yet even in less upscale establishments, middle-class migrants are more attuned to potential prejudice because of the battles they have waged on other fronts. Discrimination has a cumulative impact, and occurrences that may seem minor to outsiders tend to be interpreted in light of a lifetime of past discriminatory experiences.[35] Middle-class respondents had a greater cumulative experience with discrimination in different realms of life, which made them more attuned to perceiving it and more comfortable acknowledging it.

As middle-class migrants interact with mainstream institutions like their workplaces, they experience many forms of discrimination linked to being Latino or to their nationality, but they also become more aware of how skin color affects Latinos' opportunities. Whereas the majority of working-class migrants said that color does not affect Latinos' experiences, almost every professional migrant I spoke with agreed that it does. Their own experiences in the workplace illustrated this pattern, as those with dark skin reported the most workplace discrimination and those with light skin the least.[36] This pattern is particularly noteworthy because it occurs in a context where their ethnicity is known by colleagues and employers. In the professional world, being Latino may affect your opportunities, but color adds an extra layer of barriers.

Middle-class respondents observed how dark-skinned Latinos often fare the worst in their interactions and opportunities. Hugo, whose skin is medium-light in color, avoids many forms of racial bias. Yet he notices how his wife, whom he describes as *negra*, receives the brunt of it when they enter a high-end establishment. He personally has never received worse service than other clients in a shop, he claimed:

> But my wife has. . . . We went into a jewelry store and my wife wanted to see a watch and the Indian guy didn't really want to. He thought that if he gave us the watch we were going to run away with the watch. And the guy was real nasty. My wife got very offended and she cursed him out. (Puerto Rican migrant, IT manager)

Professional migrants also observe the dynamics of the work world around them. For instance, Angela, who works in finance and socializes with many other professional Dominicans, suspects that skin color must play some role in who ends up in this high-status group, stating, "As I see it, by my experience, all of this environment where I function professionally, I think that there are a few *morenos* and everybody is *blanco*. I don't know, but there has to be something there. . . . Of 50 Dominican people that I know, that 3 are *moreno*." It may partly be due to their social class backgrounds, Angela posited, but she also recognized the advantage of looking White. As Filomena, a lawyer with light skin, noted, "When you get here, to the U.S., you're Hispanic. But if you're a dark Hispanic, you're doubly stereotyped."

Light-skinned Latinos are more accepted socially, professional migrants maintain. Racism is partly visual, and thus even when someone's Latino ethnicity is known, it may not matter as much if she looks White. Rafaela noted:

> Wanda is my friend that works with the Italians. And she's light-skinned and has straight hair. She would easily pass as a White American person. And I don't know, I think that at least Italians, they pay attention a lot to the physical appearance and those things. Maybe with them she'd have more advantage. I've never seen a *negro* employed by Italians. (Dominican migrant, accountant)

Others note that those with light skin have more residential options and can move into White neighborhoods, an observation supported by larger studies.[37]

White appearance can, in fact, offset many of the negative stereotypes that Americans hold about Latinos. Angela has light skin and European features;

she described how her appearance allowed her to avoid discrimination that would have been targeted against her because of her nationality, as she sought to rent an apartment in an exclusive section of Queens.

> I swear that never in my life had I felt discriminated against and this was the [only] time and it was looking for this apartment. . . . I called on the phone from [an ad in] the *New York Times*. . . . I called and I have an accent obviously. The lady asked me where I'm from and I told her Dominican. She says okay, and she started to give excuses. "No, because you have two kids and it's upstairs and going up the stairs and whatever." I said, "Look, my kids know how to go up the stairs. . . . I want to see it." She started to give me pretexts. Who did I work with? What did my husband do? Was my husband Dominican too or was he American? I said, "I can't believe she is asking me those things." . . . So I said, "Well, we are going to come see the apartment." She was in love with us. "What a nice couple!" and whatever. And she says to me, "Look, I am going to give you some advice. If I were you, when people ask you, don't tell them you are Dominican." (Dominican migrant, investment banker)

Once Angela showed up at the woman's doorstep, her White appearance made her, in the landlady's eyes, an exception to the larger group of Dominicans. Angela was offered the apartment, but turned it down in disgust.

Respondents who look White describe less discrimination and feel more accepted in U.S. society. Signals of their Latino origin may still trigger negative responses from others; but even though they are not completely free from the burden of the Latino stereotype, they have tools with which to confront it. César, who looks European, noted that the infrequent experiences he does have with discrimination or prejudice usually revolve around his surname or his accent: "I've never felt that much prejudice. Of course there is some when I send a résumé and they see my last name. I have many qualifications and sometimes I feel that just because of my last name there's an issue. It's the name of any Latino and they think it's something bad. It's because of the stereotype." Because he is aware of the stereotypes associated with Latinos, César explained, if he is applying for a job, he likes to stop in so they can put a face to a name. When employers see that he looks like any other middle-class White person, the stereotypes of Latinos that his surname evokes frequently disappear. His appearance helps him get his foot in the door, and by the time he tells them where he is from, he has already established a relationship with them. His friends who "have the Hispanic look," he said, have more trouble getting their foot in the door to establish that relationship. Skin color can provide opportunities or barriers, which contribute to middle-class migrants' position in America's racial hierarchy in addition to their Latino classification.

Conclusion

Different racial schemas produce overlapping, interconnected planes of social stratification. In the Dominican Republic and Puerto Rico, a nationality schema and a continuum schema each produce different systems of ranking individuals. Because all Dominicans and Puerto Ricans fall into the higher-status location of a nationality schema in their own countries, its power as a form of stratification is more easily overlooked. Yet few Haitians in the Dominican Republic or Dominicans in Puerto Rico would deny that their nationality affects their status in those societies. The majority group in each society is more affected by color stratification within its nationality location. As Dominicans and Puerto Ricans become minorities in the United States, they are touched by intersecting status hierarchies based on both their location within a Hispanicized U.S. schema and a color schema that has long existed in the United States. Just as multiple racial schemas exist within a society, so too do they create different ways that people are simultaneously ranked and stratified.

The very fact that many racial schemas exist at the same time in a society suggests that changing cultural concepts of race do not always entail drastic changes in racial stratification. In the Hispanic Caribbean, even as some nonmigrants add Americanized schemas to their racial schema portfolios, prior forms of stratification based on existing racial schemas remain in place. Many Puerto Ricans in San Juan are coming to see themselves as Latinos, but a color hierarchy based on the earlier continuum racial schema remains strong, and has real consequences in the lives of those with darker phenotypes. The fact that a Hispanicized U.S. schema increasingly predominates over a binary U.S. schema in the United States does not mean that visible African heritage is irrelevant in the social locations that Latinos occupy.

What the importation of new racial schemas can do, however, is provide a new basis for political mobilization. In several Latin American countries, increased adoption of Black identities has led to political movements, influenced by the U.S. civil rights struggle, to demand greater rights and benefits for people of African descent.[38] In various countries, this Black mobilization has led to targeted legislation for Black populations and, in Brazil, affirmative action–style considerations in education.[39] Greater adoption of a binary U.S. schema encouraging more people to embrace Black classifications, or diffusion of Black

Pride narratives from abroad, is the type of process that could lead Puerto Ricans and Dominicans to combat racial inequality in their home societies.

Over time, as new schemas are used more often, they will play a greater role in organizing society, and the symbolic boundaries revealed in less frequently used schemas may fade in importance. Being Irish American rather than English American, a significant boundary in late-19th-century America, has little influence on socioeconomic opportunities today. But such boundary blurring rarely happens without concerted effort, and usually the deflection of stigma onto other racialized groups.

Cultural change can occur through the importation and adoption of new ideas, shifting the basis for racial hierarchy, but structural change does not necessarily follow. Racial inequality does not diminish because many people in a society come to more frequently use a new racial schema over an old one. All of these are ways of ranking individuals in society, albeit different ways. Only as new racial concepts and schemas are adopted as a way for underprivileged groups to demand rights and resources will those hierarchies become more egalitarian.

6 Performing Race Strategically

RACIAL SCHEMAS OFTEN OPERATE AT A SUBCONSCIOUS LEVEL. We may not even be aware of how we divide the world into racial categories and try to place everyone we see into the appropriate one. However, people also develop conscious ideas or concepts about different races—how they behave, for example—which are not the same as those racial schemas but are based upon them. When migrants move to a new society, they learn not only new cognitive schemas for dividing up and classifying the world, but also bits of cultural knowledge about how to behave around those new groups and how to perform their own race as well. They learn the styles, routines, and actions to signal who they are and, sometimes, who they want to be seen to be.[1] Enacting this cultural knowledge of ways of behaving to signal membership in a particular racial group—what I call *racial strategies*—can be deployed purposefully, as part of a cultural tool kit. For example, Latino migrants can use these strategies, to the extent that their appearance allows, to try to shape whether they are seen as Latino or as White or Black Americans in different situations.

Chapter 5 examined how other people's perceptions of race, especially the views of people in power, are what matter most in stratifying society. Individuals have only limited control over how they are perceived racially by others. But they can use culture and performance to try to mediate that perception. Here, I focus on "race in action"—how migrants enact race by performing it, adopting types of behavior, styles, and routines that signal who they are within a racial framework. Just as every decision about how to behave in a situation constitutes a strategy of action, these decisions can collectively constitute broader racial strategies for positioning oneself within a racial hierarchy.

The selection of American or immigrant styles of behavior can be a deliberate decision, chosen as a way of avoiding discrimination and improving one's position within a racially stratified society. Sociologist Mary Waters found that West Indian immigrants retained their immigrant identities, and even taught their children the accents and styles that would distinguish them as West Indian, to avoid the stigma of being seen as African American.[2] Similarly, Dominicans and Puerto Ricans may choose to retain or to shed the trappings of their ethnic origins by adopting the styles and behaviors of native-born Americans. But for them, which racial strategy will improve their status is influenced by their skin color. For those who are lighter and more European in appearance, choosing the cultural strategies of White Americans is likely to position them closer to Whites, and may lead others to view and treat them accordingly. For those who are darker, the cultural strategies of their Latino group signal their difference from Black Americans and tend to present them as having what they see as a higher-status position. In groups with such phenotype diversity, where a person falls on the color spectrum influences what advantages can be gained from becoming more culturally American.

How these racial strategies are understood depends on whether Latinos are viewed as a race or as a collection of ethnic groups, which in turn depends on the racial schema adopted. When Latino origin is regarded as an aspect of ethnicity, as with a binary U.S. schema, such strategies can be understood as part of cultural assimilation—migrants adopting more American ways of behaving.[3] In this sense, migrants' awareness of what part of American society—White or Black— they would be seen as assimilating into may help shape their strategies. When a Latino category is viewed racially, however, as it is by many of my respondents and by those adopting a Hispanicized U.S. schema, these behaviors take on the character of racial passing. Although few feel the need to permanently hide their Latino origins, as Blacks and others sometimes did in the days of overt discrimination before civil rights protections, many migrant respondents nonetheless view the tactic of acting White or Black in similar terms—as hiding one's roots for personal benefit. Just as "Latino" can be seen as either a race or an ethnicity depending on the schema used, migrants can experience their strategies as both a form of cultural assimilation and a way of passing for another race.

In studies of assimilation, whether immigrants and their children retain their immigrant or ethnic identities or come to see themselves as Americans is an important concern.[4] However, the way that many Dominican and Puerto Rican migrants racialize nationality categories such as "American" points to our need to distinguish their cultural behavior from their identity. Puerto Rican and

Dominican migrants can adopt many strategies of action from their new society without adopting an American identity. In their mind, "American" means *gringos* and *Morenos*, ascribed statuses they may never feel able to achieve. Although identity is an important factor that influences specific kinds of behavior, decoupling the two allows us to understand the circumstances when a person may allow her racial performance to differ from how she identifies.

Although my migrant respondents recognized that some members of their group do assimilate (or pass) into White or Black America, most respondents who added the strategies of their host society to their cultural tool kits—primarily college-educated, middle-class respondents—do not subscribe to cultural assimilation as a permanent strategy. Rather than consistently trying to present themselves as Latino, White, or Black, they often find it more advantageous to switch how they present themselves in different situations. This leads to code switching, a practice of selecting different cultural codes and ways of behaving in different circumstances.[5] It also leads to a closely related pattern that I call *situational passing*. This does not necessarily involve the active use of different codes or behaviors, but represents a strategic approach toward whether or not to communicate or withhold their Latino origin, information that generally leads others to reevaluate their initial classifications.

Most migrant respondents identified as Latino or with their nationality; none viewed themselves as American. Yet that does not mean that none of them have assimilated into American culture. Many of them have incorporated American strategies of action into their cultural tool kits. While the most assimilated among them enact those Americanized behaviors most often, others find that there are numerous occasions when it is more advantageous to draw on non-American cultural repertoires. Especially in a city like New York, where Latinos are becoming more significant as larger voting blocs, consumer groups, and cultural forces, the loss of ethnic culture is not always the best strategy.

The Presentation of Race in Everyday Life

In *The Presentation of Self in Everyday Life*, Erving Goffman compares social interaction to a performance, where an actor seeks to control the terms of the situation and the audience's impression of herself in order to lead the audience to voluntarily act in the way she desires. A wide range of verbal and nonverbal communication is used to this effect, both intentionally and unintentionally. As the actor performs her role and the audience judges it, the interaction becomes "a kind of information game—a potentially infinite cycle of concealment, discovery, false revelation, and rediscovery."[6] Like everyone else, Dominican and

Puerto Rican respondents engage in such a performance to convey their group membership to others. Using a wide range of signs—language, accent, dress, physical movement, and other social cues—they can seek to control the terms of their interaction by shaping impressions of who they are.

For Latinos, language is one of the most important signals of group membership. In interactions, it is their language that typically offers the first indication that they are not White or Black Americans. Octavio, like many others, claimed that people do not know he is Hispanic until he speaks. When migrants want to disclose their identity, they make a point of speaking in Spanish or revealing an accent in English. Conversely, sometimes migrants want to conceal their origins. Silvia, a Puerto Rican professor with an African appearance, commented: "We try to eliminate the accent so [we] sound [American]. It's not that easy but we try."

Hairstyle and dress are another way that migrants signal their race. For women in particular, hairstyles are a significant way of indicating identity and belonging. Yesenia explained that she uses these cues to judge other people's group membership: "The hair, the way they do it. . . . The difference is that Dominicans make it straight, most of them. We [Puerto Ricans] don't like it too much. I like curly like I have it." Men also use hair as a cue—for instance, whether they grow facial hair or how they comb their hair. And both men and women employ jewelry and clothing to signal whether they are Latino. Such cues, whether deliberate or not, allow respondents to manage other people's impressions. For those at the ends of the racial spectrum, it can also lead observers to view them, at least initially, as White or Black Americans or as Latinos.

The performance of race goes beyond appearance to ways of interacting, body language, and mannerisms. Migrants mentioned posture (how you hold your shoulders, for instance), how you walk (with a swagger or with your body straight), and how much personal space and privacy you give people as aspects of that performance. These subtle cues rely on the observers' familiarity with the behavior of different groups, or their stereotypes and assumptions. But like appearance, behavior can be used to manage impressions and to signal membership in a specific racial group.

Often these cues are intended to convey class more than race or ethnicity. Silvia noted that the kinds of things one could do to act more American—"dress American. The jargon, the phrases. . . . Reading. Keeping up to date of all the subjects. Knowing the history. Being able to talk, converse with Americans"—are ways of signaling education—the advantage that White Americans are seen as having—as much as race. When she behaves this way, particularly in professional settings, she said, it is not about wanting to come across as more American or Puerto Rican, but as more educated. She feels that she rarely tries to "act American," but that her comportment is often the kind that people associate more with Whites because of their higher education levels. Similarly, when César claimed that certain styles and dress lead people to classify him as Puerto Rican, he portrayed that as an image associated with lower-class status. Explaining that he often tries to look more like a White American when going to a disco or club, he said:

> If you look too ghetto at a disco, the bouncers know that, and prefer Americans who dress better. . . . If they see you dress a certain way or style, people classify it with a certain group or race. If I walk by with a wifebeater [shirt] with my pants below my waist wearing Timberlands, people think that I'm up to something. (Puerto Rican migrant, film producer)

Because Latinos are stereotyped as being poor, less professional, more likely to be "up to something" than Whites, the styles and mannerisms that people associate with acting American are often those intended to convey a higher-class status.[7] The associations between race and class are deeply ingrained, such that "performing class" is often interpreted as "performing race" as well.

Of course, skin color and aspects of appearance that are less controllable (short of cosmetic surgery) are central to observers' judgments about race and limit an actor's ability to influence those impressions. Because Dominicans and Puerto Ricans span the Black-White continuum, it is typically those who fall in the middle of this spectrum—those with brown or medium skin tones—who have the least flexibility in performing race. They are the least likely to be seen as White or Black and the most likely to be racialized as Latino, even if they are fully acculturated. César, who has a European appearance, acknowledged: "If they don't hear me speak, they don't know [I'm Hispanic]. Not dark-skinned people, but mixed, *mestizo* skin [people] have it even worse because it fits the profile. They associate them with that look from *West Side Story*. That person is not White, not Black, but *mestizo*, so it's bad." While those with medium or brown skin may feel that a Latino classification provides a higher status than being seen as Black Americans, it nonetheless gives them less ability to control impressions through the performance of race.

Cultural Assimilation, Passing, and Covering

Because a Latino classification involves cultural as well as physical cues, permanently altering behaviors that would lead people to see them as Latino is one strategy that migrants can adopt. Those whose appearance is more European or African have the option of adopting the behaviors that lead observers to regard and treat them as White or Black Americans. When "Latino" is viewed as an aspect of ethnicity, this approach is effectively cultural assimilation—the adoption of the culture or strategies of action of native-born groups within the new society. Many earlier immigrant groups, including Italians, Irish, Jews, and other European ethnics, followed such a pattern of cultural assimilation and eventually structural assimilation into White America. Early scholars of assimilation treated the culture of the host society as homogeneous, believing that immigrants would join the "mainstream" society, meaning the dominant White Anglo-Saxon culture.[8] More recent observers have noted that the culture of the host society is itself diverse and immigrants may assimilate into particular segments of it.[9] Sociologists Alejandro Portes and Min Zhou argue that the children of the post-1965 immigrants, unlike the mostly European immigrants of the turn of the 20th century, will experience a "segmented assimilation," with some communities—especially those who share racial characteristics of the native-born minorities and lack key resources—likely to assimilate into those native-born minority groups.[10] While many have debated this argument, including whether integrating into native-born minorities necessarily entails downward assimilation,[11] it remains the case that when immigrant groups with African appearance lose the indicators of their ethnic origins, they are often associated with Black Americans.[12] Similarly, light-skinned Latinos may be viewed as White Americans when they acculturate to the norms and behavior of this group while losing their Latino identification.

Yet because "Latino" is a racialized category, it can be more difficult for Latin American immigrants and their descendants to lose a Latino classification than for other immigrants to lose their ethnic labels. Even if they have adopted the cultural behavior of native-born groups, an indication of Latino origins often leads to a reclassification. In this way, even when Latinos are viewed as an ethnic group, they are "racialized ethnics," perpetually defined as foreigners even after many generations and full acculturation to American norms.[13] When Latino is viewed as a race, those who present themselves as White or Black Americans through their behavior or by withholding information about their Latino origins can be seen as racially passing.

"Passing" is a deception that allows a person to effectively present herself as different than who she understands herself to be, and to assume a role or identity that prevailing social standards would otherwise bar her from holding.[14] The classic example is light-skinned Blacks who passed as White in the pre–civil rights era to partake of socioeconomic opportunities that were limited to Whites. Passing may sometimes involve active deception, but often occurs simply through the omission of relevant information—failing to correct someone else's assumption, for example. Several of my respondents used the word "pass" to describe their co-ethnics who deny their Latino roots or who act like White or Black Americans, socialize primarily with that group, and distance themselves from their fellow Latinos. Such behavior was highly stigmatized as denying an essential aspect of the self, just as African American communities sometimes stigmatized racial passers for betraying their race and themselves.[15] For better or for worse, many respondents understand their cultural origins primordially, as an aspect of self that is rooted in their blood. Odalys harshly described this behavior as "negating what God has chosen you to be, your soil, your nation, your race, your origin."

None of my migrant respondents claimed to have lost an ethnic or Latino identity, perhaps not surprisingly, given the stigma associated with it.[16] Shedding an ethnic identity is also less common in the first generation than in later generations.[17] Yet several respondents described acquaintances—co-ethnics with light skin—whom they view as trying to become White Americans by disassociating themselves from the ethnic community and acting White. César, for instance, told me:

> I know that there are Puerto Ricans that don't want to be Puerto Ricans and don't want to know anything about it. They don't want to speak Spanish or eat the food. When a person knows that his last name is Hispanic and tries to speak Spanish to them, that person tries to block it out and not let them classify him as Hispanic. (Puerto Rican migrant, film producer)

Tomás believes it is the pressure to fit in that spurs such behavior: "Some Puerto Ricans have lighter skin and don't speak Spanish so they give up their heritage to fit in. Maybe it's a sign of giving up, but sometimes people just want to fit in so badly and so are forced to choose a side." Those who tried to blend in with non-Latino Americans would avoid use of Spanish or Americanize their names, both key ways of trying to hide their Latino origins, since such indicators can act as a proverbial one drop of blood, instantly tying them to a Latino classification.

Yet because Latinos are not formally barred from opportunities in the way that Blacks were during the Jim Crow era, there is less need to permanently hide a Latino origin. Those who look White or Black can simply adopt the behavior, lifestyle, and norms of that group and expect to be viewed and treated as a member most of the time. This is what Goffman describes as "covering."[18]

Unlike passing (attempting to hide a stigmatized identity), covering is behavior to manage a stigma by making it less obtrusive. It involves trying to play down that identity by avoiding the behavior associated with it.[19] Latinos who cover do not deny their Latino origin, but by assimilating to dominant norms, they minimize its visibility in their performance. Raquel described an instance of covering, noting its advantages for Latinos who look White:

> In this country, even though there are a lot of opportunities, . . . there's a lot of [racism]. I think that if you're Hispanic and you lean more towards your European ancestry, you're more accepted, the possibilities are better, etc. There's a guy who went to college with me. He's a reporter on Channel 41. I remember when I saw him walking through the campus, I'd say, "He's so cute!" (laughing) And I never knew he was Hispanic. I never heard him speak in Spanish, until a lot later, maybe in the last year of school. "[Jaime,] are you Hispanic?" He said, "Yes. I'm Peruvian." "And why don't you ever speak Spanish?" "Oh no, because it's not necessary. Why?" So if you look more like the mass of Whites, sometimes you mix in and shut up and, if you don't have the accent in English, there's no necessity to say. (Dominican migrant, assistant principal)

In this example, Jaime does not conceal his Peruvian identity, but he also does not flaunt it. By speaking English without an accent, "mixing in" with Whites, and "shutting up" about his origins, he receives the social advantages of Whiteness.

In order to align themselves with Whites, some Latinos were seen as distancing themselves from their co-ethnics. This occurred not only by moving in White social circles and moving into White neighborhoods, but also by using negative or harsh treatment toward co-ethnics as a signal to other Whites of the boundaries between them. Paulina suspected this was why she received much worse treatment from her Puerto Rican boss than any of the other employees did. Gloria, a retired Puerto Rican school aide with dark skin, described her former boss's harsher treatment toward co-ethnics: "The school where I worked, the principal was Puerto Rican and like they say, 'There's no worse thorn than the one from your own tree.' She was mean with her own kind . . . she was too stern. Like she copied Americans. . . . She tried to be like them." Gloria explained that her boss was friendly with all the Jewish teachers and tried to act like them, while trying to distance herself from the Puerto Ricans in order to affiliate herself more with Whites. The principal's Puerto Rican identity was well known; thus her behavior was not an instance of passing, but perhaps the fact that she was recognized as Puerto Rican was all the more reason for her to seek to differentiate herself from other Puerto Ricans through her behavior.

Very few respondents described Puerto Rican or Dominican acquaintances as adopting a Black American identity, although some suggested that it does happen. Hugo shared one example: "This girl I know was born in Puerto Rico. Her parents, one is *blanco* and the other *negro* and she is *trigueña*. . . . She came to live here in the U.S. . . . and she grew up among Blacks, among African Americans, so she feels African American." The few respondents who described such patterns view them as a result of spending time around African Americans in school, work, or neighborhoods. Some believe that it helps them to fit in or feel less foreign. For example, Adrián said:

> I think there are even some [Dominicans] that try to pass as Afro Americans as well. . . . To be more accepted I guess. . . . And I see this happens more when they have to be among Afro Americans. Because Afro Americans, they don't accept Blacks from other places. I've seen that when they refer to Africans, for example—they're not Afro Americans. And that's the case with Dominicans. But I've seen that when a Dominican works among them . . . because they're *negros* they try to pass as Afro Americans. They adopt the way of dressing, the way of talking, the music, everything. (Dominican migrant, journalist)

Dark-skinned migrants are more likely to be residentially segregated from White neighborhoods and more likely to live in primarily Black neighborhoods.[20] Acculturating to a Black American community may be more common in the second or 1.5 generations[21] than among those who migrate as teenagers or adults. Yet because most migrant respondents regarded Black Americans as lower in status than Latinos, most viewed this path as unusual and even surprising. Although respondents still frowned upon those light skinned Latinos who wanted to "become White," that approach was at least understood, as a way of escaping the racism associated with a Latino label.

Performing *Latinidad*

Although migrant respondents were well aware that some members of their ethnic group choose to assimilate and hide their Latino identities, the respondents primarily sought to retain, assert, and perform their Latino identities in many situations. There were several reasons why migrants sought to express their Latino origins by adopting the cultural codes and actions associated with their group, and found it advantageous to do so.

Among the respondents who most frequently performed their *latinidad* were those with darker skin. Like other immigrant groups with African appearance,[22] darker Latinos felt an interest in differentiating themselves from

Black Americans. Migrants never described reacting aggressively when others thought they were White Americans, but those who were mistaken for Black Americans quickly protested. Marisela described the reaction of a dark-skinned Dominican friend, originally from a region of the Dominican Republic known for its African heritage:

> I have a friend that is really *morena* [dark] and she doesn't like when they tell her, she automatically says, 'Ay, I am not American *Morena*.' She opens her mouth real big and says, 'I am *morena* Dominican!' But, you know, people confuse her because she is from San Pedro de Macoris. She is real *morena* with very bad hair like the [American] *Morenos* have, so people confuse her. (Dominican migrant, travel agent)

Language is frequently used by darker Latinos to send signals about their identity, with Spanish serving as an indicator of group membership. Yesenia said, "*Negro* Puerto Ricans don't want to be Black Americans. . . . When they come in the elevator and you think they are Black Americans and you speak English to them . . . they quickly speak Spanish to you." Among the migrant respondents, those with dark or medium skin were slightly more likely to identify their race on the open-ended question as "Latino" or "Puerto Rican/Dominican." Yet the vast majority of light-skinned migrants did so as well.[23] Overwhelmingly, respondents asserted the importance of maintaining a Latino or national identity and communicating it to others. This was equally true for those who had lived in the United States for most of their lives and claimed that it felt more like home than their countries of origin.

Some respondents, including those who have spent decades in the United States, never do acculturate. They perform their *latinidad* not deliberately, but because they have not acquired other cultural codes of behavior. Respondents who do not speak English well, especially those who never attended school in the United States and who socialize primarily with other Latinos, signal their nationality group to other Latinos, but do not pick up the skills to downplay, or "cover," their Latino origins. Most of the migrant respondents who have lower levels of education and work in low-skill jobs fall into this category. Whether deliberately, to avoid feeling excluded, or because of language barriers, those who interact primarily with other Latinos perform their *latinidad* because they have not acquired alternative cultural scripts.

Many respondents also feel it is important to emphasize their Latino origins because of the cultural view that they bring with them of their national identity as something primordial and essentialized. For them, race is closely tied to cultural attachments to a homeland and its people. Thus, even if they frequently adopt aspects of American culture, they cannot fully discard the culture of their ancestral lands without "negating their race." Because their *latinidad* is part of the essence of who they are, they do not see "becoming American" as entirely possible or desirable. Gloria, for example, is effusive in her praise for the United States. She has spent almost half a century there. But she will never stop being Puerto Rican.

> Q: *Considering the good and the bad, how happy are you that you came to the U.S.?*

I am the happiest woman of this world and I say that I will be thanking my mother until the day I die that she brought me to this country. Because I tell you that I love New York.

> Q: *And which country do you feel is your home?*

This right here . . . because I have lived the best years of my life here. I succeeded because I studied. And then I got married twice. . . . In the second one I was very happy and we lasted 32 years even though he wasn't one of mine [a Puerto Rican] but look at what good chemistry we had. . . .

> Q: *Do you feel closer to being American or Puerto Rican?*

Well, I am Puerto Rican because regardless of anything, that is my country. That's where I was born. As far as that always, if anyone talks about Puerto Rico in front of me I set them straight at least. Because that's where I saw the light for the first time. (Puerto Rican migrant, retired assistant teacher)

Despite feeling more at home in the United States, Gloria has a strong emotional attachment to her homeland and "her people," among whom her Cuban husband did not, alas, qualify. Many insist that being Puerto Rican or Dominican is "in your blood." Despite recurring political pressures for immigrants to lose their hyphenated identities and just become Americans, these Latinos' primordial view of national origins means that even becoming Americanized does not make them American.

With their primordial view of nationality, many respondents racialize the term "American," most often associating it with White non-Latinos, or *gringos*. Marcia, a Puerto Rican doctor's assistant, is proud of her U.S. citizenship, but excludes herself in her definition of "American." She says, "For me, the White person is the American. He belongs to the United States. He's the American."[24] Although Marcia also identified her own race as "White," she distinguishes herself from this American cultural group. Respondents believe that the category "American" is reserved for those from an Anglo-Saxon background.[25] By this conception of race, being American is not something one can learn (despite the fact that many earlier immigrants did just that). For them, Latinos who acculturate simply become Americanized Latinos.

In addition to respondents' primordial views of identity, the external barriers to full acceptance that they perceive reinforce a reactive Latino identity. As a racialized group, they are seen as "forever foreigners," a group of perpetual outsiders.[26] Those who are identifiable as Latino on the basis of physical appearance or surname are marginalized from the category of "real Americans." Reynaldo asserted that, despite his 40 years in the United States, he does not feel fully accepted "because they don't consider me American." Reynaldo sees "being American" as partly about social acceptance, and experiences with discrimination reveal that an American identity is being withheld. As Esperanza, a Dominican homemaker and informal day-care provider, noted laughingly, "Living in this country, I always feel Dominican." Feelings that they are not allowed to be fully American strengthen a Latino identity and, for many, encourage the signaling of that identity through behavior.

Bicultural Fluency

Many Puerto Rican and Dominican migrants do acquire American cultural codes and scripts, but believe that there are reasons for not using them exclusively. In addition to the reactive pressures pushing them to identify with and signal their Latino origins, there is also an important pull factor for migrants to retain their native cultures, language, and behavior: with the growth of the Latino community, there is a large demand for people who not only speak Spanish but understand Latino cultures. Those respondents who do pick up American cultural strategies through their interactions outside their ethnic community see it as more advantageous to learn how to navigate mainstream America without losing their own culture. This provides them with a *bicultural fluency* that allows them to move smoothly between communities and serve as mediators between Whites and Latinos. In this sense, migrants selectively acquire the cultural practices of the majority group as an additive process, without rejecting their own.[27] Others have noted that Latinos "exhibit chameleon-like behavior in different social contexts,"[28] particularly the second generation, among whom the ability to navigate mainstream and immigrant communities is considered a particular "second generation advantage."[29] Yet even in the first generation, those who acquire American strategies of action often use them selectively, switching from one set of cultural codes to another as the situation demands.

Even respondents with light skin who might be seen as White Americans often feel that it is more advantageous to straddle both cultures than to immerse themselves fully in just one. Bilingual skills in particular are in great demand. Nilda has light skin and could pass for a White American, but when applying for jobs she finds that it helps to be seen as Puerto Rican:

> When I came, at the beginning, I think that Americans had many more advantages than us. Now I think that on the contrary, it helps us a lot being bilingual. In many jobs . . . when you're bilingual, you have a better opportunity. Because that happened to me in customer service, that my English is not perfect, many young women that spoke better English applied and they gave me the opportunity of having that position for being bilingual. (Puerto Rican migrant, customer service representative)

Latinos in the United States are a tremendous potential market, and employers need staff who can speak their language, literally and figuratively. Such employees can also serve as intermediaries between non-Latino managers and the clientele.

Pedro, who also has light skin, believes that Dominicans of all skin colors do better by asserting a Dominican identity. He emphasized the size and growth of the Latino community, and the opportunities that it creates for people who can serve both a Latino market and other potential markets:

> You could navigate in two different worlds. That's the advantage. If you navigate the English world, it's something, you know, but if you can do both— Fifty years from now this is going to be totally different. . . . The U.S. is going to have a very large Hispanic population. So 50 years from now everything is going to change. It is changing. If we are 35 million now, imagine 50 years from now. Or 20. (Dominican migrant, assistant librarian)

Pedro is raising his daughter not only to be bilingual, but to understand both American and Dominican cultures. In the future, he argues, such bicultural fluency will be more valuable than just being Americanized.

Many respondents who seek to be able to navigate between the Latino and mainstream American cultures adopt lifestyles, interests, and tastes from both. Arturo, a Dominican truck driver, exemplifies this cultural agility. Neither assimilated nor immersed in an ethnic community, Arturo straddles both worlds—and keeps his foot in the door back home too. Equally comfortable in Spanish and English, he reads a variety of newspapers to keep himself up to speed on each community: the *Daily News* and a local Queens paper, the *Rich-wood Times*; *El Diario* to keep tabs on Latinos in New York; and sometimes *La Prensa* or *El Listín Diario* from the Dominican Republic. He prefers Latin music like *merengue*, *bachata*, and *balada*, but watches mainly U.S. television. CNN (in English) is on constantly in his house, or else the local news channel, New York 1. He is very interested in U.S. politics and is an astute critic of the government's domestic policies. His family eats mainly Dominican food, although a pizza box on the counter suggests an occasional American temptation. Although they have mostly stopped celebrating Dominican holidays and now celebrate only American ones (often with a Dominican twist), they still put out their Dominican flag in February to mark the Dominican independence. It is important to Arturo that he teach his young sons both Dominican and American customs. He navigates these cultural boundaries with remarkable fluency, a skill that has helped him in his work at an Italian American trucking company, where he serves as union steward. He explained:

> Most of the workforce is Latino and that's one of my advantages. That's why I run for [union] shops through all my jobs and that's why I won because I speak both languages. The guy that was there before was a White guy that only speaks English and there's a lot of guys over there that don't speak a word of English. And when they have a problem it's easier to have me in the middle that I speak both languages to solve the problem. (Dominican migrant, truck driver)

His skills in mediating between his Italian bosses and the Latino union members are in demand from both sides. His ability to switch to American cultural codes makes his bosses comfortable around him, and eager to have him as the shop steward. Arturo feels that his comfort level with White Americans as well as Latinos has helped him in his career.

Those who become truly fluent in both cultures need more than just bilingualism—they must be able to adopt the subtle mannerisms and behaviors that are appropriate to the group they are around. Code switching involves expressing internalized strategies of action from different cultural repertoires, rather than passing as a member of a group one does not identify with. Alfonso, who migrated at age 14, frequently employs code switching between the Dominican world of home and the American persona he adopts at work. As he explained, this is little more than expressing different sides of himself:

> Let's say when I'm at work and I speak proper I present myself a certain way, I have to ask questions a certain way, I think I have to walk a certain way. . . . You

have to carry yourself with your chest . . . standing up straight, you know? But if I'm around my uncles, you know, drinking Presidente [Dominican beer], and being this loud, it's different. I would say that I'm an actor. But now thinking about it, is it acting or is it just being me? Both are who I am, the Dominican here and the American here. So it's not really acting I guess.

Q: Does one feel like more of an act than the other?

I think the American [is more] like an act. I've got to deal with these rich millionaires from Manhattan trying to buy up co-op[s] and I have to talk like I own a two-million-dollar co-op and you know, be a certain way. I have to hide my accent the best I can. It's very difficult. (Dominican migrant, mortgage broker)

Although his American behavior feels more like an act, Alfonso is simply using different cultural scripts he has acquired, and the more he performs the American scripts, the more fluent he will become in that culture. Migrant respondents who have internalized aspects of American culture prefer to also remain fluent in their old culture rather than shedding it to show their full Americanness. Not only do they see full Americanness as unattainable, but they realize that bicultural fluency offers the advantage of moving more readily between the American and Latino worlds.

Situational Passing

Code switching is one way that migrants who have added different cultured capacities to their tool kits can take advantage of those that are most beneficial in a particular situation. They change their behavior, yet without necessarily signaling different identities. A person who identifies as Latino can make that identity known and yet still adopt the strategies of action associated with White America.

Many migrant respondents also adopt a closely related strategy to confront discrimination and gain a momentary advantage—what I call *situational passing*. This approach is available to migrants with light or dark skin whether they have acquired new cultural codes or not. It involves not necessarily changing their strategies of action, but selectively choosing whether or not to make their Latino origins known. The fact that many Puerto Ricans and Dominicans look like White or Black Americans allows them to take advantage of the confusion about their race by adopting different masks, depending on their utility in the moment.

With code switching, migrants and their children generally change their behavior to better fit in with whatever group they are around. They adopt the cultural behavior of their own group when around their family and other co-ethnics and adopt that of native-born groups when interacting with them. With situational passing, people do not always adopt the mask of the group they are with; rather they identify some instances when it is advantageous to reveal Latino origins around outsiders or to pass as a member of an outsider group around co-ethnics. Of course, some people may use both situational passing and code switching for the same ends, when certain aspects of performance can support the mask they have put on. But unlike those who engage only in code switching, those who are situationally passing are willing to momentarily claim or foster the impression that they are members of a group with which they do not identify. The following cases illustrate this racial strategy.

.   .   .

Through his delivery work, Arturo, the Dominican truck driver in an Italian American company, comes into contact with people of diverse backgrounds, from his Italian employers and Latino coworkers, to "redneck drivers from Mississippi" who bring in shipments, and the panoply of New York's ethnic spectrum as he makes deliveries throughout the city. As he interacts with people from these different groups, Arturo often finds himself adopting different masks. His appearance helps: he has very light skin, straight brown hair, and European features. While he identifies as Latino, the way he presents himself to others depends on what is most useful in any given context:

> A lot of people think I'm Italian, especially because my name is [Arturo] and at my job when they give me an assistant and they tell him that he's going with [Arturo] he thinks that he's going to help an Italian. . . . When they see that I put the Spanish station [on] in the truck radio, they say, "Oh, you're Spanish? I thought you were Italian". . . .

> Q: And how do you feel when they confuse you with Italians?

> (Pause) Sometimes good, sometimes bad. It all depends on my convenience. . . . If I feel it's okay for them to confuse me with an Italian at the moment, I stay Italian.

> Q: Can you pretend to be Italian?

> Yeah. Yeah. I can pretend to be Italian. A lot of people told me. . . ." You sound Italian." . . . Sometimes I try to make the Italian accent. Sometimes I stay Italian and some people, I go to make deliveries and they think I'm Italian and they start speaking Italian to me, so the words I know, I talk back. . . . I understand

a lot [of Italian]. . . . Most of the time, I stop people and tell them, "Look, I do look Italian, but I'm not Italian. I'm Dominican." . . . [But] like if I'm in an Italian neighborhood and somebody wants to beat me up and I look Italian they're not going to beat me up. In a lot of neighborhoods I think it's to my advantage that the people know that I'm a Latino.

Arturo knows a few words in Italian, which he throws in to make his Italian mask more believable. But he has not acquired particular knowledge of Italian cultured capacities. His Brooklyn accent, his name (which could be either Italian or Spanish), and his light skin lead people to see him as Italian, and Arturo simply plays along to create greater rapport with his customers. However, in some situations, his light appearance can be a disadvantage. In some of the areas where his work takes him, it is not so great to be seen as White.

My complexion is of a White person. A lot of times I walk through the streets in a neighborhood where I'm known by no one, let's say that it's a Black neighborhood, and I see a Black guy spit on the floor. And I ask my friend from work that's Black why they're spitting and he says it's because they think I am a White guy.

If the person knew he is Latino, Arturo insists, they would never do that. So whenever he can in those situations, he tries to present himself as Latino.

Arturo makes a similar judgment call of what mask to put on when he is stopped by the police.

When the police pull you over, you don't want them to know, if it's a White cop, that you're Spanish. A lot of people have that in mind: "Oh, they're going to take it out on me because I'm a Latino" and sometimes it goes to your advantage and sometimes it doesn't.

Q: What if it's a Hispanic cop?

Then I let him know. Well, he'll know when he talks to me that I'm Spanish. He'll know my accent right away. A lot of times [it] happen[s] that they think I'm a White guy and it's a Spanish cop and they end up talking back to me in Spanish.

Arturo is not shifting between different identities. He consistently identifies as Latino, and does not consider himself White in the United States, even though he could claim this identity in the Dominican Republic. Rather, he is strategically controlling his presentation of himself to others, in whatever way helps him most at the moment. By "staying Italian" when it is convenient to do so, he is passing for White, but only in that fleeting moment. In the next area he delivers to, he may decide to stay Latino.

. . .

Reynaldo, a Dominican engineer in his 50s, lives in Harlem. He identifies as Latino, yet with his dark skin and African features he could easily be seen as a Black American. He has a strong awareness of his African heritage and gets along with his African American neighbors; he lists many African Americans among his close friends. At the same time, he feels a strong connection to the Dominican community. He sports a baseball cap reading "Washington Heights," attends the Dominican parade, and tries to maintain many Dominican customs in his home, although his tastes have broadened to include American music and movies.

Reynaldo has faced a great deal of racism over his life, yet he is not one to let racial barriers get in his way. Even in a system that is unfair, he feels, you can learn how it works and figure out how to succeed within it. In high school, for example, he noticed that White students would get tracked into the honors classes, even if they did not belong there, because teachers would give them better recommendations. Recognizing this inequality was the first step to figuring out how to overcome it.

> You start to understand the process and begin [to learn] how to play your cards. You have to learn to manipulate the situation. Because if you want to go to a certain university and need a recommendation you need to know who might give it to you; who is a good person; who you can take classes with; who you can't because it doesn't matter if you're smart or not, you may have problems.

He learned early on that you have to keep your eyes open and look for ways around the obstacles, whether it is figuring out which teacher will not allow racial stereotypes to cloud her judgment or learning how to network and make the right connections to get a promotion. He takes a similarly strategic approach to how he presents himself to others.

> When someone wants me to be Black, I am. And when they want me to be Latino, I'm Latino. . . . For example, I can be Black and I could be Latino depending on where they want to put me, when it's convenient for them. . . . If they want to hire a minority [for instance]. . . . It depends on what situation you're in. There are times it's convenient to be Black American and sometimes it is convenient to be Black Latin American, Dominican. . . . If you know what that

person wants you can change so you can also use that to your favor. . . . Sometimes they want to specifically look for a Black person, but if you're Dominican you don't qualify.

Employers may be looking for a particular type of candidate when they make a minority hire, he feels. Whether it is because of quotas or because of the ethnicity of the person doing the hiring, it may be better to appear Latino in some situations and Black American in others.

Reynaldo is self-conscious that he may not be as good at passing for Black as he would like. He has had difficulty losing his accent, which he feels can be a problem because it gives his identity away.

Sometimes from our accents you can tell if someone is Latino, Dominican. But if the person doesn't have that accent you can't know. . . .

Q: *Do you know people that try to keep their accent so that people know they are Dominicans and not Black Americans?*

I think that happens. Sometimes I think of myself. . . . Yes. Psychologically, probably in the back of my head I was fighting it. [Fighting] losing my . . . accent. [But the accent] costs me too much money . . . because when you have an accent then you can get discriminated [against]. They probably think something else about you and you don't get the money you're supposed to be earning. . . . I don't want to save it now; it costs me too much.

Reynaldo is now trying to lose his accent to better control the impression he gives to others. He might face less discrimination in dealing with clients over the phone if it were not clear that he is Latino. In other situations, it might be better to appear Black than Dominican. "It depends," he said, "because they refer to Dominicans as drug dealers, so it's not advantageous in that case. It all depends on the situation you're in."

. . .

In passing for White or Black, Arturo and Reynaldo know they are putting on a mask that does not represent them but is useful to maintain for the moment. While language or accent is often a signal of identity, both are traits that Arturo and Reynaldo can nominally pick up or change without internalizing an entire set of cultured capacities associated with a different group. Situational passing is thus closely related to code switching, and is often used together with it, but it relies upon physical appearance—being able to look White or Black—for its effect.

The situational variant is a particular form of the larger phenomenon of racial passing. There have always been those who have engaged in "part-time" passing,[30] but situational passing is always fleeting. Beyond a few momentary encounters, names are usually exchanged or language must be used. The situational passer fully expects that sustained interaction will reveal her origins. It is also usually not premeditated behavior. In an era of formal segregation, even temporary passing involved some deliberate planning, if only to separate oneself from social ties that would reveal the hidden identity. The passing worker had to hide her family life from her work colleagues; the passing shopper had to avoid the company of friends to achieve her effect. Situational passing, by contrast, typically involves seizing a sudden opportunity. Rarely does an individual plan to mislead, but on finding herself alone in a shop, she may choose to withhold identifying signals or to play along with an observer's assumptions if it proves useful to do so.

This type of performance involves withholding information or creating a false impression more often than deliberate misstatement. In speaking Italian to a client, for example, Arturo makes no false statement; he does, in fact, know some Italian. Language, and the decision whether or not to use it, is the most commonly employed signal in the act of situational passing. Bernardo, who is European in appearance, will sometimes keep his mouth shut when someone assumes he is a White American. He said:

> I get away with it more with lack of action than . . . acting one way or another. I just . . . don't want to [explain to] any random person. I just sit tight, you know if I'm in line, whatever, I just don't open my mouth, because I know that's my dead giveaway, my accent. (Puerto Rican migrant, investment banker)

When he goes to Spanish Harlem to eat in a Puerto Rican restaurant, however, he makes a point of using Spanish to make his identity known in hopes of getting better service. Bernardo learned early on that people did not associate him with their stereotypes of what Puerto Ricans look like. While he found those stereotypes frustrating, he also saw the strategic promise they offered him, since their existence made people more likely to place him outside the group. He claimed, "The whole racial thing came about later when I was like, 'Hey, I can play this game too, use it to my advantage.' . . . In some situations, you don't want to deal with the person. . . . You just play along and don't give them a reason to suspect." Migrants who appear White or Black can exploit the ambiguity over how to classify Latinos in the United States, whether to obtain an advantage in an interaction or just to avoid the hassle of explaining to someone what you are.

The act of passing is itself associated with pursuing strategic advantage. Yet in this situational form, passing is not always beneficial; it is premised on the perception that the most advantageous identity varies considerably from one situation to another. Those who engage in this shifting performance must regularly assess what mask works best at a given moment. The advantages of being perceived as White are clear to many light-skinned Latinos. Thus in a restaurant or shop, or even a job interview, they may try to present themselves as White Americans. But there are many occasions where it is useful to be Latino. Their Spanish skills may improve their chances of employment. César is often assumed to be White, but is quick to emphasize being Puerto Rican on some job interviews: "Where the boss is Spanish, I play that card. I would have a quicker connection with that person because we have something in common and we can establish a conversation." Affirmative-action considerations, in hiring and education, also create a context when emphasizing Latino origins is beneficial.[31]

It is typically considered a disadvantage to be seen as Black. A Black identity is highly stigmatized, leading many dark-skinned immigrants and their children to distinguish themselves from Blacks.[32] While most of my Dominican and Puerto Rican migrants do not embrace a Black identity, they do recognize that on certain—usually brief—occasions it can be useful to pass for a Black American. When they are in the company of Blacks, for instance, it can help them be better accepted or escape racial tension. Odalys said she has observed many Dominicans pretending to be Black Americans:

> I have seen Dominicans that have acquired the look using their skin, their color and hair. Then they get braids and if they speak English they pass as Americans. . . . I think it's a smart way, many adopt it as if it were a uniform to be able to defend themselves in the area of work. Like the saying goes, "When in Rome, do as the Romans do."[33] If I worked at 125th [street in Harlem] I would adopt the whole style even if I don't like it to be able to defend myself and feel more identified with them. And I think they would accept me more. . . . And many [migrants] don't want to lose their identity [but] don't want to be looked at as Dominican. (Dominican migrant, factory worker)

Male respondents, in particular, say they sometimes find it useful to play off the stereotype of African Americans as intimidating or threatening, and create fear toward those around them by adopting that guise.

Respondents describe experiencing discriminatory or unfair treatment from African Americans as well as from Whites, particularly in shops or service establishments. For those who can look Black, not revealing their Latino identity can help them avoid such treatment. Hernando, who has dark skin, described one missed opportunity with a train operator:

> One day I was . . . coming out of school, I was going to the train and I had my pass, and there was a *Moreno* who wouldn't let me in. Because she was Afro American, she didn't want to let me in. I was speaking Spanish with my friends, and you could tell that she didn't like that, and so she was racist against me. And I said, "Wow, at least I could have looked [Black]. If hadn't talked, maybe she'd have thought I was *Moreno*." (Dominican migrant, business administrator)

In retrospect, he thought that he should have just kept his mouth shut, to pass as Black.

Some dark-skinned Latinos also pass for Black in the company of other Latinos. Not revealing that you speak Spanish can be particularly useful for listening in on what other people have to say about you. As a receptionist in a doctor's office, Marcia is sometimes on the receiving end of this tactic, as it is used by other Latino groups:

> The ones from Panama, a lot of times because of their [dark] color, speak to you in English so that later they can know if you're going to speak badly about them. Then they'll speak to you in Spanish. . . . They don't want to speak Spanish because that way we won't find out that they speak Spanish and they'll understand something that you say. . . . You get confused with Panamanians. You think they're *Morenos* from here because of their color. They have pretty dark skin . . . and they speak perfect English. (Puerto Rican migrant, doctor's assistant)

This strategy, of course, works whether you look Black or White. Riding together with several White people who had held up the elevator's ascent, Bartolomé cursed them out in Spanish to his friend; the passengers kept silent until the end of the ride before revealing that they were Latino and understood perfectly.

Names are another signal of group membership, with Spanish names providing an indicator of Latino origins. In the past, immigrants were encouraged to legally Americanize their names as a sign of their assimilation. Today, permanent change does not allow the flexibility that many immigrants desire. For example, Alfonso found a more situational version of name changing to be in his interest. He explained a new strategy he has begun to try out at work with his American clients:

> Let's say if the receptionist says "[Alfonso] there's a phone call right now, somebody wants to know the rates," I tell her to send it through, transfer to my line. Four rings, "This is [Alfred]." It's not [Alfonso] anymore. Like a month ago I started thinking about it, I don't get too much success if "This is [Alfonso]." For the sake of business, he's not really helpful. . . . I was thinking wow, my business card said [Alfonso], my last name is [Silva], you can't really hide that you're Spanish. But from doing what I do and I wanted to take it to the next level. Am I really limiting [myself] to have my first name [Alfonso]? Just call me [Alfred]. People call me [Alfred] from high school, [Alfie]. So, the past couple, you know, I probably did that like three times, and one time I thought that if I would have told this guy that my name was [Alfonso], he probably wouldn't be talking to me.

Most of Alfonso's clients are Latinos, and with them he introduces himself as Alfonso and emphasizes his Latino origin. A permanent name change would hinder Alfonso's rapport with his Latino clients. Choosing when to use the Americanized version of his name allows him to present himself to his best advantage with each new client.

Puerto Rican and Dominican migrants confront a society where one's reception is often based on racial group membership. Situational passing allows them to reclaim some measure of control in that process by turning the game to their advantage. Respondents whose appearance falls at the ends of the color spectrum recognize the unique advantage of being able to inhabit both a Latino category and a Black or White category, depending on the information they choose to reveal about themselves. Yet the effectiveness of this strategy is still shaped by the masks that an individual can reasonably put on. Being able to pass for Black is useful in many contexts, yet it does not offer the same range of opportunities as being able to pass for White. Thus, light- and dark-skinned migrants use this approach toward different ends. Passing for Black is most useful as a form of security, to blend in and avoid racial conflict with Black Americans. The situations in which appearing Black rather than Latino is an advantage in seeking a job, apartment, or other material resource are limited. Light-skinned migrants find this strategy more helpful in pursuing socioeconomic opportunities. In a society where Whites still dominate most opportunity structures, the ability to pass for White is more useful than the ability to pass for Black. Situational passing helps both light-

and dark-skinned Latinos achieve immediate gains and avoid some forms of discrimination. But it is a more useful route to upward mobility for those with lighter skin.

Conclusion

Although race is cognitive in the sense of how people divide up and organize others into groups, it is also something that people enact through their behavior. They signal who they are, and shape the way others perceive them. Much of what determines how people are racially perceived is based on physical appearance, something that structures people's lives and opportunities, over which they have relatively little control. Yet Puerto Ricans and Dominicans with European or African appearances fall into a racially ambiguous position at the intersection of culturally competing racial schemas. Although their social position and identities in the United States may be more shaped by a Hispanicized U.S. schema (or a panethnic nationality schema), leading them to see themselves racialized as Latinos, the existence of a binary U.S. schema enables them to present themselves as White or Black. To the extent that they are able to assimilate, to code-switch, or to pass, they can shape that perception in a way that is less possible for those who fall in the middle of the racial spectrum.

The selection of American or immigrant codes of behavior can be a deliberate strategy for improving a person's position in the racial structure and avoiding discrimination. The incentive to assimilate is shaped by skin color; those with lighter skin reap more benefit from assimilating than do those with darker skin and a more African appearance. Yet despite the fact that many of the Dominican and Puerto Rican respondents physically can become White, most do not. These respondents perceive that the advantages of racial status are not inherent in a static social structure but are contextual. The greatest advantages, in their eyes, accrue to those who can adopt different guises, performing the race that is most useful in a given situation.

For this reason, those respondents who do adopt American cultural codes of action do not let them replace their own culture. They seek to be fluent in the cultures of both the mainstream society and their ethnic community and to navigate between them. This strategy is part of the reactive identity that forms when the dominant group restricts the entry of those willing to pass, and it is also a reflection of their perceived interests. The growing Latino population in the United States is creating economic and social incentives for being Latino and having the cultural familiarity to cater to Latino markets. For those who question whether Latinos can be assimilated into American culture, the answer is a resounding yes. But the more telling issue is whether those who do internalize American cultural scripts decide to use them or not.

The racial strategies that these migrants adopt—assimilation, code switching, and situational passing—are ultimately private solutions for dealing with racial barriers. They allow some light-skinned Puerto Ricans and Dominicans to step across the color line either momentarily or permanently, but they leave that color line in place behind them. Those with medium and dark skin are unable to cross into Whiteness, even momentarily. While adopting the cultural behavior of the dominant White group may improve their socioeconomic opportunities, they remain racialized as Latinos—a classification that brings some advantages in terms of affirmative-action considerations, but also many barriers. The private solutions associated with racial strategies may be helpful to some individuals, but public solutions are what break down racial barriers for all.

7 Is Latino Becoming a Race?

Cultural Change and Classifications

WITH MORE THAN 50 MILLION PEOPLE, and 16.3% of the nation's population in 2010, Latinos are the largest minority and the fastest-growing population group in the United States today.[1] In 1960, they were less than 4% of the population; by 2050, they could account for nearly one-third.[2] Latinos are transforming American society and culture, including its concept of race, which has been described as "a fundamental axis" of American society.[3] Their phenotype diversity—the fact that Latinos span the Black-White color line and represent a range of colors and appearances—is central to understanding the integration experiences of all Latinos, and especially groups like Dominicans and Puerto Ricans.

Color has long been an issue as scholars have considered where Latinos will fit into American racial structures. In the period after World War II, when Puerto Rican mass migration to the mainland U.S. reached its peak, social scientists predicted that the migrant community would divide along racial lines. They noted that those with light skin experienced greater social mobility and were able to move from inner-city areas to White suburbs. Those with dark skin were often left behind in impoverished areas that they shared with Black Americans, and lighter Puerto Ricans tended to avoid social contact with their dark-skinned compatriots.[4] Sociologist Clara Rodríguez describes this early literature as predicting "that those Puerto Ricans who could pass for white would assimilate into the white communities in the United States; those who could not, would assimilate into the black community; and that a small group of standard bearers, who did not assimilate into either community, would be left to represent the Puerto Rican community."[5]

In making such predictions, social scientists believed that Puerto Rican migrants would acculturate to an American concept of race. From seeing race as a continuum with many intermediate points between White and Black, they were expected to adopt the view of a racial dichotomy in which those with any amount of African ancestry were Black. This predicted racial acculturation clearly never happened; nearly half of all Puerto Ricans today—and of all Latinos in the mainland U.S.—do not classify themselves as White or Black, and even fewer see themselves as having entered the group of White or Black Americans.

And yet, for both Puerto Ricans and Dominicans, the process of mass migration has changed the way that many migrants, their host society, and those left behind think about race and classify themselves and others. Rather than acculturating to an Americanized view of race, Latino migrants have transformed it. By bringing with them a racialized view of their nationalities, Puerto Rican, Dominican, and other Latin American migrants have fostered the view, now accepted by much of mainstream America, that they do not fit into existing White or Black categories. They have helped to create a new American racial schema, moving their host society away from a dominant binary U.S. schema—which would classify them all as White or Black, based on the one-drop rule—to a Hispanicized U.S. schema that treats White, Black, and Latino as mutually exclusive racialized groups. Despite contributing to its creation, not all of the migrants I spoke with adopt a Hispanicized U.S. schema. But those who experience structural assimilation, developing friendships and connections through mainstream institutions, come to learn how their host society classifies them and adopt its classifications. Instead of the majority assimilating into the White or Black category, leaving only a small group to represent a Latino community, most of my respondents—and large numbers of Latin Americans in the United States in general—see themselves as part of a distinct, racialized Latino group.[6]

This racialized concept of Latino panethnicity has also spread beyond the host society context where it originated and has been adopted in some migrants' home societies. The non-migrants I interviewed in Santo Domingo and San Juan cognitively internalize this concept and the ordered set of categories it fits into, even if not all of them actively use a Latino category in their daily lives. Even more strikingly, many non-migrant respondents also revealed that they have internalized Americanized concepts of Whiteness and Blackness, cultural concepts that differ significantly from those traditionally held in their societies.

How have these changes taken place? How does migration cause such change in personal and collective ideas about racial classification? I have argued that recognizing race as a form of cognitive organization and as an aspect of culture allows us to understand how such change occurs. Here, I summarize this theoretical contribution, using my empirical findings in both the sending and the receiving societies to detail how racial schemas function as an aspect of culture, and how racial schemas are created, learned, diffused, and discarded in many individual-level actions that collectively create large-scale change in cultural concepts of race. I then summarize and expand on the methodological contributions of the book, discussing how race should be measured and studied in order to advance scholarship in this area. Next, I focus on Puerto Ricans and Dominicans as two Latino groups, comparing them to one another, discussing their experiences beyond the first generation, and putting them in context through comparisons to other Latino groups in the United States. I then address larger debates about how Latinos are transforming the U.S. racial structure, focusing on what the experience of Puerto Ricans and Dominicans can tell us about future generations of Latinos and how they will be viewed racially in America. Finally, I discuss how immigration can transform concepts of race and racial structures outside of the United States, and its potential for having a global impact on how race is understood.

A Cultural Transformation of Race

Race is an aspect of culture and, therefore, of cognition. We cognitively organize bits of information about race into schematic structures as a way of making ideas and images more accessible and interpretable. When we see people, we process a great deal of information about what they look like, how they are dressed, and how they behave. Through the use of racial schemas, we mentally sort that information into a set of ordered categories and knowledge about how those categories relate to one another. These schemas reflect the symbolic boundaries that we and others draw to differentiate one group from another, to mentally distinguish who is like whom and who is part of "our group" or outside of it. Thus, often subconsciously, we assign people to categories almost every time we see them. We learn and access bits of cultural knowledge about how to interpret other people's actions based on these categories, and adopt an interactional tool kit of strategies for how to behave ourselves.

But racial schemas are not exclusive; they are dynamic, overlapping, and influenced by context. People have the ability to maintain multiple racial schemas and to decide which one is the most relevant in a particular situation. Thus, a Dominican migrant may come to learn a Hispanicized U.S. schema through her interactions with native-born Americans, and recognize that when working around her American colleagues, it makes sense to view them as White and Black and see herself as Latino, because that is how they classify her. Her behavior toward them will likely be influenced by that knowledge. Yet in her neighborhood, when around an ethnically diverse group of Latinos, she might rely on a nationality racial schema—classifying people by their nationality, with herself as Dominican and others as Mexican, Salvadoran, and the like. When the conversation focuses on appearance, or when the group composition becomes all Dominican, she might instead draw upon a continuum racial schema—using a range of color terms representing mixed appearances between Black and White—to refer to people, including herself. The concepts of race associated with each schema affect her strategies of action and her performance of race to others.

The three individuals profiled at the beginning of this book offer a glimpse of how people maintain multiple racial schemas, yet choose different ones. Agustín, Raquel, and Isandro describe different ways of thinking about a racial mixture they all share. All three have European and African ancestry and cultural roots in the Hispanic Caribbean. Although each has a distinctive way of conceptualizing and labeling what they are—as *mulato* (Agustín), Black (Raquel), and Latino (Isandro)—they are also aware of the concepts that predominate for each of the others. Agustín agrees that he *is* Black in the "macro sense," or in terms of how Blackness is understood outside his own society, and also that when Dominicans like him go to the United States, they become classified as Latinos. Raquel realizes that her view, while rooted in the history of American race relations, is a minority perspective and that most of her fellow Dominican immigrants would classify her and themselves as Latino or as her specific Latino group. Isandro concedes that if Latino is not considered a race, he would be Black and, like Raquel, he also recognizes *mulato* as a term for the mixture of White and Black that makes up his racial ancestry. These individuals and many others like them reveal that people need not adopt only a single notion of what race means or what race they are.

The mechanisms traced throughout this book are broadly applicable to many groups beyond those studied here. Conceptualizing a portfolio full of different racial schemas to choose from extends beyond the immigrant experience to broader social processes. Recently, scholars have focused on the fluidity of identities in general, and how they are contextually specific. Non-Latino adolescents, for example, are more likely to identify themselves as multiracial when filling out a survey at school, but as monoracial when asked by an interviewer at home, often with family members looking on.[7] There is also considerable fluidity in claiming a Latino identity in different contexts.[8] Such findings can be reframed as not only selecting individual identities at different moments but also choosing among the different racial schemas into which those identities fit. When a multiracial non-Latino adolescent with Black and White ancestry shifts between Black and multiracial identities, she is likely not thinking of those labels as stand-alone categories, but in terms of how Black relates to White in one particular schema and how multiracial relates to Black and White in another. Anyone who shifts between different identities is cognitively choosing different schemas and locating herself within one of their constituent categories because of the symbolic boundaries and reference groups that are momentarily triggered. Migrants moving to new societies are certainly not the only people who learn and maintain multiple racial schemas.

I have focused in this book on how new racial schemas are created, learned, diffused to new places, and adopted, as well as how old ones can fade away through disuse. New racial schemas slowly coalesce into being over time as populations create new symbolic boundaries to distance and differentiate themselves from other racially defined groups or remove symbolic boundaries that previously existed.[9] The creation of a Hispanicized U.S. schema is but one relatively recent example, brought about through immigration—including the growing presence of Latin Americans and the racial concepts that many brought with them—and the efforts of many Latinos to differentiate themselves from Black Americans at the same time that White Americans sought to distance themselves from Latinos.

New schemas that are culturally dominant can be learned through personal interaction, institutions, and the mass media. Puerto Rican and Dominican migrant respondents learned about the Hispanicized U.S. schema through interactions with native-born Americans in stores, on the street, or in many other casual encounters. Its classifications are reinforced by local media, such as newspapers and television news programs that treat White, Black, and Latino as mutually exclusive groups. In the sending societies, educational institutions were influential in teaching Dominican and Puerto Rican non-migrant respondents about race. Through their school curricula, the Dominicans learned a schema of official categories used for different types of racial mixes, while the Puerto Ricans learned the national ideology that all Puerto Ricans are a mix of Spanish, Indigenous, and African races—a lesson linked to the way many have racialized their nationality.

Schemas that are less culturally dominant require more sustained communication to learn because they are less likely to be picked up through cursory interactions. Thus, while all migrants, even those with limited English skills, acquired a Hispanicized U.S. schema through their casual encounters, only those who experienced structural assimilation and developed sustained, meaningful relationships with native-born Americans acquired the binary U.S. schema and its view that all Latinos must be Black, White, or some other race. They learned this through discussions with non-Latino friends and colleagues at mainstream colleges and workplaces. Some also learned about this schema through their college courses, but conversations afterward or other experiences discussing race crystallized these lessons into a racial concept that was relevant for their lives. Institutional forms and census questions drove the lesson home, making them realize as they completed such forms that "Latino" was not an option on the race question. Yet those who had not previously learned the lessons completed the same forms without remarking on the absence, but simply writing in "Latino" or their nationality.

The same sources can diffuse racial schemas to new places. I found that personal communications and firsthand contact between migrants and nonmigrants were most effective in spreading knowledge about U.S. schemas and categories. Non-migrant respondents with close U.S. ties who communicated or visited often, and non-migrants who had personally visited the United States, had the greatest awareness of Latino panethnicity and Americanized notions of Whiteness and Blackness. Puerto Rican respondents who served in the military also learned these concepts through their interactions with American soldiers. The mass media and institutions diffused these concepts as well; television programs on transnational Spanish-language networks that try to instill a sense of shared panethnicity were particularly influential. And Puerto Rican nonmigrants who completed government forms, such as loan or job applications, with U.S. race and Hispanic origin questions remarked that the forms' choices influenced their understanding of a Latino category. But these sources do more to reinforce than to teach outright. People are more influenced by the ideas they receive from close ties than those that come from the media or more objective sources.[10] Thus, transnational migration, accompanied by globalization processes, plays a major role in the cultural diffusion of racial schemas to new places.

Of course, people can add new racial schemas to their portfolios without using them much. We constantly acquire pieces of cultural knowledge that we learn and maintain but rarely if ever use. Often these are schemas that are less salient to the particularities of our lives, and because we are rarely in situations where they would be relevant, they are less likely to be triggered by a particular setting or interaction.

By contrast, people are more likely to use new racial schemas when their lives are structured in such a way as to make those schemas more salient more often. This relates to the symbolic boundaries that are meaningful in their lives. My middle-class migrant respondents not only learned but use a Hispanicized U.S. schema because they have regular workplace interactions with non-Latinos; the distinctions between Latino, White, and Black are the most relevant boundaries for them. The working-class migrants tend to live in a world dominated by Spanish speakers, but from a variety of national backgrounds. They use a nationality racial schema most often because the symbolic boundaries that matter most in their worlds are the differences between a Dominican or Puerto Rican and a Mexican, Honduran, Salvadoran, or Peruvian. In their daily interactions, everyone is Latino, so a Latino category is a less pertinent distinction.

In the sending societies, too, racial schemas are adopted widely when the symbolic boundaries they reference are meaningful in people's lives and routines. More Puerto Rican than Dominican non-migrant respondents adopted a Hispanicized U.S. schema or a hybrid version of it, revealing that cultural hybridization often results from diffusion. Yet their use of the categories White, Black, and Latino (either alone or together with some nationality groups) shows that the United States and its mainstream populations are salient reference groups in Puerto Rico. They have become relevant because of the long history of political colonialism (or "affiliation," depending on their party loyalties), as well as non-migrants' constant awareness of the migrant communities to which they have been linked by numerous transnational threads for the better part of a century. They are further reinforced by steady media flows from the mainland U.S., to which almost all Puerto Ricans have access. Dominicans are equally aware of these categories; they have learned that Dominicans who go to the United States are classified as Latinos and distinguished from Whites and Blacks. But they do not use this schema in their daily lives because they have not constructed the same symbolic boundaries toward Americans. The most relevant reference group in the construction of their national and racial identity, and the focus of most of their boundary work, remains their Haitian neighbors, despite increasing migration to the United States.

The situational context also matters in determining when particular racial schemas are used. A schema is triggered by the environmental cues in a particular setting, making the audience and the nature of the interaction relevant. I believe that respondents were more likely to use certain kinds of schemas with me, in a formal interview situation, than they would have in different types of interactions with other types of people. Some explained that they did not see the continuum racial schema, which represents so much of the literature on race in the Hispanic Caribbean, as appropriate in this type of setting, but they would use it in informal interactions with co-ethnics and people they knew well. This reveals the relevance of context and audience, and the particular symbolic boundaries that are referenced by both.

Racial schemas can also fade away as people stop using them as much as they formerly did. Most of my migrant respondents recalled the list of terms I showed them associated with the continuum from White to Black—including *trigueño, jabao, mulato, indio,* and *moreno*—but middle-class migrants who spend more of their time around non-Latinos often said they had forgotten what many of the terms meant and that, while they had used them before they migrated, they rarely use them now. Some of this was the result of a new sensibility, learned in the United States, that such minute aspects of racial appearance should not be so openly discussed. But those terms had also just become less salient in their lives as they came to conduct and experience more boundary work relating to new groups in their new society.

Changes in the conceptualization of race, then, occur as a combination of individual and societal level processes. Different schemas are part of a cultural repertoire in a society. Individuals learn or fail to learn, use or ignore, and keep or lose those schemas as the social structure of their lives changes and as they engage in different types of situations and interactions. A migrant may experience racial acculturation if she uses a schema associated with her new society more and more, eventually to the exclusion of all others. But she may experience a different type of racial acculturation than another migrant who increasingly adopts a different schema associated with that society (think of Raquel's use of a binary U.S. schema and Hugo's use of a Hispanicized U.S. schema). The culture to which immigrants acculturate is not homogeneous and unified, and neither is there a solitary notion of what race means in any society. Even in the United States, concepts of race are constantly evolving, and the idea that there is an "American" and a "Latin American" conception of race that are spread consistently throughout those regions overlooks the way that racial schemas compete within societies. Racial change at the macro level occurs as the cumulative effect of all those people adding, adopting, enacting, and removing racial schemas from their cognitive portfolios. When populations move in the same direction—large portions of a society adopt and use a new schema most often—societal change in racial classifications comes about.

Studying Racial Schemas

Recent work that recognizes the cognitive aspects of culture, and the cognitive turn in studying race and ethnicity, advocates a move toward conceptualizing race as an element of culture.[11] But most empirical studies continue to focus on racial identities. To understand race as a cultural phenomenon, it is necessary to consider not just how people identify themselves but also how they see and classify others. Such schemas of racial classification are the macro-level repertoires that individuals tap into when they form and perform their racial identities. Studying identity alone therefore provides only a partial picture; it is but one location in a system of related categories. Recognizing what all those categories are and how they are defined focuses attention on how individual identities are shaped through boundary work relating to the other categories in the schema. In terms of the specific strategies of action that people adopt, their judgments about the race of those they are interacting with are just as important for shaping their behavior as their own self-identification.

Using photographs to capture people's racial schemas is one way to move beyond an exclusive focus on identity. Allowing people to provide their own categories reveals a great deal about how they conceptualize race and the range of racial categories that they perceive. This technique is particularly valuable for providing comparisons across groups and examining how respondent characteristics shape the schemas that people adopt in a similar context. I found that class and nationality are important influences on the schemas that respondents use when asked to identify the race of the people in the photographs. In a similar type of context, who is doing the classifying matters as much as who is being classified.

However, the schema evoked by the photos is only one of many schemas that people use, and the answers they give are themselves influenced by the interview context and the identity of the researchers. To comprehensively study the range of racial schemas that people adopt, and under what circumstances, researchers must use a variety of approaches, involving different question types, formats, and research methods. In interviews, in addition to asking open-ended questions and offering no guidance about the type of categories or schemas to use, the researcher can elicit particular schemas and the range of categories that respondents include within them. Anthropologist Clarence Gravlee does this very effectively by asking Puerto Rican respondents to classify the color of people in a range of drawings, evoking a particular schema (what I call the continuum racial schema) that relates to their concepts of color.[12] In a similar vein, a particular context or audience can be cued rather than a particular schema, for example by asking respondents how they would classify the race of each person if they saw them on the street or in a business office, in Santo Domingo or New York, if they were describing their race to a co-ethnic friend or to a White or Black American. Open-ended questions can also be combined with forced-choice questions, asking people to use a specific set of categories in classifications, thereby measuring their recognition of a schema rather than recall. This is what I did by showing a list of terms associated with the continuum racial schema when respondents did not use this schema on their own, and asking them to apply the terms to the photos. Forced-choice questions can help respondents recognize some of the schemas they unconsciously adopt, or use without consciously thinking of them as racial categories.[13] Of course, this approach puts an additional burden on researchers to provide a full range of options, and makes discovery of unexpected new schemas unlikely.

It is also advantageous to combine research methods in the study of racial schemas, either through mixed-method research designs or through the cumulative knowledge that is gained through different scholars studying a given topic. I combined my qualitative interviews with observations during my fieldwork. A more rigorous ethnographic approach, use of focus groups, and analysis of written documentation all have their own advantages (and disadvantages) for revealing what types of racial schemas people use in different settings and for different audiences. Ethnography is particularly useful for revealing the schemas that people actually use and the strategies of action that different racial schemas lead to, but it does not reveal the range of schemas within their portfolios that they do not use and the reasons for not using them. With interviews, we can ask people how they behave in different circumstances, but the results are affected by respondents' self-consciousness about their actions. In this book, I have focused more on the range of schemas, their meanings, and the circumstances of their use than on the full range of actions they can produce; future work on this aspect of how people use racial schemas will be particularly valuable.

Future work should also examine the wider universe of racial groups that are included in people's cognitive schemas. The specific photographs that a study uses set the boundaries for what types of individuals are classified. In this study, I focused on people who range phenotypically from Black to White, to explore how classifications along this axis vary in the sending and receiving societies. Yet this approach excluded categories that also factor into the cognitive schemas that respondents use, such as Asians and Native Americans. A valuable extension of this work will consider a fuller range of the racial diversity that Puerto Ricans, Dominicans, and other groups actually experience.

The Rainbow People:
Puerto Ricans and Dominicans Compared

With their considerable color diversity, Puerto Ricans have been described as "the Rainbow People"[14]—an expression that applies equally well to Dominicans. This expression is particularly poignant not just because Puerto Ricans and Dominicans have varied phenotypes—many groups do—but because they straddle the particular color line that has mattered most in U.S. history. This makes these groups especially valuable cases for a study on changing concepts of race and racial acculturation among migrants to the United States.

It is important to consider both how Dominicans and Puerto Ricans compare to each other and how they compare to other Latino groups. The two Hispanic Caribbean societies have much in common, including a similar history of racial *mestizaje* of the same population groups, residential concentration on the East Coast, and transnational migration patterns. Yet this is one of the first comprehensive studies to explicitly compare Puerto Ricans' and Dominicans' migration experiences.[15] As a "free associated state," Puerto Rico is legally part of the United States, but there is little doubt among Puerto Ricans that it is a very different society and culture.[16] The unique nature of Puerto Ricans' political status has not only excluded them from much of the immigration literature but also prevented relevant comparisons, such as the social and cultural integration of these groups and how it relates to their race.

I found both similarities and cultural differences in the racial schemas that Puerto Rican and Dominican non-migrants used to classify the photographs, related to educational status. Among respondents with lower levels of education, both groups shared the same predominant schema: a nationality racial schema. The differences emerged among those with higher education; there, Dominican respondents used a limited version of a continuum schema based on specific mixes of races, while Puerto Ricans continued to use nationality labels, but attributed to them a racialized meaning that was not held by their less-educated co-ethnics. In both societies, those with higher education defined race in terms of physical and biological characteristics rather than cultural ones, and found educational institutions particularly influential in shaping these views. Thus, despite the different schemas used by those with higher education, there remain many parallels in how people across these societies understand what race is.

The unique political status of Puerto Ricans distinguishes their migration experience from that of Dominicans in some ways, yet is less relevant in others. Among migrant respondents, Puerto Ricans' citizenship brings security and some incentive to conduct boundary work between themselves and other Latino groups. Unlike Dominicans, Puerto Ricans need not fear deportation if they are arrested, and they can bring their passports along to job interviews to document their legality for employers. Their political status led many of my Puerto Rican respondents to emphasize their national identities, while Dominican respondents tended to emphasize panethnic identities and advocated affiliating with other Latino groups. Yet in other ways, the integration experiences of Puerto Rican and Dominican migrants in the mainland U.S. are quite comparable. I found similar patterns in the racial schemas that both groups used there. Those with lower education levels primarily used a nationality schema to identify the photographs, while those with higher education were more likely to use a U.S. racial schema, a result that indicated how social mobility and structural integration promote the adoption of Americanized notions of race. And in spite of Puerto Ricans' efforts to emphasize their nationality, respondents from both groups see themselves treated in similar ways by Americans. Both feel they are excluded from a White category in the United States, and both tend to distinguish themselves from a Black category. They see themselves occupying the same location in the American racial hierarchy—a middle location between Black and White. I contend that Dominicans' growing awareness of this middle location, spurred by the growth of the overall Latino population in New York and their racial integration after a major migration flow in the 1990s, helps explain the significant shift since 1990 among Dominicans from selecting "Black" on the U.S. Census to selecting "Other" race (see Table 1, in Chapter 1). It is not only Dominicans' and Puerto Ricans' own experiences that shape the perception of a Latino race in America. The growth of other Latino groups has helped create that perception for both native-born Americans and themselves.

Puerto Ricans' political status also matters a great deal when it comes to considering how racial schemas created in the United States are diffused transnationally and adopted in the sending societies. Among non-migrant respondents, Puerto Ricans had greater cultural contact with American society because of their long-standing political affiliation. This occurs through the back-and-forth movement and ongoing participation of migrants in Puerto Rico, the U.S. institutional infrastructure present in Puerto Rico because of the affiliation, and the American media presence that it fosters. America's political and cultural presence in Puerto Rico thus serves a dual function: it helps to spread racial concepts and it also establishes Americans as a racial point of reference. The symbolic boundaries that distinguish Latinos from non-Latino Americans have become meaningful in their daily lives. Dominican non-migrants, despite their transnational connections to migrants in the United

States and the diffusion of the same racial schemas, have not adopted the same definition of Americans as the primary racial "other."

Yet when Puerto Ricans and Dominicans are compared to other U.S. Latino groups, they often appear more similar to each other than different. In terms of socioeconomic outcomes, these two groups tend to be at the low end of the distributions compared to other Latinos, a finding that is sometimes attributed to the large percentage of Dominicans and Puerto Ricans with African heritage who are likely to be the target of discrimination.[17] In 2004 Dominicans had the lowest median household incomes (about $30,000) and the highest poverty rates (28%) of all Latino groups; after Hondurans, Puerto Ricans had the third worst outcomes among Latinos (about $34,000 and 24%, respectively).[18] Dominicans have the lowest rate of home ownership (24%, compared to 48% for all Latinos)[19] and one of the lowest rates of English proficiency of all Latinos, with only about half of Dominican children speaking only English at home by the third generation.[20] Puerto Ricans are sometimes described as "involuntary migrants"—like native-born minorities, they came to be part of the United States through conquest and colonialism, rather than by choice.[21] Involuntary migrant groups typically experience some of the worst socioeconomic outcomes. Yet Dominicans, despite migrating voluntarily, are sometimes lumped together with Puerto Ricans, because of their physical and cultural resemblance and settlement in similar regions, leading some to argue that the stigma associated with Puerto Ricans is applied to Dominicans as well.[22] In fact, while most second-generation Latino groups achieve upward socioeconomic mobility compared to their immigrant parents, there is some evidence that Dominicans and Puerto Ricans are at greater risk of downward mobility.[23]

Clearly, Puerto Ricans' political status distinguishes them from Dominicans and other Latino groups in some important ways, yet this alone does not facilitate a smooth integration into American society.[24] Puerto Ricans' experiences in the mainland U.S. are in many ways more similar to those of Dominicans than they are different. These similarities argue for the inclusion of Puerto Ricans in more literature on the cultural and social impacts of immigration. Their citizenship status should be treated as a variable in studies of groups' integration, rather than a cause for their exclusion.

Latinos and the Racial Structure of the United States

The growing presence of Latino immigrants in the United States, a group that does not fit easily into the earlier Black-White divide, has led many to question how Latinos are reshaping the American color line. Where Latino immigrants fit within this racial structure, when they arrive and over generations, has the potential to remap racial configurations in the United States. Although Dominicans and Puerto Ricans are only a portion of this community, examining how they conceptualize race, their location in the U.S. racial structure, and how their presence has affected American classifications raises important issues for this discussion.

First, their experience points toward the necessity of distinguishing between structural assimilation and racial incorporation. These components of immigrant integration tend to get confounded because of the implicit comparison to the European immigrants who came to the United States at the turn of the 20th century. For most of those earlier immigrant groups, structural assimilation went hand in hand with incorporation into the White majority. But these processes do not necessarily coincide. Immigrants and their descendants can even enter into the core institutions and personal networks of American society yet still be distinguished as a racially distinct group that is never regarded as being fully American.[25]

My research points to the fact that Latinos are largely viewed and treated as a separate racial group that falls between Whites and Blacks in the racial hierarchy. The Hispanicized U.S. schema, which treats White, Black, and Latino as mutually exclusive racial groups, is becoming culturally dominant over a binary U.S. schema, as represented by how the census measures race and treats Hispanic or Latino origin as an aspect of ethnicity, assigning most Latinos to a Black or White race. Latinos fit into a distinct racial group that tries to differentiate itself from Blacks and is not accepted into the realm of Whiteness. Continued Latin American immigration perpetuates this middle tier, fueling public perception of a distinct Latino group and keeping the group identity alive.[26] This does not mean that the Latino category is internally homogeneous or that no one is able to move out of it. It does not even mean that the group boundaries are as difficult to cross as those of other racial groups, like Blacks. But because the category is increasingly seen in racial rather than ethnic terms, the options for doing so are more limited.

Although Latinos' socioeconomic outcomes fall behind those of Whites overall—for instance, the median household income of U.S.-born Latinos was 73% of White household income in 2000[27]—Latinos have experienced upward mobility and some degree of structural assimilation over time. Among younger birth cohorts, larger percentages of Latinos hold jobs in top-tier (high-paying) occupations.[28] Second-generation Latino groups in New York exceed their parents' level of education.[29] Latinos are less residentially segregated from Whites than are Blacks, and they tend to adopt sociopolitical and racial attitudes that are more similar to those of Whites than to those of Blacks.[30] This has led some to conclude that Latinos are becoming White or that a new Black/non-Black divide has replaced the old Black/White divide, with Latinos falling on the non-Black side.[31]

Yet not only my first-generation respondents but also Latinos in the second, third, and even later generations regularly confront social boundaries that tell them they are not White, and in some cases, not fully American.[32] Unless they choose to hide or withhold it, any information about their Latino origins can cause a readjustment in how they are seen by others. Even those who check "White" on the census race question view this response, when combined with a Latino origin on the preceding question, as qualitatively different from a White American identity. The two questions cannot be meaningfully separated, as the answer to one changes the meaning that many intend on the second. This fact limits our ability to use the percentages checking "White" or "Black" as an indicator of Latinos' acceptance of American racial classifications.

In large part, what has led scholars to view Latinos as White or almost-White is their social proximity to Whites and group boundaries that are generally more permeable than those experienced by Blacks. Intermarriage has long been viewed as a litmus test for the nature of group boundaries, with intermarriage between groups revealing low social distance between them. Latinos have a high rate of intermarriage; in 2000, 14% of Latinos were intermarried, compared with 7% of Blacks.[33] Out of all marriages involving one Latino spouse, about 30% are to a non-Latino person.[34] In particular, the rate of Latino intermarriage with Whites is higher than the rate of Black-White intermarriage; 90% of intermarried Latinos marry Whites, compared with 69% of intermarried Blacks.[35] Latino intermarriage rates also increase for later generations: from 1999 to 2001, only 6% of first-generation Latinos intermarried, compared with 19% of the second generation, and 32% of the third and later generations.[36] As a result, Latino group boundaries are seen as fading over time, and doing so more rapidly than Blacks' group boundaries.[37]

Intermarriage is also important because it is a key factor in the racial identification of later generations. With high rates of interracial marriage, larger percentages of younger generations of Latinos will have multiracial origins and increased options for their identity. Approximately 63% of the children with one Latino and one non-Latino parent are identified as Latino on the 2000 Census.[38] And while 36% of children from Latino-White intermarriages were identified as White and non-Latino in 1990, only 26% of those from Black-White intermarriages were identified as White.[39] This pattern also holds when the children are old enough to identify themselves. In a study of multiracial adults in California, those from Latino-White intermarriages were more likely to identify as White than those from Black-White intermarriages.[40] Studies of Mexican Americans have also found that those whose parents intermarried are less likely to identify or be identified by their parents as Mexican.[41] Furthermore, intermarriage is likely to affect how people are seen by others. It influences phenotype, can lead to names that do not indicate Latino origins, and generally results in a set of cultural codes from a non-Latino background that may send mixed signals to observers. Intermarriage, then, allows the offspring of Latinos to identify or be seen as the race of their non-Latino parent, thus permitting a loss of Latino ethnic or panethnic classification across generations in a family.[42]

Yet there is another way to view intermarriage: it can be regarded as the only significant way that people of Latin American descent move out of the Latino category. While the children of Latinos who do marry non-Latinos are more likely to lose a Latino identifier, the children of Latinos who do not intermarry are extremely unlikely to lose theirs, even in the third or later generations. Compared with 63% of children with one Latino parent, more than 98% of children with two Latino parents were identified as Latino.[43] When a Mexican American man marries either a Mexican American or a Mexican immigrant woman, the child's Mexican identification is "virtually assured."[44] In fact, even in the fourth and later generations—those whose parents and grandparents are all born in the United States—almost all children 17 and younger (98.4%) are identified as Mexican when both parents identify as Mexican.[45] In a study of a Mexican American age cohort over time, Richard Alba and Tariqul Islam found a general decline in the percentage of people who selected "Mexican" on the Latino-origin census question from 1980 to 2000. They also found that about 3% to 4% of the Mexican-origin population have Mexican ancestry but identify as non-Latino (most identify as White). Yet because many in this group also report some European ancestry, they inferred that these are the descendants of intermarriages. The other pattern that they found for the disappearance of Mexican Americans from the group was that some seemed to shift to a panethnic Latino or Hispanic identity rather than a Mexican one.[46] These findings suggest that those who feel able to identify as non-Latino White, and who enter the White mainstream, are likely the products of intermarriage, while others remain identified as Latino.

From this perspective, intermarriage may be seen less as a litmus test for blurring group boundaries and more as an exit route from a racialized group.

The Latino race does have more porous boundaries than the Black race does. But as with other racialized boundaries, a person may still have to decide to actively cross that boundary in order to have his or her children experience racial mobility. The idea of intermarriage as a strategy for racial improvement has deep roots in Latin America; Carl Degler described the presence of an intermediate category in Brazil as providing a "mulatto escape hatch" from the stigma of Blackness, positioning intermarriage as a way for Afro Brazilians to help their children move up in the racial hierarchy.[47] Such strategies of "improving the race" by marrying lighter are still common in the Hispanic Caribbean. Whether deliberate or not, the pattern of intermarriage among U.S. Latinos leading to movement into a White racial category resembles these intergenerational strategies for racial mobility based on mate selection. Without intermarriage, and the ability for multiracial Latinos to identify with the race of a non-Latino parent, losing a Latino identity appears more like racial passing than ethnic assimilation. Intermarriage, then, is truly a "Latino escape hatch" for many families.

Many factors influence the likelihood that Latinos will intermarry, including language, education, and occupational status.[48] Those who are upwardly mobile are more likely to intermarry, and thus can improve their children's status, not just through social mobility but by providing them with racial options. Yet another factor that likely affects intermarriage and whom those individuals marry is skin color. An important component of mate selection is interaction, and skin color affects Latinos' residential options. Puerto Ricans and Cubans with darker phenotypes tend to move to neighborhoods with fewer Whites, compared to those with lighter phenotypes.[49] I found similar differences in interaction among migrants in this study. In the social networks they reported, respondents with darker skin had significantly more social ties to Blacks than to Whites.[50] An analysis in the *New York Times* showed that in 2009, Latinos who identified as Black were more likely to marry non-Latino Blacks than to marry Latinos who identified as White. Similarly, Latinos who identified as White were much more likely to marry non-Latino Whites than to marry Latinos who identified as Black.[51] Racial self-identification is not necessarily a good proxy for skin color,[52] and at least one study of U.S. Mexicans found that skin color was not associated with the choice of a White or Mexican partner in 1990.[53] But this *New York Times* finding suggests the need to examine whether light-skinned Latinos overall are in fact more likely today to marry Whites and dark-skinned Latinos to marry Blacks, and how those patterns affect the racial classification of their children.

Although I maintain that Latinos are increasingly crystallizing into a middle tier in the racial hierarchy between Blacks and Whites, Latinos as a group are also stratified by skin color. A "pigmentocracy" has been found within many Latino nationality groups, including those who range from European to Indigenous phenotypes.[54] Yet Americans have always reserved the lowest racial status for people of African descent, and it is here that Puerto Ricans and Dominicans provide the most analytical leverage for understanding the American racial hierarchies. Most U.S. Latino groups have relatively small African-descended populations; if a new Black/non-Black color line were emerging, this characteristic would place Latinos as a group on the non-Black side, in terms of proportions alone. The experiences of the group would be heavily weighted toward the experiences of Mexicans, South Americans, and Central Americans. Yet those Latinos with an African appearance, including many later-generation Dominicans and Puerto Ricans, are still likely to fall on the Black side of that line, unless they actively maintain strategies to position themselves as Latinos for multiple generations. Research on West Indians suggests that the prospects for maintaining those ethnic strategies dim beyond the second generation.[55] It is likely that many third- or later-generation Latinos with African phenotypes will make efforts to maintain their Spanish language and Spanish names to signify their *latinidad*. This may be why Dominicans have one of the lowest English proficiency rates by the third generation. But those who do not make efforts to signify their Latino origins will come to be seen as fairly indistinguishable from Black Americans.

A study of skin color among U.S. Mexicans in 1989–1990 found evidence of many of these patterns. It found a pigmentocracy such that Mexicans with light skin had superior outcomes to medium or dark Mexicans in education, household income, and occupational status. It also found that light Mexicans were socially closer to Whites; they socialized with them more and had more positive attitudes toward them and the United States in general. Mexicans with dark skin showed evidence of emphasizing their ethnic ties. They were most likely to assert a *mexicano* identity, they were more likely than those with light skin to speak Spanish at home, and they held more favorable views of Mexican immigrants than did those with medium skin. However, those with medium skin color in some ways showed even more interest in differentiating themselves from Blacks and their darker co-ethnics. They had more negative attitudes toward Blacks than both their lighter and their darker peers, they were least likely to live among co-ethnics, and they were more likely than both of those groups to be Spanish-language dominant.[56] If those with medium skin are distancing themselves the most from those who are darker, it may be because they see such boundary work as a real option. Those with dark skin, while trying to emphasize their ethnic roots, may ultimately have more difficulty moving further away from Blacks, either physically or socially.

The emerging racial structure that I see taking shape around Latinos consists of a distinctive, racialized Latino group forming a middle tier between Whites and Blacks, but with relatively porous boundaries. Those porous boundaries allow movement into the White group primarily through the "Latino escape hatch" of intermarriage (although with small numbers in the first and second generation whose parents have not intermarried moving in by "passing"), and movement into the Black group for smaller numbers of later-generation Latinos of African descent who do not emphasize their Latino origins. This most closely resembles the model put forth by sociologist Eduardo Bonilla-Silva, who has described the American racial hierarchy as moving from a bi-racial model to a tri-racial model,[57] which has been described as roughly "White, Brown, and Black."[58] Generational status is an important aspect of this model, as the U.S.-born are more likely to intermarry, and also, I expect, because darker Latinos in later generations will be less active in signaling their membership in the Latino middle tier than those in earlier generations. I also suspect that those later-generation Latinos who do move into the Black group tend to be not merely those with dark skin—a description that applies to those with darker but more Indigenous phenotypes[59]—but those with more African phenotypes. The concentration of Indigenous phenotypes within the "Brown" middle tier is likely to create an association between such appearance and a Latino classification, one that can incorporate a range of skin tones within that spectrum. While I expect there to be color stratification even within the Latino tier, those later-generation Latinos with more African phenotypes are most likely to be grouped with Black Americans in the racial hierarchy.

The predictions of early social scientists about Puerto Rican migrants—that those who could pass for White would assimilate into the White community, those who could not would assimilate into the Black community, and a small group would be left to represent Puerto Ricans—may not have occurred in terms of their self-identification or their cultural assimilation. But in terms of their racial incorporation—how they are viewed by Americans and positioned within the racial structure of American society—and with the exception of the relative numbers being sorted into the three paths, this is precisely what is happening for Puerto Ricans, Dominicans, and other Latinos groups with significant African ancestry.

Despite the expressions of public concern over how Latino immigrants are unassimilable and pose a cultural threat to the nation,[60] Latinos do not fundamentally challenge our traditional models of acculturation.[61] Even among the first-generation Puerto Ricans and Dominicans I interviewed, there was evidence of people adopting the language, culture, and behavior of the dominant society. Many even experienced structural assimilation into mainstream institutions and social circles. But these patterns do not necessarily entail a loss of the language, culture, and behavior of their own community. Immigrants can garner advantages from the ability to navigate both mainstream and immigrant cultures and retain their fluency in each.

Yet while Latinos do add aspects of American culture to their interactional tool kits, they have challenged and transformed the American racial structure. I believe that the fears of those who see Latinos as unassimilable or who pass laws to detain anyone who "looks" illegal are more racial than they are cultural. The greater concern is about the changing color of American society—the "browning" of America—not about its cultural character. The fault here lies not with Latinos but with America's unwillingness to treat them as fully American.

U.S. Racial Policies and Measuring Race

Given the way that Latino immigration is reshaping American racial structures, what are the implications for race-based policies and laws? Policies such as affirmative action and government structures for monitoring employment discrimination like the Equal Employment Opportunity Commission (EEOC) rely on federal data about the racial composition of the nation and how the different groups are doing. Yet these data represent only one racial schema out of the many that people use and that affect their lives and opportunities. Our current standards for data collection need not only to better reflect the reality of how Latinos' race is understood in the United States, but also to develop new measures that can capture other crucial bases of racial discrimination that are currently missed—particularly color.

Census race data are the primary source of information on the changing racial demographics of the nation. Based on the Office of Management and Budget's federal standards for data collection, these data currently represent a version of what I have called the binary U.S. schema. This schema increasingly does not represent the way that most U.S. Latinos view their race; neither does it represent the way they are seen by others. It is clear that many Latinos, in both the first and later generations, consider their race to be Hispanic, Latino, or a particular Latino-origin category. Even though the 2010 Census placed an instruction immediately before the questions on Latino origin and race informing people that "For this census, Hispanic origins are not races," a sizable percentage of Latinos—36.7%—still checked "Other" race and many wrote in "Latino" or a national-origin group.[62] Given that the race question now allows people to "check all that apply," some have suggested adding "Hispanic/Latino" as an option on the race question to permit people to select it together with other racial categories if they choose.[63]

One of the primary arguments made against this solution is the loss of information that about half of all Latinos now provide in completing the race question—primarily whether they select "White" or "Black." When "Latino" is provided as an option on the race question, the percentage selecting another race category diminishes to less than one-third.[64] This fact, of course, indicates that many of those people selecting "White" or "Black" under the OMB formulation would not do so if given another option. But nonetheless, it creates concern about losing information about other aspects of Latinos' race, such as how they look or fit into U.S. standards of White and Black.

The problem, though, is that racial self-identification is not a good proxy of Latinos' appearance. The Dominicans and Puerto Ricans I interviewed complete the census race question in a variety of different ways. Some people complete it by the racial standards of their home countries. Thus, following the Puerto Rican maxim that "if you're not Black (i.e., not "pure" African, because you have some racial mixture), you're White," Salvador—a restaurant worker with dark skin and Indigenous features—identified himself as White on the census question, although I believe many Americans would see him as Black. Others interpret the question as asking for their subjective self-identifications, regardless of appearance. This led Raquel, who has light skin and mainly European features, and whom I viewed as White, to classify herself as Black. Overall, among my migrant respondents, 72% of Dominicans and 36% of Puerto Ricans identified their race on the census question in a way that differed from how I viewed them, based on their appearance alone.[65] While this certainly does not represent all Latinos, the truth is that we really do not know what the race question is measuring for Latinos if it is not measuring their understanding of their race. Studies have found significant inequalities between Latinos who check "White" or "Black" on the census.[66] Yet it is possible that a White racial designation on the census follows from higher socioeconomic outcomes rather than indicating an appearance that causes those higher outcomes. The Latin American belief that "money whitens" may lead people who have achieved upward mobility to feel more able to check the "White" box.[67]

The obvious solution to this problem is to directly measure what we are interested in: racial appearance. After all, appearance, not how people subjectively self-identify, is the basis on which discrimination occurs. There are many aspects to appearance, of course, but a measure of skin color would allow us to evaluate the extent of color inequalities and discrimination nationwide. I argue that federal data collection should add a "Latino/Hispanic" category to the multiple-option race question and add a separate measure of color.[68] Color is clearly an important dimension of how race is lived for Latinos in the United States, as well as many other groups, yet we do an inadequate job of measuring and considering it in our policies and provisions to combat racial discrimination.

The Civil Rights Act of 1964 and subsequent equal employment legislation prohibited discrimination based on "race, color, religion, or national origin."[69] Yet legal structures primarily focus on discrimination on the basis of racial or ethnic group membership, while claims of discrimination based on color are given less legal legitimacy and are often unsuccessful. In an important study of employment discrimination cases involving Latinos, legal scholar Tanya Hernández argues that judges inappropriately view the fact of racial or ethnic diversity in a workplace as evidence against discrimination, while failing to see other characteristics aside from minority status, such as color, as legally relevant.[70] By this logic, if there are Dominicans in the workplace, the employer cannot be discriminating against Dominicans, even if all of the Dominican employees are light-skinned. Suits claiming discrimination on the basis of color, including claims of discrimination against Latinos by other Latinos, are rarely successful because the legal system is not set up to recognize or deal with this very real type of discrimination. It recognizes only one type of racial schema, although we have seen that there is racial stratification along many intersecting racial schemas at once.

A focus on color inequality is important for many groups other than Latinos. Not only have color gradations long affected status among Black Americans, Native Americans, and many Asian groups, but they are also relevant for the growing multiracial populations in the United States. In 2010, 9 million people, or 2.9% of the population, identified themselves as being of more than one race. Since 2000, the mixed-race population has grown by about 32%.[71] Phenotype is important to the way multiracial people identify their own race,[72] and it may well shape their experiences with discrimination. The particular population segments that are contributing most to the nation's growing diversity are ones where skin color varies considerably within groups, and may shape social experiences as much as ethnic or racial group membership.

Affirmative action and anti-discrimination legislation try to minimize the extent to which race delimits people's opportunities. Yet these policies and legal structures focus on a model of race that does not capture the complexity of how it is lived by many people, especially Latinos. Racial policies need to keep pace with the way race is being transformed in the United States. That means recognizing not only how Latinos and others view their race but also how the presence of new, racially diverse groups, and the variety of racial schemas that they bring with them, gives new importance to racial schemas other than the ones that the government has measured in the past.

Immigration and Race Outside the United States

Latin American immigration to the United States also affects race outside of the country. The transformation of the U.S. racial structure results in large part from immigration—not just the physical presence of new immigrants but also the cultural change in concepts of race that mass migration promotes. Latin American immigrants bring with them a racialized view of their nationality, which in the United States translates into a racialized view of both national-origin groups and a Latino panethnic group. But this cultural change is not restricted to immigrant-receiving societies, as I found in Puerto Rico, where a racialized view of a Latino panethnic group was also adopted.

It is particularly striking that at the same time that Americans are adopting "Latin Americanized" racial concepts—in the form of both a three-tier racial structure and a greater acceptance of mixed-race populations and multiracial identity—some people in Latin American sending societies are also adopting Americanized ways of thinking about race. Some of my non-migrant respondents in both Puerto Rico and the Dominican Republic adopt an understanding of Blackness and Whiteness as traditionally defined by the one-drop rule in the United States. Other Latin American societies have recently seen Black social movements and race-based policies that reflect a dichotomous view of race.[73] Brazil, which has traditionally used mixed-race classifications, in 2001 began to establish affirmative-action policies for Black students in higher education based on a dichotomous Black-White classification.[74] Other countries, including Colombia, Nicaragua, Ecuador, Honduras, Guatemala, and Bolivia, have adopted legislation granting rights and recognition to their Black populations, challenging long-standing national ideologies of *mestizaje*.[75] Transnational networks, international organizations, and the model of civil-rights-era racial mobilization in the United States have been influential in some of these changes.[76] While I do not see evidence of Black social mobilizations gaining force in Puerto Rico or the Dominican Republic, the schemas and concepts that flow globally from one society to another create a potential for new racial affiliations and political movements in the long term—whether based on Black classifications or a sense of pan–Latin Americanism that is fueled by panethnic identities abroad.

Given the movement of some in the United States and Latin America to adopt racial schemas and structures that are more similar to one another, it is interesting to consider where such transnational racial change might lead. Will societies' cultural and institutionalized concepts of race, like structural aspects of nation-states, converge as they are influenced by a world cultural order?[//] It is unlikely that a single model of racial classification will become dominant everywhere; the difference between which schemas are actively adopted in Puerto Rico and which are adopted in the Dominican Republic suggests that context and local symbolic boundaries play too important a role for convergence around a single schema. However, immigration and globalization will likely lead societies to develop increasingly similar cultural repertoires of race, causing the individuals across them to develop a more similar collection of schemas within their racial schema portfolios. The variation will come in which schemas individuals are led to activate by the social structure of their lives. Much like the way social class led my migrant respondents into different types of interactions, where different symbolic boundaries were most salient, the structured dimensions of social life everywhere bring individuals into situations that influence the racial schemas they use, even if the various options in their portfolios become more alike.

As societies become more globalized, and as transnational migration weaves sending and receiving societies more closely together, the racial structures of one become more relevant for the other. Analyzing race as a system of cognitive organization and as an aspect of culture helps us understand how it can change at both the micro level and the macro level, for immigrants, for their host societies, and for the societies they leave behind. Latin American immigration to the United States is transforming concepts of race because, in many ways, it is not just people, but race itself that migrates.

Reference Matter

Appendix:
Notes on Methodology

As a teacher of research methods, I love to introduce my students to the way that knowledge is produced, not just the end results. Much of qualitative research is best learned through experience, so I find it extremely valuable to learn what challenges other scholars have faced in their research and how they overcame them. I hope that these notes and reflections will prove useful to students and other scholars.

Designing the Study

Because I was interested in whether experiences in the host society affect migrants' conceptions of race, I focused on people who spent their formative years in Puerto Rico or the Dominican Republic but had been in the United States long enough for their ideas about race to be influenced by their experiences. I therefore restricted the sample to people in the New York metropolitan area who were born in Puerto Rico or the Dominican Republic, who came to the U.S. at age 14 or older, and (initially) who had lived there for at least 7 years. This meant that my respondents would be age 21 or older. I excluded migrants who had lived anywhere besides the mainland U.S. and their country of origin, as well as those who had returned to their home country for more than six months after migrating.

For the non-migrant samples, I focused on people whose views were formed within Puerto Rico or the Dominican Republic. I restricted the interviews to adults (21 or older) who had not lived outside of their home country for more than six months. To capture respondents who may be considered ethnically Dominican or Puerto Rican, I included only those who identified both parents as being of these respective nationalities. Because one focus of the original study was on social networks and how individuals rely on them to find work, I tried to make the labor market context as comparable as possible to that of the migrants who lived or worked in the New York metropolitan area. I therefore interviewed only non-migrants who lived or worked in San Juan or Santo Domingo. Some non-migrant respondents had, in fact, moved to the capital from other parts of their country, just as some migrants to the United States originated in rural areas. The diversity of experiences that people bring with them from other geographic regions of the country is part of the urban experience in the cities where I did my research.

To make the migrant and non-migrant samples as similar as possible, and also to explore factors that I expected would influence the process of racial acculturation, I sought variation in age, sex, occupational status, and skin color across all four sample groups. For the migrant samples, I also sought variation in age at arrival in the mainland U.S. and the amount of time they had spent there. For each sample, my goal was to interview 30 respondents who fell roughly evenly into the categories specified in the left-hand column of Table A. The table shows the resulting distribution of the samples across these criteria.

Table A. Distribution of sampling characteristics among respondents

	Non-migrant Puerto Ricans	Non-migrant Dominicans	Migrant Puerto Ricans	Migrant Dominicans
Age				
21–35	11	11	5	16
36–50	11	11	9	10
Above 50	8	8	14	6
Sex				
Male	15	15	14	13
Female	15	15	14	19
Occupational status				
High	10	11	13	11
Medium	11	8	5	8
Low	9	11	10	13
Color				
Light	13	11	14	11
Medium	11	7	10	12
Dark	6	12	4	9
Age at migration				
14–18			16	22
19–25			10	4
Above 25			2	6
Time in the U.S.				
3–13 years[a]			4	11
14–20 years			5	10
Above 20 years			19	11
Total	30	30	28	32

[a]Aside from 3 respondents, this group ranges from 7 to 13 years of age.

I defined high occupational status as managerial and professional specialty occupations. Medium occupational status consists of technical, sales, and administrative support occupations. And low occupational status consists of service occupations; production, craft, and repair occupations; operators, fabricators, and laborers. Respondents who were unemployed at the time of interview were classified according to their most recent occupation. Homemakers were classified according to the occupation of their partner or spouse. Individuals on long-term disability or welfare receipt were classified as low status.

For the purposes of sample distribution, respondents' skin color refers to their observed skin color, as I perceived it on a scale from 1 (lightest) to 10 (darkest). Light skin color corresponds to my ratings 1–3; medium to 4–6; and dark to 7–10. To provide a concrete measure of how I applied this scale, I used it to rate the photographs before the fieldwork began. I determined the color score I would assign to the respondent upon first sight and did not allow the interview or the respondent's self-identification to alter that assessment. Although it was possible to screen respondents for the other quota characteristics over the phone, that did not work for skin color. As much as possible I tried to fill the quota groups for color while canvassing or using other methods where I saw potential respondents before setting up an interview. In Puerto Rico and the Dominican Republic, I sometimes relied on personal contacts to help me fill the more elusive color groups.

For the amount of time migrants had spent in the mainland U.S., my original distribution criteria were 7–13 years, 14–20 years, and more than 20 years. I initially expected that migrants who had lived there for longer amounts of time would be more likely to adopt a U.S. racial schema. Yet I was surprised to find that almost everyone, even the most recent arrivals, saw themselves racialized as Latinos and that many already identified panethnically. This led me to question how quickly new schemas could be adopted and to relax my original criteria to explore this question. I first decided to interview one person who had been in New York for only 6 years, then 5 years, and then finally 3 years. In each case, the patterns were the same as those of the respondents who had made New York their home for nearly half a century. At that point, I started to ask respondents how quickly after arriving they began to realize that they were classified as Hispanic or Latino. Respondents told me that they learned how they were classified within the first few months after arrival or, in many cases, were alerted to it by their U.S. ties even before they arrived. Some flexibility in sampling criteria proved necessary to be able to understand this process.

Any study involving both sending and receiving societies must address the issue of immigrant selectivity—in what ways those who immigrate differ from those who stay behind. Part of the reason for focusing on the sending country capitals, to which many people migrate from rural areas, was to approximate some of the motivation characteristics that also lead people to immigrate. Matching the migrant and non-migrant samples on key demographic characteristics was also intended to make them roughly comparable. To gauge the significance of immigrant selectivity, I asked non-migrants about their interest in immigrating to the mainland U.S. and about the influence of race and race relations there on their interest in moving. Most Dominican non-migrants said they wanted to move to the United States to improve their economic situation and only the lack of visas prevented them from doing so. They had high levels of awareness of U.S. racial hierarchies, and some of them expressed concern about how they would be received, but this generally mattered little to their feelings about moving. Many of the Puerto Rican non-migrants said they would consider moving to the mainland U.S. at some point. This was particularly true of younger respondents. More of the older and middle-class Puerto Ricans (and a couple of the Dominicans) said they had no interest in migrating, but that was only because they were settled, comfortable, and had their family around them. About two or three respondents in each society expressed a distaste for American culture and society as their primary reason for not wanting to move. Similarly, among the migrants, many said they were well aware before they migrated of the racial hierarchies in the United States and how they would be perceived, but that this had little impact on their decision. Although it is likely that the migrant and non-migrant samples differ in terms of motivation, drive, and other unmeasured characteristics that influence a decision to move to a new society, I found no evidence that the issues I focus on in this study—cognitive concepts of race, racial structures and attitudes, or racial strategies—contributed to their feelings about migrating.

I was fortunate to be able to hire native Spanish-speaking research assistants for this research. Although I speak Spanish, and my fluency improved over the course of the project, I am not a native speaker. I felt that having a native speaker present would help me catch more of the nuances of meaning around the racial terminology that people used, especially the colloquial terms used to describe race or color. In Puerto Rico and the Dominican Republic, my research assistants were natives of the country. In New York, my research assistants were Puerto Rican, Cuban, and Ecuadorian. My assistants in the sending societies were also invaluable cultural informants. They helped me navigate the cities, geographically and socially, often giving me background on particular neighborhoods, groups, and recent events.

Finding Respondents

A common approach to finding respondents in ethnic communities is to use snowball sampling, asking one respondent to refer me to others who met my criteria. But my partial focus on respondents' social networks made this approach problematic; with this technique, the networks of many respondents would have been interconnected.

I initially thought I could locate my New York samples through a large random sample of second-generation Puerto Ricans and Dominicans. The Immigrant Second Generation in Metropolitan New York study included a random sample of 429 second-generation Puerto Ricans and 427 second-generation Dominicans. All of these respondents were between 18 and 32 years old in 1999 and were living in New York City or its close suburbs. These samples were obtained by a random-digit dialing telephone survey that screened for respondents matching the sample selection criteria. Of those surveyed, 41 Puerto Ricans and 43 Dominicans participated in an additional in-depth interview in 1999 and were asked to take part in a follow-up in-depth interview in 2002. At the end of each second-wave interview, second-generation Dominican and Puerto Rican respondents were asked for the names of friends or relatives in the first generation who might be willing to be interviewed for my project. Individuals who participated only in the 1999 telephone survey were contacted by phone and asked for similar referrals. When the named second-generation contact had moved, we asked current residents who were Puerto Rican or Dominican to refer first-generation contacts or, if they met the study criteria, to participate themselves. No more than one contact was interviewed from each referral "seed" to reduce the likelihood that social networks were interconnected.

I did find some respondents this way, but it became clear that this strategy was generating only a certain kind of respondent. Members of the second generation generously provided contact information for their parents, aunts, and uncles, but few of them knew anyone else who was first generation. As a result, I quickly filled my quotas for older respondents and those who had been in the United States for many years. But younger respondents and more-recent arrivals proved more elusive.

I therefore decided to broaden my tactics and combine several approaches to finding respondents. Different strategies proved more successful in some sites than others and for locating certain types of respondents. Together, these methods helped me fill the various quotas for my sample distributions. In all three locations, I found some respondents by canvassing particular neighborhoods and passing out flyers in public locations, including malls, shops, and buses, or posting flyers on bulletin boards. I struck up conversations with as many people as possible during my fieldwork and recruited some of the people I came into contact with over the course of my daily interactions in restaurants, shops, and other public places. In San Juan and Santo Domingo, I knocked on doors in some neighborhoods, always accompanied by a research assistant as a safety precaution.

Some respondents were referred by personal contacts, either by my research assistants or by staff in the research institutes with which I was affiliated. Often the chain of connections linking the respondent to me was several degrees removed.[1] This distance was facilitated by the use of forwarded e-mails about the project. People I e-mailed for referrals frequently passed the request on to others, who often forwarded it in turn. Not all the people located in this way were computer-literate. For example, one person in New York who received the e-mail referred me to her Puerto Rican housecleaner. This approach did have some unintended consequences, however. At one point during my New York fieldwork, someone posted my e-mail description on Craigslist, and I received several e-mail messages from interested participants. I was initially reluctant to accept respondents located in this unintended way. However, I found that it was particularly useful for finding younger respondents, a group that had been especially difficult to discover among Puerto Rican migrants. I therefore accepted a small number of respondents who learned of the project this way if they fell into the quota groups that were proving to be more difficult to reach. For all respondents recruited through e-mail or personal contacts, I ensured that no two were referred to me by the same individual.

Finally, in order to find some respondents with high occupational status, I contacted professional organizations, which contacted their membership on my behalf. In only one case did I accept two respondents from the same organization, and that was because the circumstances made it clear that the two members did not know each other. In other cases, I interviewed only one member of each professional group, while asking additional members who responded to refer me to other individuals who met the criteria and were not associated with the group.[2] To achieve a balance between those who were and were not involved in such professional groups, I also ensured that not all of my respondents with high occupational status in any sample group were located through professional organizations.

Whenever respondents were recruited over the phone, my research assistants made the initial phone call. I believed that potential respondents might be more comfortable talking to a native Spanish speaker and, ideally, a member of their own ethnic group. This strategy did go a long way toward building rapport with respondents, and it may have given them a chance to ask blunt questions about my motives and interests. Potential respondents were always told that I was a graduate student at Harvard University doing my dissertation research. It is possible that the Harvard name may have helped open some doors, although only one respondent ever indicated that this was the case. After our interview, Juanita told me that her son was interested in learning how to get into Harvard, and I spent some time talking with him about it. With the professional respondents and organizations, I suspect that the mere fact of a student taking an interest in the experiences of their community played more of a role in recruiting respondents.

The most difficult aspect of conducting research in multiple locations was the amount of time it took to figure out what worked and what did not in each location. I started the fieldwork in New York because I was familiar with the location and because I expected my access to large random samples of Puerto Ricans and Dominicans to allow me to hit the ground running. When I realized that I could not find all my respondents through these referrals, I experienced a frustrating hiatus, realizing that I would have to find new ways of recruiting respondents. I began to talk to anyone I could for additional suggestions on ways to find people. I met with several local academics, spoke with neighbors, friends, and just about anyone who was willing to listen. It took a while for these efforts to pay off, but after a period of trying different approaches, leaving numerous phone messages and waiting for returned calls, setting up appointments and rescheduling those that were canceled, I found that the interviews took on a momentum of their own. In each location, as soon as the momentum got going and my efforts were proving successful, it became time to start all over somewhere else. There are entry costs to getting established in multiple research sites, and researchers should factor in these considerations when planning comparative research across locations.

Assembling the Photographs

My primary goal in creating a set of photographs was to collect images of real people who would represent the range of typical phenotypes found in Puerto Rico and the Dominican Republic. It was not necessary that every image be of someone who was actually Puerto Rican or Dominican, but I did seek out locations to take photographs where I expected to find people from these groups.

I submitted a separate application to my institutional review board for the project of compiling a photographic instrument. This included a consent form that explained the purpose of taking the photos, how they would be used in the interview and in subsequent publications and talks, and an offer of $5 to each person in exchange for allowing me to take and possibly use his or her photograph. After receiving approval, I set out for Jamaica Plain, a Dominican neighborhood in Boston, to approach people on the street for the project. I was fortunate to be accompanied by a Venezuelan friend, both because his extroverted personality made it easier to approach strangers on the street and because his presence provided an extra safety measure. I encourage all researchers to consider such safety precautions when canvassing neighborhoods or knocking on doors, regardless of the area.

We took approximately 20 photos in Jamaica Plain, mostly of people we approached on the street. Several others were either employees or customers in stores we entered. Most people we approached were happy to participate, although one person—who declined to be photographed—was very suspicious and thought we might be from a government agency. Having a university identification card is very useful in this type of situation, although I doubt it dissolved his concerns. I supplemented these photographs with a few others of people I knew and store employees in a shop that I frequented. After relocating to New York to begin my fieldwork, I decided that I needed some additional photographs to provide more variety. However, my first few efforts to approach people in New York on the street as I had in Jamaica Plain were completely unsuccessful. Following advice from local scholars, I went to the campus of a city college that had a large Latino student population. There I found many additional people who agreed to have their photos taken, and a few who were interested enough in the study that they volunteered to participate in pilot interviews.

I did not ask about the racial or ethnic identity of each person I photographed, although some people volunteered this information as I was taking their picture. Since I was interested in the classifications that people make and how they arrive at those decisions, I did not want to be armed with knowledge of whether their classifications were "right." In fact, this was a central preoccupation of many of my respondents. After we finished going through the photographs, the first question many of them asked was "Did I get it right?" It was some small consolation to be able to tell them that I honestly did not know and that I was not trying to test them.

I consulted with two people to whittle my collection of 45 photographs down to 20 that best represented the range of phenotypes common in the Hispanic Caribbean and that best represented the variety of terms in Table 3 (in Chapter 1). One, a female Puerto Rican migrant, was one of my research assistants. The other, a male Dominican migrant, was a respondent for a pilot interview who was particularly perceptive about race and color, so I asked him afterward if I could hire him as a consultant to decide on the final photos I would use. Both fit the criteria for my target population. With each of them, I talked through the continuum terms that might be used to describe the photos in Puerto Rico and the Dominican Republic.

Designing the Questions

To avoid reinventing the wheel and to maintain some consistency with earlier studies, I found it helpful to start with the interview guides of a few previous investigations that related to my topic. Some of these I was lucky to obtain from scholars at my university. Another excellent source for interview questions is UMI Dissertation Services. Many dissertations, including those that later evolved into award-winning books, include their interview guides. I combined a few questions from these different sources with many of my own.

A Puerto Rican research assistant translated the interview guides into Spanish, and offered advice about what questions might be problematic or confusing. Later, a Dominican research assistant went over the questions and suggested wording changes that would be more appropriate for that population. The initial pilot phase before beginning any interviews was fairly extensive. Many of the questions I tried out simply did not work or were interpreted in very different ways than I intended. I found it useful to do more pilot interviews in San Juan and Santo Domingo, both for the additional questions that were specific to non-migrant interviews and for the opportunity to tailor the interviews to those particular populations.

A challenge for comparative qualitative research is to keep questions roughly the same, so they are asked of different groups in similar ways, while still having enough flexibility to test new ideas. My solution to this was to maintain the wording and order of my primary questions for the most part, while allowing myself more leeway on subsequent probes and follow-up questions. When I found important new avenues of inquiry in this way, I added them to the interview guide so I could ask them in a standardized way.

I gave respondents the Spanish version of questions 5 and 6 (Hispanic origin and race) from the 2000 Census on a sheet of paper and asked them to complete the questions. In some interviews, I varied the timing of these questions to examine whether their placement in the interview would affect the open-ended responses. However, I did not find any differences based on the placement of these questions before or after the photos and other open-ended questions. I also asked respondents to identify their own race in open-ended terms, as well as how they believe Americans would classify them, and how different people in their home country have described their race. Later, I asked them to describe their color using a scale from 1 to 10, with 1 representing the lightest person they could imagine and 10 representing the darkest person. To anchor how each respondent applied the scale, I also asked them to use it to describe the appearance of some of the people in the photos. The list of continuum terms that I showed respondents toward the end of the interview consisted of the following terms in a single vertical column: Negro, Azulito, Prieto, Pardo, Grifo, Moreno, De color, Cenizo, Mulato, Trigueño, Mestizo, Indio, Piel canela, Café con leche, Blanco con raja, Jabao, Colorao, Rosadito, Rubio, Cano, Jincho, Blancusino, Blanquito, Blanco.[3]

After the interview, I asked a number of demographic questions and completed an interview summary sheet. Placing this at the end avoided the issue of having short-answer questions affect respondents' willingness to answer expansively in our open-ended discussion. To measure their income, I gave respondents a card with a series of income ranges next to letters and asked them to tell me the letter that corresponded to their household income. This avoided discomfort with the question and also allowed me to change the range of incomes to appropriate levels in Dominican pesos for interviews in Santo Domingo.

In migrant interviews, I then gave respondents a series of questions to complete to measure their attitudes toward other U.S. racial groups, taken from the Multi-City Study on Urban Inequality. I asked them to put the questions in an envelope and seal it before handing it back, so they would be assured that I would not look at their answers in front of them. Finally, with all respondents, as soon as I left and had an opportunity to sit down, I completed a form about my perceptions of the respondents' appearance, including their skin color using the 10-point scale, how Americans might see them, their hair color and texture, their eye color, their facial features, and a prose description of their overall appearance.

Measuring Social Networks

Partway through the interview, I asked respondents about their social networks. I used a *name generator* approach, which enumerates "alters," or ties that lie within a network, by asking respondents to list people with whom they share a certain relation. I asked them to list up to five people who had helped them find jobs; their best friend and three additional good friends; a current romantic partner and up to three previous partners;[4] up to three additional friends from work or school; and up to three people they are friendly with from organizations they participate in, such as church, a club, or a voluntary organization.

I then used a *name interpreter*, a series of questions designed to elicit information about the alters, including alters' demographic characteristics and relationship with the respondent. The names or initials of alters were written on a sheet next to a given letter. To ensure the confidentiality of this information, I asked respondents to read off the letter rather than the name in response to questions about the alters. The tape recorder was shut off during the name-generation process, and at the end of the interview the list of names was left with the respondent. This technique made respondents more comfortable with providing information about their friends and also reduced interview time by allowing respondents to list the letters for all the alters who matched given criteria, rather than repeating questions for each alter.

Respondents were asked to state the race of each alter in open-ended terms. Many responded by listing national or ethnic identifiers such as Puerto Rican or Dominican. However, if respondents did not do so, the ethnicity of each tie was asked as a follow-up question. After prefacing the question by explaining that many Dominicans or Puerto Ricans vary greatly in their appearance, I asked respondents to describe the color of each alter on the 10-point scale. Asking respondents to describe their own color with the scale immediately after this question made what might have been an awkward question relatively unobtrusive.

The respondents' ratings with this scale do not capture the full complexity of how some Puerto Ricans and Dominicans perceive "color," which incorporates physical features as well as skin color. European features are conceptually entwined with concepts of lightness, while African features may lead one to apply a "darker" color rating, regardless of skin tone. Although respondents also rated their own skin color using the scale from 1 to 10, their ratings of their color often differed from mine. External observations are more appropriate when the concern is with how perceptions of physical appearance shape opportunities controlled by others. For this reason, I use my descriptions of the respondent's appearance throughout the book, rather than their color ratings.[5]

Conducting the Interviews

I told respondents that I preferred to conduct the interviews in Spanish, unless they had a strong preference for English (two respondents did). Even with respondents who were fluent in English, this provided greater comparability in the types of terminology they used to discuss race. I always gave respondents the option of deciding where they would like to be interviewed. Most chose their own homes. In both San Juan and Santo Domingo, I had access to office space through the research institutes I was visiting, and many interviews were conducted there. But in New York I did not have any institutional affiliation, and when respondents did not want to be interviewed in their homes, we had to find a public location that would be relatively quiet. I usually asked respondents to recommend a quiet public place in their neighborhood. A few interviews were conducted in cafés or in some of New York's enclosed "public spaces" built into office buildings. None of the respondents seemed uncomfortable with the public aspect of these spaces, or the potential for eavesdroppers. I do recommend checking out the conditions of such spaces ahead of time, as some were noisy, some were freezing, and it can take a while to find a good public interview environment.

I offered respondents an honorarium for their participation. This seemed only fair, given that I was asking people to share their time and experiences with me, and because most interviews were long, lasting about two and a half hours on average. Initially I offered $20 per interview in New York, but I was not having a lot of luck finding respondents. In one of my many conversations with local scholars, a colleague told me that her recent project had offered $75 per respondent for follow-up interviews in a longitudinal study. It occurred to me that what I was offering might be too little to be worth New Yorkers' time. I raised the amount of the honorarium to $40, and eventually to $50. I was quite concerned that offering what seemed to me to be a large amount of money might act as an excessive incentive, perhaps leading some people to agree to an interview who might not otherwise have wanted to do so. There were only one or two instances in which I feared that this might have been a factor (as I explain below). But I did my best to tell people ahead of time what the interview would cover and to ask repeatedly if they were comfortable discussing this type of information. I also reminded them several times throughout the interview that they could skip any questions or stop the interview at any time. Only one respondent asked to draw the interview to a close, but this seemed more related to the fact that an hour and a half of interviewing after a long day of work was more than she had the attention span for.

I tried to match the honorarium amounts to the local context in Puerto Rico and the Dominican Republic so that I would not be offering too strong an incentive. In Puerto Rico, I paid $20 per interview, eventually raising this amount to $30 toward the end for the types of respondents I was having difficulty locating. In the Dominican Republic, I paid RD$500, or approximately $17. One man in Puerto Rico had indicated over the phone that he had never lived outside of Puerto Rico, but when he arrived for the interview it turned out that he had lived abroad for a year and was not eligible. Judging from his reaction when I explained, I worried that he might have been primarily interested in the honorarium. In this case, I felt the ethical thing to do was to interview him anyway, as I suspected that he might have been uncomfortable if I had simply offered him an honorarium without interviewing him first. Afterward, he seemed proud to have been able to help us with the study. I never transcribed that interview, but I believe that when resources allow, it is important not to make potential participants feel that their experiences are less valuable or interesting to a foreign researcher just because they do not fit particular research criteria.

The Insider/Outsider Issue and Bicultural Interviewing

Throughout the research, I tried to be as reflexive as possible of how my various identities—for instance, as a White American with no Latin American ancestry, as a woman, as a person pursuing a doctoral degree at an elite university—shaped the context of the interviews and everything else I witnessed during my fieldwork. I was honestly surprised to find that in Puerto Rico and the Dominican Republic many people initially assumed from my appearance that I was a native. While I expected to be easily recognizable as American, many of the stereotypes people held of Americans seemed to work in my favor for visually blending in. I was told that Americans are believed to have blond hair, blue eyes, and no *nalgas* (or rear ends). Since I defied these perceptions, people often said they did not realize I was American until I opened my mouth to speak, at which point my accent made it instantly clear. In some ways, then, I had the opportunity in the Hispanic Caribbean to experience what many of my migrant respondents experienced in New York, the shifting of other people's classifications on the basis of coded signals such as language and accent. To my knowledge, however, I was never confused for a Puerto Rican or Dominican in New York, where there was generally much greater awareness of differences in appearance, styles, and mannerisms.

Nonetheless, despite a few initial assumptions, my role as researcher was that of a cultural outsider, a position that has both advantages and disadvantages. Race is a very sensitive topic among Dominicans and Puerto Ricans, and many are reluctant to discuss it. When Jorge Duany and his research team asked respondents in the Barrio Gandul section of San Juan to describe their race, many were embarrassed or uncomfortable; several just shrugged and pointed to their arm to suggest that their skin color was obvious. Such reactions led Duany and his team to abandon the question and to use interviewer perceptions to describe the respondent's race instead.[6] While I feared I would experience the same reaction, I was pleasantly surprised to find that I did not. My status undoubtedly helped me broach this difficult topic. While some respondents may have thought my questions about race strange, most saw me as an ignorant outsider interested in their community's perceptions, and they were willing to enlighten me.

At the same time, respondents almost certainly expressed their racial identities differently around me than they would have around a co-ethnic. In particular, I believe their use of categories such as Latino or Hispanic, or their adoption of a nationality schema rather than a continuum schema for the photographs was tied to circumstances of having me as part of the audience. Initially, I feared that I was getting the "wrong" answer, and I began varying whether my research assistant or I led the interview, to test for American/Latino interviewer effects. The majority of my research assistants were of the same nationality as the respondents; in New York, those who did not share nationality did share Latino panethnicity.

As the fieldwork progressed, I realized that having both a cultural insider and an outsider present could be a major advantage from an analytical perspective. I began to develop a research protocol that I call *bicultural interviewing*. Rather than simply alternating interviewers, the crux of bicultural interviewing is that the insider and the outsider both attend an interview and compare perspectives and insights. I discussed the interviews with the research assistants to get their perspectives on how well the responses resonated with their observations of their society and how they felt the responses might have differed if I, as an American, had not been present. I tape-recorded many of these discussions and used them as part of my data. But more than simply treating these as additional data points, I found that these conversations shaped my analytical standpoint. Thus my research assistants also served as cultural informants, helping me to see the data through their eyes and to better understand my own role as observer.

These conversations typically occurred after an interview, when my research assistant and I would repair to a quiet location, set up the recorder, and begin to discuss the interview we had just conducted. I usually began by asking about anything I was unsure

I fully understood, and from there the discussion flowed into the major themes that had come up in the interview, and how it compared to other interviews. As my research assistants provided a "local" perspective on those themes, I would probe and sometimes challenge them, just as they would sometimes challenge me. Sometimes this led to our sorting respondents' experiences into different types or groupings, and working back through earlier interviews to make sense of them in light of new issues that had come up. In many ways, these conversations also served as oral "memos," focusing the interview themes into analytical categories, while also coming to understand those themes from different perspectives.

This approach is particularly useful for a study on a culturally sensitive topic like race. While it is always possible that respondents will give an answer they believe the interviewer wants or expects to hear, in-depth probing can reveal the extent to which these views are deeply held and the meaning that people attribute to these categories. This helped to highlight for me precisely how Puerto Rican and Dominican respondents may have multiple ways of understanding and classifying race, all of which are deeply held, yet evoked in different ways and for different audiences. It was my conversations with my research assistants, and particularly their views on how respondents reconciled the different race terms they revealed, that helped me shift my analytical lens from viewing these different terms as inconsistencies to viewing them as the maintenance of multiple racial schemas.

Reactions to Studying Race

Some respondents were surprised and perhaps a bit uncomfortable by the level of detail in my questions about race and classification. This was particularly evident in my earliest interviews. One of the first interviews was with Alberto, an older Puerto Rican man in Brooklyn. He and his wife were very friendly when we arrived and proudly showed us around their home. The interview started out well, and Alberto spoke at great length about his experiences coming to New York and living there for almost 50 years, as well as the discrimination he had faced as a Puerto Rican. We had mentioned on the phone, and described at the beginning of the interview, that we would be talking about race, and he seemed fine with classifying the photos openly. But when we got to the discussion of the continuum terms and how they are used, Alberto became uncomfortable. He insisted that he judges everyone equally and would never use terms like these. When I asked him to apply the color terms to the photos, he became evasive. For each photo, he would say something like, "This looks like an intelligent person. They're healthy and strong. They look like they could do any kind of work they wanted to." This was his way of indicating that he did not judge people on the basis of color. Despite our repeated assurances to the contrary, Alberto seemed to think that we would judge him as a racist for even using these terms. At the end of the interview, although he offered us refreshments and continued to be polite, his wife came into the room from the kitchen and, after some casual conversation, asked if I had any identification to show who I was. She said she had been on the phone with her daughter, who was worried about exactly who we were and why we were asking questions. I showed her my university identification card, gave her a business card with my local number on the back, and pointed out on their copy of the consent form where my phone number and the phone number of the university's Human Subjects Committee were written. They were clearly embarrassed and apologized for even asking for this, and while I tried to reassure them that I was not offended, they went out of their way after this exchange to be polite and friendly, keeping up the chitchat for quite some time and offering more refreshments.

The experience with Alberto and his wife made it clear that I needed to be much more explicit in my descriptions to respondents about what we would be covering in the interview. It was not enough simply to say that we would be talking about race. From that point on, I took care to explain on the phone and in person that we would be talking about how people classify each other's race and what those decisions are based on, and to ask if this was a topic they felt comfortable discussing. I began to introduce the sections on classifying the photos and discussing the continuum terms with an explanation of why I was asking about this, why it was valuable, and I reminded them that they could skip any questions they wanted to. I never had another interview where the respondent seemed as uncomfortable as Alberto. Clearly it is not just the wording of the questions themselves that is important, but also how they are introduced and explained.

Many of the respondents said they enjoyed the interview and saw the identification of the photos and the discussion of continuum terms as a type of game. Several indicated that they had never paid attention to these issues before and felt that they had learned something from the interview. But there were also a few respondents—especially in New York—who seemed to think that even talking about race and color differences was the same as racism. I found this to be particularly true among more religious participants. In such circumstances, it is important to explain why it is valuable to study race, and what the study is for. Respondents deserved to know that their participation was contributing to something valuable and not just helping a nosy researcher get a degree or advance her career. Embarrassed reactions can be normalized; I felt that some of my respondents were looking to me for assurance that they were not racist. Explaining that everyone classifies other people into groups and that this is why it is valuable to understand how those classifications are made can help assuage such concerns.

Observations, Notes, and Analysis

I draw heavily on interview data in this book because I want to allow respondents' views and experiences to come across in their own words. But the analyses that shaped the book were very much formed by participant observation as well. I took several hundred pages of field notes based on my observations, interactions, and experiences in these sites. My notes focused particularly on any use of race terms or language, as well as any interactions I observed that seemed connected to race. But they also captured other aspects of the life and culture of these places that seemed connected to the substantive frame of the project.

As a participant observer, I was able to gather much richer and fuller accounts in Puerto Rico and the Dominican Republic than in New York. In both of the former locations, I was immersed in the communities of interest, in each case living with local residents and interacting with potential subjects every time I walked out the door. In New York I lived with my own family on the Upper West Side during my fieldwork. The cost of housing in New York made this a necessity. But it did come at the expense of more detailed immersion and observations, which I would have been able to acquire if I had had the opportunity to live with a Dominican or Puerto Rican family, or in a neighborhood like Washington Heights or Spanish Harlem.

My standard procedure was to come home each evening and "dump" my reflections and experiences from the day into a stream-of-consciousness log, including my descriptions of any relevant observations that were not tied to the interviews. If I had conducted an interview that day, I first wrote up a set of notes on the interview, which included a description of the interview location; my impressions of the interview (how it went, how the respondent acted, anyone else who was present); a profile of the respondent; and a description of the conceptions of race that he or she expressed.

The interview notes gave me an opportunity to reflect on the themes and patterns that were emerging. I also kept a separate file of analytical memos, which were more thematically organized and served as a canvas on which I could jot down initial observations and thoughts, add subsequent observations that spoke to the theme, and eventually work out what I thought was going on. I went back and forth between these memos and the interview tapes and transcriptions, my participant observation field notes, and my interview notes. I copied any relevant information from the other locations into the memos and added a reflective commentary with questions to myself and initial hypotheses until the patterns became clearer.

I initially planned to ask my research assistants to transcribe the interviews they had been present for, but it soon became clear that they did not have time to transcribe as well as help locate respondents and participate in the interviews. The cost of having Spanish-language interviews professionally transcribed and translated was simply prohibitive for a graduate student. And I was reluctant to transcribe the interviews myself, both because of time constraints and because I thought a native Spanish speaker would do a better job of catching any words or expressions that I might have missed in the interview.

I ended up putting an advertisement on a job listing Web site at Columbia University. I interviewed several native Spanish speakers who were bilingual in Spanish and English and gave them sample recordings to try to transcribe and translate. I purchased several transcription machines cheaply on eBay and discount equipment sites, and after I selected my transcribers I lent each one a transcription machine so they could work whenever the hours suited them. The flexibility of the job seemed to appeal to students, and I was surprised by the number of excellent and highly qualified candidates who were eager to do some transcription work from home whenever they had time. Later, after I finished my fieldwork, I found additional transcribers/translators through a similar Web site at Harvard University and through Craigslist. They did simultaneous translation and transcription into English. Ideally, a two-step process could have provided for back translation and checks, but my budget would not allow this. As much as possible, I tried to match Dominican and Puerto Rican translators to transcripts from respondents of that nationality. However, some interviews were transcribed and translated by people of different Latino nationalities. Each assistant signed a confidentiality agreement that held him or her to the same obligations as researchers to protect the confidentiality of the data.

I entered the transcripts into Atlas.ti, an analysis software program that allows for coding and sorting of qualitative data. I also eventually entered my interview notes and participant observation field notes. First I developed and applied a set of descriptive codes that identified key topics or specific questions in the interview. After this, I developed a set of analytical codes that related to the patterns, hypotheses, and explanations that I saw in the data. I also employed some "in vivo codes"[7] whenever interesting ideas or categories came from the words of the respondents themselves. The process of coding was tightly intertwined with additional memo writing. I wrote memos in Atlas.ti that connected codes to one another and that helped me make sense of patterns and themes I recognized as I was coding the data.

After coding, I did some of the "sorting and sifting" in Atlas.ti using its query tool. This allowed me to specify the base group (e.g., Dominican migrants) and call forth all quotations assigned a particular code, which was especially useful for comparing the responses of subgroups on specific themes. However, I often wanted to examine variation by characteristics within these groups, such as gender differences or color differences in the types of racial schemas that respondents adopted for the photographs. To get a broader overview of these patterns, I entered basic information about responses into a spreadsheet. This helped me visualize some patterns more easily, such as the different types of schemas that people were using. The sort feature of the spreadsheet then allowed me to examine, for example, how those schemas corresponded to people with different education levels in each group. Once I identified general patterns this way, I went back to the qualitative data to read through the different passages from respondents in these subgroups and flesh out more of the nuances in their responses.

Many of the different stages of analysis overlapped. I began coding my interview data while I was still in the field, as soon as the first transcripts were available, but I did end up going back over them later after I had developed more of my analytical frames. Taking notes and writing memos while I was still in the field was invaluable, as it allowed me to change or add questions according to preliminary patterns I was seeing. But I was simply too busy and too exhausted during the data-collection phase to do as much coding and analysis as I would have liked. If I were planning this project now, I might take a break between the fieldwork sites to analyze the first set of interviews before conducting some of the later ones.

The most important lesson for all qualitative researchers is that no project is ever without its share of difficulties and challenges. Honest reflection and description of the challenges faced and the ways they were handled gives readers and other researchers a chance to evaluate or even try to replicate aspects of the study. And hopefully it will also provide valuable lessons and reassurance to those starting out on projects of their own.

Notes

Chapter 1

1. The names of all respondents have been replaced by pseudonyms. In cases where respondents mention their names to make a particular point (e.g., that it can be interpreted as either a Latino or an Italian name), I have used pseudonyms that I believe convey that same meaning.

2. I have deliberately capitalized the racial categories "White," "Black," and "Indigenous" throughout this book. Common grammatical usage does not capitalize these terms, even though other racial categories such as "Asian" and "American Indian" are typically capitalized, as are ethnicities, nationalities, religions, and other social constructions. I believe this grammatical exception is a holdover from a conception of race, and particularly of Whiteness and Blackness, as natural and generic, much like age and sex (which are also not capitalized). One of the underlying assumptions of this book is that not only are these categories socially constructed, but their very meaning and membership may change as a result of social processes such as immigration. Therefore, I believe it is appropriate that these social categories take their rightful place in our language with other proper nouns.

3. In this book, I retain Spanish terms referring to race or color that do not have immediate English equivalents. I keep gender agreement only when they refer to specific people. The term *moreno* can mean both a dark-skinned person in general and an African American specifically. I use *moreno* for the former, and the capitalized *Moreno* for the latter. Respondents often used the terms *blanco* and *negro* both to describe skin color and to refer to White or Black Americans. I keep these in Spanish in the former case, and translate them as "White" or "Black" in the latter.

4. F. James Davis, *Who Is Black? One Nation's Definition* (University Park, PA: Pennsylvania State University Press, 1991); Joel Williamson, *New People: Miscegenation and Mulattoes in the United States* (New York: Free Press, 1980).

5. John D. Skrentny, "Culture and Race/Ethnicity: Bolder, Deeper, and Broader," *Annals of the American Academy of Political and Social Science* 619 (2008): 59–77; Howard Winant, "Race and Race Theory," *Annual Review of Sociology* 26 (2000): 169–85.

6. I use the terms "Latino" and "Hispanic" interchangeably in this book. Although there are noteworthy historical and symbolic differences between them, most of my respondents used them as synonyms.

7. Sharon M. Lee and Barry Edmonston, "Hispanic Intermarriage, Identification, and U.S. Latino Population Change," *Social Science Quarterly* 87 (2006): 1263–79.

8. Lynette Clemetson, "Hispanics Now Largest Minority, Census Shows," *New York Times*, January 22, 2003, online edition.

9. Samuel P. Huntington, *Who Are We? The Challenges to America's National Identity* (New York: Simon and Schuster, 2004), p. 256.

10. Carl Hulse, "Senate Votes to Set English as National Language," *New York Times*, May 19, 2006, online edition; ACLU, "English-Only Amendment Would Endanger Lives, Discriminate and Create 'Second-Class' Citizens, ACLU Says" (press release, June 7, 2007, accessed March 22, 2011, at www.aclu.org).

11. Kari Gibson, "English Only Court Cases Involving the U.S. Workplace: The Myths of Language Use and the Homogenization of Bilingual Workers' Identities," *Second Language Studies* 22 (2004): 1–60.

12. Randal C. Archibold, "Arizona Enacts Stringent Law on Immigration," *New York Times*, April 23, 2010, online edition.

13. Richard Rodríguez, *Brown: The Last Discovery of America* (New York: Penguin Books, 2002).

14. U.S. Census Bureau, *Overview of Race and Hispanic Origin: 2010* (2010 Census Briefs, 2011).

15. E.g., Clara E. Rodríguez, *Changing Race: Latinos, the Census, and the History of Ethnicity in the United States* (New York: NYU Press, 2000); Benjamin Bailey, "Dominican-American Ethnic/Racial Identities and United States Social Categories," *International Migration Review* 35 (2001): 677–708; José Itzigsohn and Carlos Dore-Cabral, "Competing Identities? Race, Ethnicity, and Panethnicity among Dominicans in the United States," *Sociological Forum* 15 (2000): 225–47.

16. Orlando Patterson, "Race by the Numbers," *New York Times*, May 8, 2001, p. A27.

17. Laura E. Gómez, *Manifest Destinies: The Making of the Mexican American Race* (New York: NYU Press, 2007); Eileen O'Brien, *The Racial Middle: Latinos and Asian Americans Living beyond the Racial Divide* (New York: NYU Press, 2008).

18. George Yancey, *Who Is White? Latinos, Asians, and the New Black/Nonblack Divide* (Boulder, CO: Lynne Rienner Publishers, 2003); Herbert J. Gans, "The Possibility of a New Racial Hierarchy in the Twenty-first-Century United States," in *The Cultural Territories of Race: Black and White Boundaries*, ed. Michèle Lamont, pp. 371–90 (Chicago: University of Chicago Press, 1999); Jennifer Lee and Frank D. Bean, *The Diversity Paradox: Immigration and the Color Line in 21st Century America* (New York: Russell Sage Foundation, 2010).

19. Eduardo Bonilla-Silva, "From Bi-Racial to Tri-Racial: Towards a New System of Racial Stratification in the USA," *Ethnic and Racial Studies* 27 (2004): 931–50; Reanne Frank, Ilana Redstone Akresh, and Bo Lu, "Latino Immigrants and the U.S. Racial Order: How and Where Do They Fit In?" *American Sociological Review* 75 (2010): 378–401; Tyrone A. Forman, Carla Goar, and Amanda E. Lewis, "Neither Black nor White? An Empirical Test of the Latin Americanization Thesis," *Race and Society* 5 (2002): 65–84; Edward Murguia and Rogelio Saenz, "An Analysis of the Latin Americanization of Race in the United States: A Reconnaissance of Color Stratification among Mexicans," *Race and Society* 5 (2002): 85–101.

20. Author's analysis of 2008 American Community Survey, www.census.gov.

21. Clara Rodriguez, "Puerto Ricans: Between Black and White," *New York Affairs* 1 (1974): 92–101; Itzisohn and Dore-Cabral, "Competing Identities?"; Frank Moya Pons, *The Dominican Republic: A National History* (Princeton, NJ: Markus Wiener Publishers, 1998).

22. Peter Wade, "Race and Class: The Case of South American Blacks," *Ethnic and Racial Studies* 8 (1985): 233–49; Peter Wade, *Blackness and Race Mixture: The Dynamics of Racial Identity in Colombia* (Baltimore: Johns Hopkins University Press, 1993); Christina Sue and Tanya Golash-Boza, "Blackness in Mestizo America: The Cases of Mexico and Peru," *Latino(a) Research Review* 7 (2009): 30–58. Although Brazil had an extremely developed slave trade, it is very distinctive from other Latin American nations. Its long and relatively peaceful colonial history under the Portu-

guese makes its colonial history unique and places Brazilian immigrants to the United States, as non-Spanish speakers, in an ambiguous relationship toward other Hispanics or Latinos. For these reasons, the nations of the Hispanic Caribbean provide a better avenue for comparative research. See Robert J. Cottrol, "The Long Lingering Shadow: Law, Liberalism, and Cultures of Racial Hierarchy and Identity in the Americas," *Tulane Law Review* 76 (2001): 11–79. Edward E. Telles, *Race in Another America: The Significance of Skin Color in Brazil* (Princeton, NJ: Princeton University Press, 2004); Stanley R. Bailey, *Legacies of Race: Identities, Attitudes, and Politics in Brazil* (Stanford, CA: Stanford University Press, 2009).

23. Edward E. Telles and Edward Murguia, "Phenotypic Discrimination and Income Differences Among Mexican Americans," *Social Science Quarterly* 71 (1990): 682–96.

24. Clara E. Rodríguez, "The Effect of Race on Puerto Rican Wages," in *Hispanics in the Labor Force: Issues and Policies*, ed. Edwin Melendez, Clara Rodríguez, and Janis Barry Figueroa, pp. 77–98 (New York: Plenum Press, 1991).

25. R. S. Oropesa, Nancy S. Landale, and Meredith Greif, "From Puerto Rican to Pan-Ethnic in New York City," *Ethnic and Racial Studies* 31 (2008): 1315–39.

26. Nancy Morris, *Puerto Rico: Culture, Politics, and Identity* (Westport, CT: Praeger, 1995).

27. Elizabeth Aranda, "Struggles of Incorporation among the Puerto Rican Middle Class," *Sociological Quarterly* 48 (2007): 199–228.

28. Recognizing the duality of Puerto Ricans' position in the mainland United States, Pérez y González refers to them as "(im)migrants." María E. Pérez y González, *Puerto Ricans in the United States* (Westport, CT: Greenwood Press, 2000).

29. Ibid.; Morris, *Puerto Rico*; Jorge Duany, *The Puerto Rican Nation on the Move: Identities on the Island and in the United States* (Chapel Hill: University of North Carolina Press, 2002).

30. For simplicity, I use "United States" to refer to the mainland United States. Most Puerto Ricans themselves adopt this terminology, thereby distinguishing their island from the rest of the United States.

31. Silvio Torres-Saillant and Ramona Hernández, *The Dominican Americans* (Westport, CT: Greenwood Press, 1998); Pérez y González, *Puerto Ricans in the United States.*

32. In this, Puerto Rico and the Dominican Republic differ from Cuba, the other country of the Hispanic Caribbean, whose migrant population has historically been concentrated in Miami.

33. The cultural connections that Puerto Ricans and Dominicans share, despite their much-touted tensions, were driven home to me during my fieldwork as I watched the 2003 Miss Universe pageant—a culturally important event in these communities—with a Puerto Rican family in San Juan. They had been rooting vociferously for the Puerto Rican candidate, Carla Tricoli. However, once she was eliminated, they threw their support behind the Dominican finalist, Amelia Vega. After Vega won the competition, the family's 25-year-old daughter exclaimed with satisfaction, "Well, if Carla had to be out of it, then I'm at least happy that the Dominican candidate won, because the Dominican Republic is like the sister of Puerto Rico."

34. Nina Glick Schiller, Linda Basch, and Cristina Blanc-Szanton, "Transnationalism: A New Analytic Framework for Understanding Migration," *Annals of the New York Academy of Sciences* 645 (1992): 1–24; 7.

35. E.g., José Itzigsohn, "Incorporation and Transnationalism among Dominican Immigrants," *Caribbean Studies* 32 (2004): 43–72; Peggy Levitt, *The Transnational Villagers* (Berkeley: University of California Press, 2001); Jorge Duany, *Quisqueya on the Hudson: The Transnational Identity of Dominicans in Washington Heights* (New York: CUNY Dominican Studies Institute, 1994); Duany, *Puerto Rican Nation on the Move*; Adrian D. Pantoja, "Transnational Ties and Immigrant Political Incorporation: The Case of Dominicans in Washington Heights, New York," *International Migration* 43 (2005): 123–46; Carlos Antonio Torre, Hugo Rodríguez Vecchini, and William Burgos, eds.,

The Commuter Nation: Perspectives on Puerto Rican Migration (Rio Piedras: Editorial de la Universidad de Puerto Rico, 1994).

36. Levitt, *Transnational Villagers.*

37. Michiel Baud, "'Constitutionally White': The Forging of a National Identity in the Dominican Republic," in *Ethnicity in the Caribbean: Essays in Honor of Harry Hoetink,* ed. Gert Oostindie, pp. 121–51 (London: Macmillan Education, 1996); Ginetta E. B. Candelario, *Black behind the Ears: Dominican Racial Identity from Museums to Beauty Shops* (Durham, NC: Duke University Press, 2007).

38. Bailey, "Dominican-American Ethnic/Racial Identities."

39. David Howard, *Coloring the Nation: Race and Ethnicity in the Dominican Republic* (Oxford: Signal Books, 2001).

40. U.S. Census Bureau, Census 2000 Summary File 1, 100-Percent Data, American Factfinder, 2000, www.census.gov.

41. Stephen Cornell and Douglas Hartmann, *Ethnicity and Race: Making Identities in a Changing World* (Thousand Oaks, CA: Pine Forge Press, 1998).

42. Brubaker, Loveman, and Stamatov summarize this incipient cognitive turn in concepts of ethnicity, race, and nation. Rogers Brubaker, Mara Loveman, and Peter Stamatov, "Ethnicity as Cognition," *Theory and Society* 33 (2004): 31–64. See also Karen A. Cerulo, "Establishing Sociology of Culture and Cognition," in *Culture in Mind: Toward a Sociology of Culture and Cognition,* ed. Karen A. Cerulo, pp. 1–12 (New York: Routledge, 2002); Eviatar Zerubavel, *Social Mindscapes: An Invitation to Cognitive Sociology* (Cambridge, MA: Harvard University Press, 1997); Roy D'Andrade, *The Development of Cognitive Anthropology* (New York: Cambridge University Press, 1995).

43. Paul DiMaggio, "Culture and Cognition," *Annual Review of Sociology* 23 (1997): 263–87.

44. There are many definitions of culture. For an overview, see Mario Luis Small, David J. Harding, and Michèle Lamont, "Reconsidering Culture and Poverty," *Annals of the American Academy of Political and Social Science* 629 (2010): 6–27. For the purposes of this study, I find it useful to think of culture as a tool kit of strategies of action that individuals maintain. These strategies of action include habits, skills, and styles that are based on symbolic meanings and worldviews. Ann Swidler, "Culture in Action: Symbols and Strategies," *American Sociological Review* 51 (1986): 273–86; Ann Swidler, *Talk of Love: How Culture Matters* (Chicago: University of Chicago Press, 2001). I conceptualize cultural tool kits as micro-level phenomena. There are a number of strategies of action "out there" in different societies, making up a macro-level cultural repertoire. An individual's tool kit is his or her collection of the particular strategies of action he or she is aware of and understands.

45. I refer to race in this section, although the arguments here apply to ethnicity as well.

46. D'Andrade, *Development of Cognitive Anthropology;* Susan T. Fiske, "Schema-Based versus Piecemeal Politics: A Patchwork Quilt, but Not a Blanket, of Evidence," in *Political Cognition: The 19th Annual Carnegie Symposium on Cognition,* ed. Richard R. Lau and David O. Sears, pp. 41–53 (Hillsdale, NJ: Lawrence Erlbaum Associates, 1986); Ronald W. Casson, "Schemata in Cognitive Anthropology," *Annual Review of Anthropology* 12 (1983): 429–62.

47. Loic Wacquant, "Towards an Analytic of Racial Domination," *Political Power and Social Theory* 11 (1997): 221–34; Rogers Brubaker, *Ethnicity without Groups* (Cambridge, MA: Harvard University Press, 2004); Frederik Barth, introduction to *Ethnic Groups and Boundaries: The Social Organization of Culture Difference,* ed. Frederik Barth, pp. 9–38 (Boston: Little, Brown, 1969).

48. Brubaker, Loveman, and Stamatov, "Ethnicity as Cognition."

49. Brubaker, *Ethnicity without Groups;* Herbert Gans, personal communication, 2006.

50. DiMaggio, "Culture and Cognition"; Brubaker, Loveman, and Stamatov. "Ethnicity as Cognition."

51. Brubaker, *Ethnicity without Groups;* Shyon Baumann, "Evaluation and Classification as an

Institutional Cultural Resource" (paper presented at the annual meeting of the American Sociological Association, Atlanta, 2010).

52. Andreas Wimmer, "The Making and Unmaking of Ethnic Boundaries: A Multilevel Process Theory," *American Journal of Sociology* 113 (2008): 970–1022.

53. Hazel Markus and Robert B. Zajonc, "The Cognitive Perspective in Social Psychology," in *The Handbook of Social Psychology*, ed. Gardner Lindzey and Elliot Aaronson, pp. 137–230 (New York: Random House, 1985); Roy G. D'Andrade, "Some Propositions about the Relations between Culture and Human Cognition," in *Cultural Psychology: Essays on Comparative Human Development*, ed. James W. Stigler, Richard A. Shweder, and Gilbert H. Herdt, pp. 65–129 (Cambridge: Cambridge University Press, 1990).

54. For immigrants, the process of moving to a new place and learning new ways can be thought of as an "unsettled period" in their life, a time when they are constructing more cultural "stuff" and new lines of action. Swidler, "Culture in Action"; Swidler, *Talk of Love*.

55. E.g., Everett M. Rogers, *Diffusion of Innovations* (New York: Free Press, 1995); Michael Schudson, "How Culture Works: Perspectives from Media Studies on the Efficacy of Symbols," *Theory and Society* 18 (1989): 153–80; David Strang and John W. Meyer, "Institutional Conditions for Diffusion," *Theory and Society* 22 (1993): 487–511.

56. DiMaggio, "Culture and Cognition."

57. Schudson, "How Culture Works"; William A. Gamson, *Talking Politics* (New York: Cambridge University Press, 1992).

58. Some studies use photo elicitation with a set of closed-ended options, effectively measuring how people apply a particular racial schema but not which schema they choose to use. E.g., R. Stanley Bailey, "Unmixing for Race Making in Brazil," *American Journal of Sociology* 114 (2008): 577–614; David R. Harris, "In the Eye of the Beholder: Observed Race and Observer Characteristics" (Population Studies Center Research Report No. 02–522, 2002); Melissa Herman, "Do You See What I Am? How Observers' Backgrounds Affect Their Perceptions of Multiracial Faces," *Social Psychology Quarterly* 73 (2010): 58–78.

59. Some have used drawings that systematically vary physical characteristics like skin tone, hair, nose, and lips. See Marvin Harris, "Referential Ambiguity in the Calculus of Brazilian Racial Identity," *Southwestern Journal of Anthropology* 26 (1970): 1–14; Clarence C. Gravlee, "Ethnic Classification in Southeastern Puerto Rico: The Cultural Model of 'Color,'" *Social Forces* 83 (2005): 949–70. However, such measured variation leads respondents to focus on the particular characteristics that are clearly varied from one drawing to another, rather than approximating the process whereby individuals make these classifications every day.

60. Vaisey argues that forced-choice survey questions are better able to identify the cultural scripts motivating behavior than open-ended questions. I argue that both are needed to identify the range of racial schemas that people maintain, but that closed-ended questions will be more valuable for identifying schemas that are less frequently used. See Stephen Vaisey, "Socrates, Skinner, and Aristotle: Three Ways of Thinking about Culture in Action," *Sociological Forum* 23 (2008): 603–13.

61. In discussing the literature on race in Latin America and the United States, I use the language of "models" of race because this research does not discuss cognitive schemas. Yet I do not see racial "models" and "schemas" as distinctive phenomena. A model is a form of cognitive organization, and schemas are the mental structures that process information and represent a person's understanding of racial organization in that way.

62. Because my focus is on Latinos, I limit myself to ways of classifying people along the Black-White continuum. In discussing U.S. racial schemas, therefore, I do not address the more comprehensive schemas that include Asians, Native Americans, and other populations.

63. For example, H. Hoetink, *The Two Variants of Caribbean Race Relations: A Contribution to the Sociology of Segmented Societies* (London: Oxford University Press, 1967); Howard, *Coloring the Nation*; Duany, "Reconstructing Racial Identity"; Clara E. Rodríguez, "Challenging Racial Hegemony: Puerto Ricans in the United States," in *Race*, ed. Steven Gregory and Roger Sanjek, pp. 131–45 (New Brunswick, NJ: Rutgers University Press, 1996); Jim Sidanius, Yesilernis Peña, and Mark Sawyer, "Inclusionary Discrimination: Pigmentocracy and Patriotism in the Dominican Republic," *Political Psychology* 22 (2001): 827–51; Peter Wade, *Race and Ethnicity in Latin America* (Chicago: Pluto Press, 1997); José Itzigsohn, *Encountering American Faultlines: Race, Class, and the Dominican Experience in Providence* (New York: Russell Sage Foundation, 2009).

64. H. Hoetink, "'Race' and Color in the Caribbean," in *Caribbean Contours*, ed. Sidney W. Mintz and Sally Price, pp. 55–84 (Baltimore: John Hopkins University Press, 1985), p. 58.

65. Duany, *Puerto Rican Nation on the Move*.

66. Some argue that while a large variety of terms make up the racial continuum, a much smaller group of classifications forms most people's "cognitive map," and greater consensus exists around the meaning and use of these functional terms. See Harris, "Referential Ambiguity"; Gravlee, "Ethnic Classification in Southeastern Puerto Rico"; Wade, *Race and Ethnicity in Latin America*; Eduardo Seda Bonilla, *Los Derechos Civiles en la Cultura Puertorriqueña*, 5th ed. (Rio Piedras, Puerto Rico: Ediciones Bayoan, 1991).

67. There is evidence that this standard is slowly changing with the prevalence of interracial marriage and greater acceptance of multiracial identities. Some observers identify racially ambiguous individuals as multiracial, although a Black classification is still the norm. See Kerry Ann Rockquemore and David L. Brunsma, *Beyond Black: Biracial Identity in America* (Thousand Oaks, CA: Sage, 2002); Herman, "Do You See What I Am?"; Harris, "In the Eye of the Beholder"; Wendy D. Roth, "The End of the One-Drop Rule? Labeling of Multiracial Children in Black Intermarriages," *Sociological Forum* 20 (2005): 35–67.

68. Rodriguez, "Puerto Ricans"; Sidanius, Peña, and Sawyer, "Inclusionary Discrimination."

69. Raymond L. Scheele, "The Prominent Families of Puerto Rico," in *The People of Puerto Rico*, ed. Julian H. Steward, pp. 418–62 (Urbana: University of Illinois Press, 1956), p. 425.

70. Rodriguez, "Puerto Ricans."

71. Isar P. Godreau, "Peinando Diferencias, Bregas de Pertenencia: El Alisado y el Llamado 'Pelo Malo,'" *Caribbean Studies* 30 (2000): 82–134.

72. Ibid.

73. This expression (*raza por atras de negro que se le cuelga*) is one of many used to suggest that aspects of a person's body reveal Blackness somewhere in their family tree. A more common Dominican expression is *negro atras de las orejas* ("black behind the ears") from a 19th-century poem by Juan Antonio Alix, implying that almost all Dominicans have African heritage somewhere in their family history, or a little bit of Black in their appearance. In Puerto Rico, "*Y tu abuela, dondé esta?*" ("And your grandmother, where is she?"), a line from a popular poem by Fortunato Vizcarrondo, implies that the grandmother is hidden from view because her Black appearance would give away the family's African roots. These expressions are frequently adopted in music, theater, and public discourse on racial identity. See Candelario, *Black behind the Ears*; Arlene Torres, "La Gran Familia Puertorriqueña 'El Prieta de Beldá' (The Great Puerto Rican Family Is Really Really Black)," in *Blackness in Latin America and the Caribbean: Social Dynamics and Cultural Transformations*, vol. 2, ed. Norman E. Whitten, Jr., and Arlene Torres, pp. 285–305 (Bloomington: Indiana University Press, 1998).

74. There is considerable overlap between the concepts of nationality and ethnicity when discussing both migrants and non-migrants. "Nationality" refers to membership in a nation, either subjective or legal belonging. "Ethnicity" refers to common ancestry and memories of a shared history. Yet for many people, nationality becomes ethnicity when they relocate to a new society. I refer

to this racial schema in terms of nationality, although its concept of race applies to ethnicity and even panethnicity in some circumstances.

75. Rodríguez, *Changing Race.*

76. Ramon Grosfoguel and Chloé S. Georas, "The Racialization of Latino Caribbean Migrants in the New York Metropolitan Area," *CENTRO: Journal of the Center for Puerto Rican Studies* 8 (1996): 191–201; Duany, *Puerto Rican Nation on the Move;* Anayra O. Santory-Jorge, Luis A. Avilés, Juan Carlos Martínez-Cruzado, and Doris Ramírez, "The Paradox of the Puerto Rican Race: The Interplay of Racism and Nationalism under U.S. Colonialism," in *Twenty-first Century Color Lines: Multiracial Change in Contemporary America,* ed. Andrew Grant-Thomas and Gary Orfield, pp. 157–77 (Philadelphia: Temple University Press, 2009).

77. Julian Pitt-Rivers, "Race in Latin America: The Concept of 'Raza,'" *Archives Européennes de Sociologie* 14 (1973): 3–31.

78. Using the expression *la raza* on its own to mean "our people" is most closely associated with Mexico or Mexican Americans. For example, in October 2010, San Francisco State University changed the name of its Raza studies department to Latino/Latina studies to recognize the growing diversity of its Latino/a students, because students saw the term *raza* as pertaining primarily to the Mexican experience. See Noemy Mena, "Department with Strong Campus Roots Alters Name," *Golden Gate Xpress,* San Francisco, accessed October 20, 2010, at xpress.sfsu.edu/Archives/Life/015404.html.

79. Silvio Torres-Saillant, "The Tribulations of Blackness: Stages in Dominican Racial Identity," *Latin American Perspectives* 25 (1998): 126–46.

80. Ernesto Sagás, "The Development of *Antihaitianismo* into a Dominant Ideology during the Trujillo Era," in *Ethnicity, Race, and Nationality in the Caribbean,* ed. Juan Manuel Carrión, pp. 96–121 (San Juan: Institute of Caribbean Studies, University of Puerto Rico, 1997).

81. Howard, *Coloring the Nation.*

82. Santory-Jorge et al., "Paradox of the Puerto Rican Race."

83. The stronger concept of *la raza dominicana,* relative to *la raza puertoriqqueña,* may stem from a stronger Dominican national identity through the state's efforts to differentiate Dominicans from the neighboring Haitian people. While Puerto Ricans have always had a strong cultural identity, their national identity has long been divided by the issue of the island's political status, with the nation divided into those who advocate statehood, those who prefer to maintain the status quo, and the small but vocal minority who promote independence. See Ernesto Sagás, *Race and Politics in the Dominican Republic* (Gainesville: University Press of Florida, 2000); Juan Flores, *From Bomba to Hip-Hop: Puerto Rican Culture and Latino Identity* (New York: Columbia University Press, 2000).

84. E.g., *Insularismo,* in Antonio Pedreira, *Obras completas* (San Juan: Editorial Edil, 1969); José Luis González, *El País de Cuatro Pisos y Otros Ensayos* (Rio Piedras, PR: Huracán, 1980); Rubén Ríos-Ávila, *La raza cómica del sujeto en Puerto Rico* (San Juan: Editorial Callejón, 2002).

85. Santory-Jorge et al. found that in a representative sample of the Puerto Rican island, 37% of respondents openly identified as Puerto Rican. When asked directly if they believed in the existence of a Puerto Rican race, 78.5% of respondents said they did. Landale and Oropesa found that half (52.5%) of the mothers they surveyed in Puerto Rico identified their race openly as Puerto Rican. The authors conclude that the concepts of race and ethnicity are quite blurred in Puerto Ricans' self-identifications. Nancy S. Landale and R. S. Oropesa, "White, Black, or Puerto Rican? Racial Self-identification among Mainland and Island Puerto Ricans," *Social Forces* 81(2002): 231–54; Santory-Jorge et al., "Paradox of the Puerto Rican Race."

86. José Vasconcelos, "La Raza cósmica," in *Obras completas,* pp. 903–42 (México, DF: Colección Laurel, Libreros Mexicanos Unidos, 1957).

87. See Cornell and Hartmann, *Ethnicity and Race.*

88. Physical characteristics are part of the shared ancestry that is associated with ethnicity. Groups that are defined racially, like African Americans, can also create their own culture, and by doing so become an ethnic group as well. Ibid.

89. Barth, Introduction, *Ethnic Groups and Boundaries.*

90. Brubaker, *Ethnicity without Groups*; Wimmer, "Making and Unmaking of Ethnic Boundaries"; Brubaker, Loveman, and Stamatov, "Ethnicity as Cognition." Other scholars treat race as a special case of ethnicity; see Milton M. Gordon, *Assimilation in American Life: The Role of Race, Religion, and National Origins* (New York: Oxford University Press, 1964); Mara Loveman, "Is 'Race' Essential?" *American Sociological Review* 64 (1999): 891–98; Orlando Patterson, *The Ordeal of Integration: Progress and Resentment in America's "Racial" Crisis* (Washington, D.C.: Civitas, 1997).

91. Victoria Hattam, *In the Shadow of Race: Jews, Latinos, and Immigrant Politics in the United States* (Chicago: University of Chicago Press, 2007).

92. Davis, *Who Is Black?*

93. Piri Thomas, *Down These Mean Streets* (New York: Vintage Books, 1967).

94. Earl Shorris, *Latinos: A Biography of the People* (New York: Norton, 1992), p. 146.

95. There are numerous sources that treat White, Black, and Latino/Hispanic as mutually exclusive categories. Just a few popular media outlets that do so include the *New York Times*, ABCnews.com, *USA Today*, and the *Los Angeles Times*: for example, Rachel L. Swarns, "Hispanic Teenagers Join Southern Mainstream," *New York Times*, December 31, 2006, online edition; Dean Schnabner, "Why It Costs More to Adopt a White Baby," *ABC News*, March 12, 2010, online edition; Haya El Nasser, "U.S. Hispanics Outliving Whites, Blacks," *USA Today*, December 14, 2010, online edition; "The Latino Paradox," editorial, *Los Angeles Times*, November 14, 2010, online edition. Academic journal articles also do so in such varied fields as economics, engineering, law, medicine, psychology, and sociology: for example, George J. Borjas, "The Substitutability of Black, Hispanic, and White Labor," *Economic Inquiry* 21 (2007): 93–106; Amy L. Stuart, Sarntharm Mudhasakul, and Watanee Sriwatanapongse, "The Social Distribution of Neighborhood-Scale Air Pollution and Monitoring Protection," *Journal of the Air and Waste Management Association* 59 (2009): 591–602; Ryan D. King, Kecia R. Johnson, and Kelly McGeever, "Demography of the Legal Profession and Racial Disparities in Sentencing," *Law and Society Review* 44 (2010): 1–31; P. R. Spradling, J. T. Richardson, K. Buchacz, A. C. Moorman, and J. T. Brooks, "Prevalence of Chronic Hepatitis B Virus Infection among Patients in the HIV Outpatient Study, 1996–2007," *Journal of Viral Hepatitis* 17 (2010): 879–86; E. Michael Foster and Ariel Kalil, "Living Arrangements and Children's Development in Low-Income White, Black, and Latino Families," *Child Development* 78 (2007): 1657–74; Pat António Goldsmith, "Schools' Racial Mix, Students' Optimism, and the Black-White and Latino-White Achievement Gaps," *Sociology of Education* 77 (2004): 121–47. Examples from popular Web sites, blogs, and institutional press releases include: Ray Suarez, "Race, Ethnicity, Wealth, and Poverty," *Huffington Post*, October 6, 2010; Alwyn Cassil, "Health Insurance Gap Persists among Latino, Black, and White Americans" (news release, Centre for Studying Health System Change, October 28, 2004); Circle of Moms Web site, Moms of biracial babies/children, accessed December 1, 2010, at www.circleofmoms.com; AfroRomance Web site, accessed December 1, 2010, at www.afroromance.com.

96. For evidence that *Latinos* consider Hispanic/Latino to be a race, see Lorena Carrasco, "Collecting Data from Spanish Speakers Using the ACS CAPI Instrument: Current Practices and Challenges" (U.S. Census Bureau internal report, 2002); E. Kissam, E. Herrera, and J. M. Nakamoto, "Hispanic Responses to Census Enumeration Forms and Procedures" (report prepared for the Bureau of the Census, Suitland, MD, 1993). For evidence that *non-Latinos* consider Hispanic/Latino to be a race, see E. Gerber, M. De la Puente, and M. Levin, "Race, Identity, and New Question Op-

tions: Final Report of Cognitive Research on Race and Ethnicity" (U.S. Census Bureau report, February 24, 1998); Laurie Schwede, "Report to the Office of Management and Budget on Third-Person Reporting of Hispanic Origin and Race in a Group Quarters/Establishment Census" (U.S. Bureau of the Census, Statistical Research Division, 1997).

97. The Equal Employment Opportunity Commission instructs employers to identify their employees as White, Black, Hispanic, Asian or Pacific Islander, and American Indian or Native Alaskan. See www.eeo1.com/EEO1Inst.htm.

98. This way of conceptualizing Whiteness and Blackness is more important than the actual terms used (e.g., "Caucasian" or "Anglo-Saxon" instead of "White").

99. Some examples of unique variants include using the terms "Nuyorrican" or "Dominican-york" (which combine cultural origins and nationality/birthplace) within a nationality schema, or combining nationalities with larger regions like "Caribbean" or "Central American."

Chapter 2

1. An exception is Nadia Y. Kim, *Imperial Citizens: Koreans and Race from Seoul to LA* (Stanford, CA: Stanford University Press, 2008).

2. Michèle Lamont, *Money, Morals, and Manners: The Culture of the French and the American Upper-Middle Class* (Chicago: University of Chicago Press, 1992); Michèle Lamont and Virág Molnár, "The Study of Boundaries in the Social Sciences," *Annual Review of Sociology* 28 (2002): 167–95; Wimmer, "Making and Unmaking of Ethnic Boundaries."

3. The patterns were the same for education and occupational status. While I discuss the results by education level, I view these patterns as related to social class.

4. Respondents in the higher education category are typically those with a four-year college degree or more; in the mainland U.S. and Puerto Rico, a bachelor's degree is generally needed to obtain professional status. However, I include in the higher education category Dominican non-migrants who have some years of college toward a bachelor's degree (*licenciatura*). Completing a bachelor's degree is much less common in the Dominican Republic. In 2002, 19.4% of Dominicans aged 20 or older had reached a university level of education, and only 10.1% of those aged 25 or older had completed a university degree; see República Dominicana Oficina Nacional de Estadística, "Resultados Definitivos, VIII Censo Nacional de Población y Vivienda 2002, Características Educativas," vol. 4 (Santo Domingo, Rep. Dom.: Secretariado Técnico de la Presidencia, 2004). It is common for Dominicans to be enrolled in a college program for many years, even a decade, and many never finish. Those with any college experience are at the high end of the educational distribution in the country, and it is possible to obtain some professional positions, such as schoolteacher or librarian, without a college degree.

5. See Chapter 1, note 73.

6. Another connotation of the word *raza* refers to the breed of a dog.

7. Word repetition is often used for emphasis, but also to indicate authenticity or purity. See Flores, *From Bomba to Hip-Hop*, p. 22.

8. Human Rights Watch, "Illegal People" (online report, 2002), accessed March 11, 2011, at http://www.hrw.org/legacy/reports/2002/domrep/domrep0402-02.htm; United Nations, "World Population Prospects: The 2006 Revision" (Department of Economic and Social Affairs, Population Division, 2007).

9. These efforts are described at length elsewhere. See Howard, *Coloring the Nation*; Sagás, *Race and Politics in the Dominican Republic*; Silvio Torres-Saillant, *Introduction to Dominican Blackness* (New York: CUNY Dominican Studies Institute, City College of New York, 1999).

10. Howard, *Coloring the Nation*; Sagás, *Race and Politics in the Dominican Republic*; Candelario, *Black behind the Ears*.

11. Michael Omi and Howard Winant, *Racial Formation in the United States: From the 1960s to the 1980s* (New York: Routledge, 1986). See also Anthony W. Marx, *Making Race and Nation: A Comparison of South Africa, the United States, and Brazil* (Cambridge: Cambridge University Press, 1998); Melissa Nobles, *Shades of Citizenship: Race and the Census in Modern Politics* (Stanford, CA: Stanford University Press, 2000); Telles, *Race in Another America*; Ian F. Haney López, *White by Law: The Legal Construction of Race* (New York: NYU Press, 1996).

12. School textbooks and curricula play a significant role in shaping racial meaning. See Sheridan Wigginton, "Character or Caricature: Representations of Blackness in Dominican Social Science Textbooks," *Race, Ethnicity, and Education* 8 (2005): 191–211; Ann Morning, "Reconstructing Race in Science and Society: Biology Textbooks, 1952–2002," *American Journal of Sociology* 114 (2008): S106–37.

13. Most students attend public school in Puerto Rico and the Dominican Republic. Of the total Puerto Rican student population, 82.4% was enrolled in public elementary or high schools in 2000; U.S. Census Bureau, Census 2000 Summary File 3, Sample Data, American Factfinder, 2000, available at www.census.gov. In 2002, 66.4% of Dominicans aged 5–19 attended public school. The lower percentage partly reflects lower rates of school attendance in general (Républica Dominicana Oficina Nacional de Estadística, Censo Nacional 2002).

14. *Ciencias sociales* (Santo Domingo: La Secretaría de Estado de Educación y Cultura, 1997).

15. Ibid., p. 154, my translation.

16. Howard also finds a class difference in Dominicans' racial categories, with only high-status Dominicans identifying as *mulato* or *negro*, while those with lower status tend to identify as *indio*. He argues that those of higher status feel socially and financially secure enough to accept their African ancestry without fear of racial discrimination. This is likely true, but my interviews show that state educational structures play a role in leading them to accept this heritage, by teaching them that this is the way to understand race. See Howard, *Coloring the Nation*.

17. Robin E. Sheriff, *Dreaming Equality: Color, Race, and Racism in Urban Brazil* (New Brunswick, NJ: Rutgers University Press, 2001).

18. See also Isar P. Godreau, "La Semántica Fugitiva: 'Raza,' Color y Vida Cotidiana en Puerto Rico," *Revista de Ciencias Sociales* 9 (2000): 52–71.

19. Sheriff's Afro-Brazilian respondents, as well as people of African descent in Peru, assert that these terms are not race, but only describe color. Gravlee argues that this taxonomy is best understood as a cultural model of color. Sheriff, *Dreaming Equality*; Tanya Golash-Boza, "Does Whitening Happen? Distinguishing between Race and Color Labels in an African-Descended Community in Peru," *Social Problems* 57 (2010): 138–56; Gravlee, "Ethnic Classification in Southeastern Puerto Rico."

20. Marvin Harris, Josildeth Goles Consorte, and Bryan Byrne, "Who Are the Whites? Imposed Census Categories and the Racial Demography of Brazil," *Social Forces* 72 (1993): 451–62.

21. David R. Harris and Jeremiah Joseph Sim, "Who Is Multiracial? Assessing the Complexity of Lived Race," *American Sociological Review* 67 (2002): 614–27; Kimberly McClain DaCosta, *Making Multiracials: State, Family, and Market in the Redrawing of the Color Line* (Stanford, CA: Stanford University Press, 2007).

22. Sidanius, Peña, and Sawyer, "Inclusionary Discrimination." See also Scheele, "Prominent Families of Puerto Rico"; Melvin M. Tumin and Arnold S. Feldman, *Social Class and Social Change in Puerto Rico* (Indianapolis: Bobbs-Merrill, 1971).

23. Matilde could be using a continuum schema on her social network and the people she lists just happen to fall at the far ends of the spectrum. However, her color ratings place many of those she lists as Black as intermediate in color (6 or 7). Someone using a continuum schema would likely have used intermediate categories between White and Black for people described this way.

Chapter 3

1. I am not able to directly examine whether migrants' concepts of race changed relative to their pre-migration concepts. My analysis is based on group differences between the migrants and non-migrants I studied. I do, however, explore subjective change in the migrants' self-reports of how their conceptions have changed since moving to the United States.

2. Haney López, *White by Law*; Davis, *Who Is Black?*

3. U.S. Office of Management and Budget, "Revisions to the Standards for the Classification of Federal Data on Race and Ethnicity," *Federal Register Notice*, October 30, 1997, online edition.

4. See www.eeo1.com/EEO1Inst.htm.

5. U.S. Department of Education, "Submission for OMB Review; Comment Request," *Federal Register* 72 (2007): 59266–79.

6. Jorge J. E. Gracia and Pablo De Greiff, eds., *Hispanics/Latinos in the United States: Ethnicity, Race, and Rights* (New York: Routledge, 2000); Jorge J. E. Gracia, *Race or Ethnicity? On Black and Latino Identity* (Ithaca, NY: Cornell University Press, 2007); Hattam, *In the Shadow of Race.*

7. Ramón Grosfoguel, "Race and Ethnicity or Racialized Ethnicities? Identities within Global Coloniality," *Ethnicities* 4 (2004): 315–36; Victor M. Rodríguez, "The Racialization of Puerto Rican Ethnicity in the United States," In *Ethnicity, Race, and Nationality in the Caribbean*, ed. Juan Manuel Carrión, pp. 233–73 (San Juan: Institute of Caribbean Studies, University of Puerto Rico, 1997). This position is also consistent with that made for Asians as "racialized ethnics." See Mia Tuan, *Forever Foreigners or Honorary Whites? The Asian Ethnic Experience Today* (New Brunswick, NJ: Rutgers University Press, 1998).

8. Gordon, *Assimilation in American Life.*

9. Ibid., p.66.

10. Robert E. Park and Ernest W. Burgess, *Introduction to the Science of Sociology* (Chicago: University of Chicago Press, 1921), pp. 736–37.

11. Carmen Teresa Whalen and Victor Vazquez-Hernandez, eds., *The Puerto Rican Diaspora: Historical Perspectives* (Philadelphia: Temple University Press, 2005); Sherri Grasmuck and Patricia R. Pessar, *Between Two Islands: Dominican International Migration* (Berkeley: University of California Press, 1991).

12. Although some migrant respondents claimed they were classified by Americans as Latinos or by their nationality, respectively, many used these terms interchangeably, at one moment saying they were seen as Dominican and at another as Latino.

13. See the distinction between Appearance-Based and Interaction-Based Observed Race in Wendy D. Roth, "Racial Mismatch: The Divergence between Form and Function in Data for Monitoring Racial Discrimination of Hispanics," *Social Science Quarterly* 91 (2010): 1288–311.

14. See Agustin Laó-Montes and Arlene Dávila, eds., *Mambo Montage: The Latinization of New York* (New York: Columbia University Press, 2001); Frances Negrón-Muntaner, ed., *None of the Above: Puerto Ricans in the Global Era* (New York: Palgrave Macmillan, 2007); Oropesa, Landale, and Greif, "From Puerto Rican to Pan-Ethnic"; Pantoja, "Transnational Ties."

15. I asked a similar question about how a child with one White parent and one Black parent would be classified in their home country; most respondents said it would depend on the child's appearance, although some gave intermediate categories such as *mulato*. Among migrants with lower education, most gave similar responses for an American child as for a Dominican or Puerto Rican child, indicating that they have little practical awareness of the one-drop rule in the United States.

16. Haney López, *White by Law.*

17. Noel Ignatiev, *How the Irish Became White* (New York: Routledge, 1995); David R. Roediger, *Working toward Whiteness: How America's Immigrants Became White: The Strange Journey from Ellis Island to the Suburbs* (New York: Basic Books, 2005).

18. Clara E. Rodríguez, "Racial Classification among Puerto Rican Men and Women in New York," *Hispanic Journal of Behavioral Sciences* 12 (1990): 366–79.

19. A few respondents mentioned that their difficulty with completing the census race question, and the conflict that created for them, was precisely what drew them to participating in this study.

20. Clara Rodríguez finds that New York Puerto Ricans who marked "White" were significantly higher in socioeconomic status than those who marked "Other" and wrote in a Spanish descriptor. She questions whether racial identification is a cause or a consequence of socioeconomic status. People with lighter skin may be more successful in the labor market, or those who are successful may come to see themselves as White (see Rodríguez, "Racial Classification"). My middle-class respondents speak to this question. They understand that "Latino" or their nationality is not a recognized option and feel they should check the category to which they come closest; for most, this category is "White" because light color does have economic advantages. But checking "White" on the census form is also in part a *consequence* of socioeconomic status—because education and status affect their understanding of the question (that "Latino" is not acceptable) and how they feel they should answer.

21. Roth, "Racial Mismatch."

22. Rodríguez, *Changing Race*; Bailey, "Dominican-American Ethnic/Racial Identities; Itzigsohn and Dore-Cabral, "Competing Identities?"

23. Mary E. Campbell and Christabel L. Rogalin, "Categorical Imperatives: The Interaction of Latino and Racial Identification," *Social Science Quarterly* 87 (2006): 1030–52.

24. Although no other research compares the open self-identification of Puerto Rican and Dominican migrants, studies on each group respectively confirm the greater tendency of Puerto Ricans to list national identities and Dominicans to list panethnic identities. See José Itzigsohn, Silvia Giorguli, and Obed Vazquez, "Immigrant Incorporation and Racial Identity: Racial Self-Identification among Dominican Immigrants," *Ethnic and Racial Studies* 28 (2005): 50–78; Landale and Oropesa, "White, Black, or Puerto Rican?"

25. Oropesa, Landale, and Grief suggest that a Puerto Rican identity is stigmatized because of the group's high poverty rate and residential segregation, explaining why those with non-Latino neighbors and friends prefer a panethnic identifier to a Puerto Rican identity. Yet my Puerto Rican respondents expressed considerable pride in their national origin. I believe that those with non-Latino neighbors and friends, instead of selecting a panethnic identifier out of shame or stigma, do so because of the greater salience of a Latino panethnic boundary in social interactions with non-Latinos. See Oropesa, Landale, and Greif, "From Puerto Rican to Pan-Ethnic."

26. Jorge Duany, *Los Dominicanos en Puerto Rico: Migración en la Semi-periferia* (Río Piedras, P.R.: Ediciones Huracán, 1990).

27. Rodríguez, "Challenging Racial Hegemony"; Bailey, "Dominican-American Ethnic/Racial Identities"; Landale and Oropesa, "White, Black, or Puerto Rican?"; Itzigsohn, Giorguli, and Vazquez, "Immigrant Incorporation and Racial Identity"; David Howard, "Reappraising Race? Dominicans in New York City," *International Journal of Population Geography* 9 (2003): 337–50.

28. Bonilla-Silva, "From Bi-Racial to Tri-Racial"; Frank, Akresh, and Lu, "Latino Immigrants and the U.S. Racial Order."

Chapter 4

1. This chapter builds upon ideas presented in Wendy D. Roth, "'Latino before the World': The Transnational Extension of Panethnicity," *Ethnic and Racial Studies* 32 (2009): 927–47, available at www.tandfonline.com; Wendy D. Roth, "Transnational Racializations: The Extension of Racial Boundaries from Receiving to Sending Societies," in *How the United States Racializes Latinos:*

White Hegemony and Its Consequences, ed. José A. Cobas, Jorge Duany, and Joe R. Feagin, pp. 228–44 (Boulder, CO: Paradigm Publishers, 2009).

2. Both Puerto Rico and the Dominican Republic experience frequent transnational communication and movement back and forth. See, e.g., Elizabeth M. Aranda, *Emotional Bridges to Puerto Rico: Migration, Return Migration, and the Struggles of Incorporation* (New York: Rowman and Littlefield, 2007); Luis E. Guarnizo, "Los Dominicanyorks: The Making of a Binational Society," *Annals, AAPSS* 533 (1994): 70–86; Duany, *Puerto Rican Nation on the Move*; Duany, *Quisqueya on the Hudson*; Itzigsohn, "Incorporation and Transnationalism"; Levitt, *Transnational Villagers*; Torre, Rodríguez Vecchini, and Burgos, eds., *The Commuter Nation*.

3. In discussing transnationalism, I adopt the broad approach that incorporates informal social practices, including phone calls, correspondence, remittances, and visits. This is appropriate for studying concepts of race and ethnicity, which can be transmitted through informal interactions. José Itzigsohn, Carlos Dore Cabral, Esther Hernández Medina, and Obed Vázquez, "Mapping Dominican Transnationalism: Narrow and Broad Transnational Practices," *Ethnic and Racial Studies* 22 (1999): 316–39.

4. See Robert Courtney Smith, *Mexican New York: Transnational Lives of New Immigrants* (Berkeley: University of California Press, 2006).

5. E.g., Mary C. Waters, *Black Identities: West Indian Immigrant Dreams and American Realities* (Cambridge, MA: Harvard University Press, 1999); Nancy Foner, ed., *Islands in the City: West Indian Migration to New York* (Berkeley: University of California Press, 2001); Philip Kasinitz, John H. Mollenkopf, Mary C. Waters, and Jennifer Holdaway, *Inheriting the City: The Children of Immigrants Come of Age* (New York and Cambridge, MA: Russell Sage Foundation and Harvard University Press, 2008); Itzigsohn, *Encountering American Faultlines*; Nancy Foner and George M. Fredrickson, eds., *Not Just Black and White: Historical and Contemporary Perspectives on Immigration, Race, and Ethnicity in the United States* (New York: Russell Sage Foundation, 2004).

6. See Kim, *Imperial Citizens*.

7. Although studies of cultural diffusion generally focus on new technologies and concrete practices, the spread of innovations may also include abstract ideas and concepts, such as race and ethnicity. See Rogers, *Diffusion of Innovations*; Alberto Palloni, "Diffusion in Sociological Analysis," in *Diffusion Processes and Fertility Transition: Selected Perspectives*, ed. John Casterline, pp. 66–114 (Washington, DC: National Academies Press, 2001); Barbara Wejnert, "Integrating Models of Diffusion of Innovations: A Conceptual Framework," *Annual Review of Sociology* 28 (2002): 297–326; David Strang and Sarah A. Soule, "Diffusion in Organizations and Social Movements: From Hybrid Corn to Poison Pills," *Annual Review of Sociology* 24 (1998): 265–90; Strang and Meyer, "Institutional Conditions for Diffusion."

8. Levitt, *Transnational Villagers*. For an in-depth discussion of how gender is transformed transnationally, see Smith, *Mexican New York*.

9. Suzanne Oboler, *Ethnic Labels, Latino Lives: Identity and the Politics of (Re)Presentation in the United States* (Minneapolis: University of Minnesota Press, 1995).

10. See Yen Le Espiritu, *Asian American Panethnicity: Bridging Institutions and Identities*, (Philadelphia: Temple University Press, 1992).

11. Ibid.; Félix Padilla, *Latino Ethnic Consciousness: The Case of Mexican Americans and Puerto Ricans in Chicago* (South Bend, IN: University of Notre Dame Press, 1985); Stephen Cornell, *The Return of the Native: American Indian Political Resurgence* (New York: Oxford University Press, 1988); Joane Nagel, "American Indian Ethnic Renewal: Politics and the Resurgence of Ethnicity," *American Sociological Review* 60 (1995): 947–65.

12. Milagros Ricourt and Ruby Danta, *Hispanas de Queens: Latino Panethnicity in a New York City Neighborhood* (Ithaca, NY: Cornell University Press, 2003), p. 10.

13. Padilla, *Latino Ethnic Consciousness*, p. 144.

14. Miguel Tinker Salas, "El Inmigrante Latino: Latin American Immigration and Pan-Ethnicity," *Latino Studies Journal* 2 (1991): 58–71; 67.

15. Latin Americans from many countries developed a sense of continental solidarity during periods of common political goals or threat. They also recognize cultural and historical commonalities among the peoples of the region. See Arlene M. Dávila, "Mapping Latinidad: Language and Culture in the Spanish TV Battlefront," in *Globalization on the Line: Culture, Capital, and Citizenship at U.S. Borders*, ed. Claudia Sadowski-Smith, pp. 147–65 (New York: Palgrave, 2002); Félix Padilla, "Latin America: The Historical Base of Latino Unity," *Latino Studies Journal* 1 (1990): 7–27. Such sentiments are a separate trend from the identities emerging reactively out of the U.S. context, although they do reinforce one another.

16. Among non-migrant respondents, 70% of Puerto Ricans and 23% of Dominicans used panethnic categories to classify photos; these figures are not representative of a larger population.

17. In this quote Pablo refers to photo 14.

18. Joshua Meyrowitz, *No Sense of Place* (New York: Oxford University Press, 1985); Akhil Gupta and James Ferguson, "Beyond 'Culture': Space, Identity, and the Politics of Difference," *Cultural Anthropology* 7 (1992): 6–23.

19. Espiritu, *Asian American Panethnicity*.

20. Arlene M. Dávila, *Latinos, Inc.: The Marketing and Making of a People* (Berkeley: University of California Press, 2001); Dávila, "Mapping Latinidad."

21. TableBase, "Latin American Television," p. 147 (2001); Univisión, "Six-Month Old Univisión Station, WLII-TV Puerto Rico, Overtakes Competition and Becomes #1 Station in the Market" (Univisión press release, October 22, 2002).

22. TableBase, "Global Cable Television," p. 181 (2000).

23. "La Tormenta Lider en Puerto Rico TOP 50," Foros Perú Website, 2007, http://www.tele novelasperu.com/forostv/showthread.php?t=21352.

24. Antonio V. Menéndez Alarcón, *Power and Television in Latin America: The Dominican Case* (Westport, CT: Praeger, 1992).

25. TableBase, "Global Cable Television."

26. Luis Eduardo Guarnizo, "The Emergence of a Transnational Social Formation and the Mirage of Return Migration among Dominican Transmigrants," *Identities* 4 (1997): 281–322.

27. Rogers, *Diffusion of Innovations*; Peggy Levitt, "Social Remittances: Migration Driven Local-Level Forms of Cultural Diffusion," *International Migration Review* 32 (1998): 926–48.

28. Panethnic categories also receive some institutional support in Puerto Rico, primarily through the presence of a U.S. Hispanicity question on the census and federal forms.

29. In 1872, the Dominican Samaná peninsula was leased to a private U.S. corporation. In 1905, the United States took over Dominican customs offices and established control over the country's finances, and the right to interfere in Dominican politics to protect its own interests. U.S. military forces have twice occupied the Dominican Republic, running the nation under martial law from 1916 to 1924 and again from 1965 to 1966. Legal reforms during U.S. occupation encouraged foreign economic involvement. U.S. capital still dominates most major private sectors of the Dominican economy. See Moya Pons, *Dominican Republic*; Jan Knippers Black, *The Dominican Republic: Politics and Development in an Unsovereign State* (Boston: Allen and Unwin, 1986).

30. Howard, *Coloring the Nation*; Sagás, *Race and Politics in the Dominican Republic*.

31. All of these respondents had ties that they described as being in the middle of the color scale.

32. Silvio Waisbord, "When the Cart of Media Is before the Horse of Identity: A Critique of Technology-Centered Views on Globalization," *Communication Research* 25 (1998): 377–98; Schudson, "How Culture Works."

33. Rogers, *Diffusion of Innovations.*

34. Duany, *Puerto Rican Nation on the Move.*

35. Jorge Duany, "Reconstructing Racial Identity: Ethnicity, Color, and Class among Dominicans in the United States and Puerto Rico," *Latin American Perspectives* 25 (1998): 147–72; p. 153.

36. Schudson, "How Culture Works."

37. For discussion of how census bureaus advance particular concepts of race, see Nobles, *Shades of Citizenship.*

38. Of the Puerto Rican population over 18, 5.5% were in the U.S. Armed Forces in 2000 or were veterans. Approximately 17,000 people in Puerto Rico were in the National Guard or the Reserve Forces in 1996. U.S. Census Bureau, Census 2000 Summary File 3; U.S. Office of the Assistant Secretary of Defense, Reserve Affairs, "Official Guard and Reserve Manpower Strengths and Statistics—Summary End Fiscal Year 1996."

39. Howard, *Coloring the Nation;* Sagás, *Race and Politics in the Dominican Republic.*

40. Bonilla-Silva, "From Bi-Racial to Tri-Racial."

41. Peggy Levitt and Nina Glick Schiller, "Conceptualizing Simultaneity: A Transnational Social Field Perspective on Society," *International Migration Review* 38 (2004): 1002–39.

42. Ramón Grosfoguel, *Colonial Subjects. Puerto Rican Subjects in a Global Perspective* (Berkeley: University of California Press, 2003); Juan Manuel Carrión, "The Construction of Puerto Rican National Identities under U.S. Colonialism," in *Ethnicity, Race, and Nationality in the Caribbean,* ed. Juan Manuel Carrión, pp. 159–91 (San Juan: Institute of Caribbean Studies, University of Puerto Rico, 1997); Santory-Jorge et al., "Paradox of the Puerto Rican Race."

Chapter 5

1. This chapter expands upon arguments developed in Wendy D. Roth, "'There Is No Discrimination Here': Understanding Latinos' Perceptions of Color Discrimination through Sending-Receiving Society Comparison," in *Racism in the 21st Century: An Empirical Analysis of Skin Color,* ed. Ronald E. Hall, pp. 205–34 (New York: Springer, 2008).

2. See Moya Pons, *Dominican Republic;* Sagás, *Race and Politics in the Dominican Republic;* Howard, *Coloring the Nation;* Torres-Saillant, *Introduction to Dominican Blackness.*

3. These were precisely the fears preyed upon to defeat presidential candidate José Francisco Peña Gómez, a dark-skinned Dominican of Haitian ancestry. His defeat has been interpreted as a representation of Dominican racial and national prejudice. See Sagás, *Race and Politics in the Dominican Republic;* Levitt, *Transnational Villagers.*

4. Edward Paulino, "Dominican Apartheid: Dominico-Haitianos and Their 21st-Century Struggle for Citizenship and Dignity" (paper presented at the Latin American Studies Association International Congress, San Juan, Puerto Rico, March 15–18, 2006).

5. Levitt, *Transnational Villagers.*

6. In the 2006 American Community Survey, 70,000 people in Puerto Rico identified themselves as Dominican, almost 2% of the population. It is likely there are many more who are undocumented. See U.S. Census Bureau, Puerto Rico Community Survey, American Factfinder.

7. See Mark Q. Sawyer and Tianna S. Paschel, "'We Didn't Cross the Color Line, the Color Line Crossed Us': Blackness and Immigration in the Dominican Republic, Puerto Rico, and the United States," *Du Bois Review* 4 (2007): 303–15.

8. Jay Kinsbruner, *Not of Pure Blood: The Free People of Color and Racial Prejudice in Nineteenth-Century Puerto Rico* (Durham, NC: Duke University Press, 1996); Hoetink, *Two Variants;* Samuel Betances, "The Prejudice of Having No Prejudice in Puerto Rico, Part I." *The Rican* 2 (1972): 41–51; Tumin and Feldman, *Social Class and Social Change;* Scheele, "Prominent Families of Puerto Rico." For sources on Latin America more broadly, see Magnus Mörner, *Race Mixture in the History*

of Latin America (Boston: Little, Brown, 1967); Carl N. Degler, *Neither Black nor White: Slavery and Race Relations in Brazil and the United States* (New York: Macmillan, 1971); Andrés Villarreal, "Stratification by Skin Color in Contemporary Mexico," *American Sociological Review* 75 (2010): 652–78.

9. Mark Q. Sawyer, Yesilernis Peña, and Jim Sidanius, "Cuban Exceptionalism: Group-Based Hierarchy and the Dynamics of Patriotism in Puerto Rico, the Dominican Republic, and Cuba," *Du Bois Review* 1 (2004): 93–113.

10. Francisco Rivera-Batiz, "Color in the Tropics: Race and Economic Outcomes in the Island of Puerto Rico" (unpublished paper, Teacher's College, Columbia University, 2004); Duany, *Puerto Rican Nation on the Move.* The association between racial self-identification and racial appearance is unreliable in Puerto Rico, however, where 80% of the population identified itself as White in 2000.

11. Sidanius, Peña, and Sawyer, "Inclusionary Discrimination."

12. Ronald E. Hall, "A Descriptive Analysis of Skin Color Bias in Puerto Rico: Ecological Applications to Practice," *Journal of Sociology and Social Welfare* 27 (2000): 171–83; Norman E. Whitten and Arlene Torres, *Blackness in Latin America and the Caribbean: Social Dynamics and Cultural Transformations* (Bloomington: Indiana University Press, 1998); Antonio V. Menéndez Alarcón, "Racial Prejudice: A Latin American Case," *Research in Race and Ethnic Relations* 7 (1994): 299–319.

13. I maintain that the cultural stigma against seeing oneself as a victim of color-based discrimination leads to a significant underreporting of relevant experiences. See Roth, "'There Is No Discrimination Here.'"

14. Nearly half of non-migrant respondents with dark skin (47%) described such experiences, compared to about one-fifth of those with light skin (23%).

15. Rodríguez, "Challenging Racial Hegemony"; Ronald E. Hall, "The 'Bleaching Syndrome': Implications of Light Skin for Hispanic American Assimilation," *Hispanic Journal of Behavioral Sciences* 16 (1994): 307–14; Evelyn Nakano Glenn, "Consuming Lightness: Segmented Markets and Global Capital in the Skin-Whitening Trade," in *Shades of Difference: Why Skin Color Matters*, ed. Evelyn Nakano Glenn, pp.166–87 (Palo Alto, CA: Stanford University Press, 2009).

16. The fact that people do marry across color lines is frequently cited as evidence that there is no racism in these societies. This view typically associates "racism" with more overt, institutionalized racism, such as the Jim Crow U.S., rather than more covert forms. See Roth, "'There Is No Discrimination Here.'"

17. Advertised on http://www.hoy.com.do/vivir, accessed July 6, 2010.

18. Glenn, "Consuming Lightness"; Jyotsna Vaid, "Fair Enough? Color and the Commodification of Self in Indian Matrimonials," in *Shades of Difference: Why Skin Color Matters*, ed. Evelyn Nakano Glenn, pp. 148–65 (Palo Alto, CA: Stanford University Press, 2009).

19. E.g., W. E. B. Du Bois, *The Souls of Black Folk* (New York: Vintage Books, 1903); St. Clair Drake and Horace R. Cayton, *Black Metropolis: A Study of Negro Life in a Northern City* (Chicago: University of Chicago Press, 1945 [1993]); Charles H. Parrish, "Color Names and Color Notions," *Journal of Negro Education* 15 (1946): 13–20; E. Franklin Frazier, *Black Bourgeoisie* (Glencoe, IL: Free Press, 1957); Kathy Russell, Midge Wilson, and Ronald Hall, *The Color Complex: The Politics of Skin Color among African Americans* (New York: Harcourt Brace Jovanovich, 1992); Cedric Herring, Verna M. Keith, and Hayward Derrick Horton, eds., *Skin Deep: How Race and Complexion Matter in the "Color Blind" Era* (Chicago: University of Illinois Press, 2004); Margaret L. Hunter, *Race, Gender, and the Politics of Skin Tone* (New York: Routledge, 2005).

20. A. E. Kerr, *The Paper Bag Principle: Class, Colorism, and Rumor in the Case of Black Washington, D.C.* (Knoxville: University of Tennessee Press, 2006).

21. Verna M. Keith and Cedric Herring, "Skin Tone and Stratification in the Black Community," *American Journal of Sociology* 97 (1991): 760–68. But see Aaron Gullickson, "The Significance

of Color Declines: A Re-analysis of Skin Tone Differentials in Post–Civil Rights America," *Social Forces* 84 (2005): 157–80.

22. Russell, Wilson, and Hall, *The Color Complex.*

23. Margaret Hunter "'If You're Light You're Alright': Light Skin Color as Social Capital for Women of Color," *Gender and Society* 16 (2002): 175–93; JeffriAnne Wilder, "Revisiting 'Color Names and Notions': A Contemporary Examination of the Language and Attitudes of Skin Color among Young Black Women," *Journal of Black Studies* 41 (2010): 184–206.

24. Parrish, "Color Names and Color Notions"; Wilder, "Revisiting 'Color Names and Notions.'"

25. Richard Fry, "The Changing Pathways of Hispanic Youths into Adulthood" (Pew Hispanic Center Report, 2009); Richard Fry, "Hispanics, High School Dropouts, and the GED" (Pew Hispanic Center Report, 2010); Rakesh Kochhar, Ana Gonzalez-Barrera, and Daniel Dockterman, "Through Boom and Bust: Minorities, Immigrants, and Homeownership" (Pew Hispanic Trust Report, 2009); Rakesh Kochhar, "Unemployment Rises Sharply among Latino Immigrants in 2008" (Pew Hispanic Trust Report, 2008).

26. See Dennis H. Sullivan and Andrea L. Ziegert, "Hispanic Immigrant Poverty: Does Ethnic Origin Matter?" *Population Research and Policy Review* 27 (2008): 667–87; Grosfoguel and Georas, "Racialization of Latino Caribbean Migrants." In terms of educational outcomes, Puerto Ricans and Dominicans do rank higher than several Latino groups, including Mexicans, Salvadorans, and Guatemalans, while the Dominican second generation has higher percentages with at least some college education than all Latino groups except Cubans and Colombians. See Fry, "Changing Pathways"; Fry, "Hispanics, High School Dropouts, and the GED"; Cynthia Feliciano, "Does Selective Migration Matter? Explaining Ethnic Disparities in Educational Attainment among Immigrant Children," *International Migration Review* 39 (2005): 841–71.

27. Telles and Murguia, "Phenotypic Discrimination"; Christina Gómez, "The Continual Significance of Skin Color: An Exploratory Study of Latinos in the Northeast," *Hispanic Journal of Behavioral Sciences* 22 (2000): 94–103; Rodolfo Espino and Michael M. Franz, "Latino Phenotypic Discrimination Revisited: The Impact of Skin Color on Occupational Status," *Social Science Quarterly* 83 (2002): 612–23; Edward Murguia and Edward E. Telles, "Phenotype and Schooling among Mexican Americans," *Sociology of Education* 69 (1996): 276–89; Jennifer L. Hochschild and Vesla Weaver, "The Skin Color Paradox and the American Racial Order," *Social Forces* 86 (2007): 643–70; Scott J. South, Kyle Crowder, and Erick Chavez, "Migration and Spatial Assimilation among U.S. Latinos: Classical versus Segmented Trajectories," *Demography* 42 (2005): 497–521; G. Edward Codina and Frank F. Montalvo, "Chicano Phenotype and Depression," *Hispanic Journal of Behavioral Sciences* 16 (1994): 296–306.

28. Nancy A. Denton and Douglas S. Massey, "Racial Identity among Caribbean Hispanics: The Effect of Double Minority Status on Residential Segregation," *American Sociological Review* 54 (1989): 790–808.

29. Among migrant respondents, 75% of those with dark skin, 64% of those with medium skin, and 68% of those with light skin described some experience they believed to be discriminatory; 46%, 32%, and 25%, respectively, described experiences with workplace discrimination.

30. For a similar finding across ethnic groups, see Kasinitz et al., *Inheriting the City.*

31. Jennifer L. Hochschild, *Facing Up to the American Dream: Race, Class, and the Soul of the Nation* (Princeton, NJ: Princeton University Press, 1995).

32. Discrimination on the basis of a Latino classification is also more culturally palatable to Dominicans and Puerto Ricans than that on the basis of color, given the internalized stigma associated with African heritage in their home societies. See Roth, "'There Is No Discrimination Here.'"

33. E.g., Jimy Sanders, Victor Nee, and Scott Sernau, "Asian Immigrants' Reliance on Social

Ties in a Multiethnic Labor Market," *Social Forces* 81 (2002): 281–314; Alejandro Portes, ed., *The Economic Sociology of Immigration: Essays on Networks, Ethnicity, and Entrepreneurship* (New York: Russell Sage Foundation, 1995); Roger Waldinger, *Still the Promised City? African Americans and New Immigrants in Postindustrial New York* (Cambridge, MA: Harvard University Press, 1996).

34. Workplace discrimination was reported by 60% of college-educated migrant respondents and by only 10% of those with lower education.

35. Joe R. Feagin and Melvin P. Sikes, *Living with Racism: The Black Middle-Class Experience* (Boston: Beacon Press, 1994).

36. Among college-educated migrants, 75% of those with dark skin reported workplace discrimination, compared with 63% of those with medium skin, and 50% of those with light skin.

37. South, Crowder, and Chavez, "Migration and Spatial Assimilation"; Denton and Massey, "Racial Identity among Caribbean Hispanics."

38. Nobles, *Shades of Citizenship*; Bailey, "Unmixing for Race Making"; Bailey, *Legacies of Race*; Tianna S. Paschel and Mark Q. Sawyer, "Contesting Politics as Usual: Black Social Movements, Globalization, and Race Policy in Latin America," *Souls* 10 (2008): 197–214; Tianna S. Paschel, "The Right to Difference: Explaining Colombia's Shift from Color Blindness to the Law of Black Communities," *American Journal of Sociology* 116 (2010): 729–69.

39. Bailey, *Legacies of Race*; Paschel and Sawyer, "Contesting Politics as Usual."

Chapter 6

1. In a similar way, people often subconsciously (or semi-subconsciously) try to organize everyone they see into categories of male and female. While this is separate from the cultural tools of knowing what the categories "female" and "male" are supposed to be like in a particular cultural context, and sometimes enacting those categories to achieve a certain goal, it is very much related to the cognitive organization that people engage in every day.

2. Waters, *Black Identities*.

3. Cultural assimilation is often studied as an intergenerational process. But it is also important to consider the extent to which the first generation adopts the cultural behavior of the host society, particularly the factors that lead them to *want* to assimilate or to retain immigrant cultural strategies.

4. E.g., Waters, *Black Identities*; Tomás R. Jiménez, *Replenished Ethnicity: Mexican Americans, Immigration, and Identity* (Berkeley: University of California Press, 2010); Rubén G. Rumbaut, "Severed or Sustained Attachments? Language, Identity, and Imagined Communities in the Post-Immigrant Generation," in *The Changing Face of Home: The Transnational Lives of the Second Generation*, ed. Peggy Levitt and Mary C. Waters, pp. 43–95 (New York: Russell Sage Foundation, 2002); Nazli Kibria, *Becoming Asian American: Second-Generation Chinese and Korean American Identities* (Baltimore: Johns Hopkins University Press, 2002); Vivian Louie, "Growing Up Ethnic in Transnational Worlds: Identities among Second-Generation Chinese and Dominicans," *Identities: Global Studies in Culture and Power* 13 (2006): 363–94; Richard Alba and Tariqul Islam, "The Case of the Disappearing Mexican Americans: An Ethnic-Identity Mystery," *Population Research and Policy Review* 28 (2009): 109–21.

5. Prudence L. Carter, *Keepin' It Real: School Success beyond Black and White* (Oxford: Oxford University Press, 2005); Andrew Molinsky, "Cross-Cultural Code-Switching: The Psychological Challenges of Adapting Behavior in Foreign Cultural Interactions," *Academy of Management Review* 32 (2007): 622–40.

6. Erving Goffman, *The Presentation of Self in Everyday Life* (New York: Anchor Books, 1959), p. 8.

7. In the literature on African Americans, "acting White" is also associated with behavior signaling a higher class or educational status or an achievement orientation. Carter, *Keepin' It Real*;

Karolyn Tyson, William Darity, Jr., and Domini R. Castellino, "It's Not 'a Black Thing': Understanding the Burden of Acting White and Other Dilemmas of High Achievement," *American Sociological Review* 70 (2005): 582–605.

8. E.g., Gordon, *Assimilation in American Life*; Lloyd W. Warner and Leo Srole, *The Social Systems of American Ethnic Groups* (New Haven: Yale University Press, 1945).

9. Alejandro Portes and Min Zhou, "The New Second Generation: Segmented Assimilation and Its Variants," *Annals of the American Academy of Political and Social Science* 530 (1993): 74–98; Kathryn M. Neckerman, Prudence Carter, and Jennifer Lee, "Segmented Assimilation and Minority Cultures of Mobility," *Ethnic and Racial Studies* 22 (1999): 945–65; Waters, *Black Identities*; Alejandro Portes and Rubén G. Rumbaut, *Legacies: The Story of the Immigrant Second Generation* (Berkeley: University of California Press, 2001); Richard Alba and Victor Nee, *Remaking the American Mainstream: Assimilation and Contemporary Immigration* (Cambridge, MA: Harvard University Press, 2003).

10. Portes and Zhou, "The New Second Generation."

11. Neckerman, Carter, and Lee, "Minority Cultures of Mobility"; Alba and Nee, *Remaking the American Mainstream*; Kasinitz et al., *Inheriting the City*; Mary C. Waters, Van C. Tran, Philip Kasinitz, and John H. Mollenkopf, "Segmented Assimilation Revisited: Types of Acculturation and Socioeconomic Mobility in Young Adulthood," *Ethnic and Racial Studies* 33 (2010): 1168–93.

12. Waters, *Black Identities*; Nina Glick Schiller and Georges Eugene Fouron, *Georges Woke Up Laughing: Long-Distance Nationalism and the Search for Home* (Durham, NC: Duke University Press, 2001).

13. Tuan, *Forever Foreigners*; Grosfoguel, "Race and Ethnicity or Racialized Ethnicities?"; Tanya Golash-Boza and William A. Darity, Jr., "Latino Racial Choices: The Effects of Skin Colour and Discrimination on Latinos' and Latinas' Racial Self-Identifications," *Ethnic and Racial Studies* 31 (2008): 899–934.

14. Brooke Kroeger, *Passing: When People Can't Be Who They Are* (New York: PublicAffairs, 2003). Randall Kennedy, *Interracial Intimacies: Sex, Marriage, Identity, and Adoption* (New York: Vintage Books, 2003).

15. Kennedy, *Interracial Intimacies*.

16. The research design adopted in this study was unlikely to capture respondents who had fully shed an ethnic or Latino identity. First, I focus on the first generation, which is less likely to identify as an unhyphenated American than are later generations. Although my interview criteria defined the population of interest as people born in Puerto Rico and the Dominican Republic (rather than those who identified as Puerto Rican or Dominican), those who feel little or no connection to their ethnic identity are less likely to participate in this kind of study. Second, my geographical criteria may also be relevant. The study was restricted to those who live or work in the New York metro area, yet several respondents suggested that co-ethnics who lose their ethnic identity may be more likely to move out of the city to White suburbia. Finally, because of the stigma associated with "denying one's roots," those who have lost an ethnic identity are likely reluctant to discuss it openly. A separate study design would be required to focus on people who lose their ethnic identity completely.

17. Latino ethnic or panethnic identification is very high in the first generation. See Brian Duncan and Stephen J. Trejo, "Intermarriage and the Intergenerational Transmission of Ethnic Identity and Human Capital for Mexican Americans," *Journal of Labor Economics* 29 (2011): 195–227.

18. Erving Goffman, *Stigma: Notes on the Management of Spoiled Identity* (New York: Jason Aronson, 1963 [1974]).

19. Kenji Yoshino, *Covering: The Hidden Assault on Our Civil Rights* (New York: Random House, 2006).

20. South, Crowder, and Chavez, "Migration and Spatial Assimilation."

21. The 1.5 generation consists of immigrants who arrive as children. They are foreign-born, but socialized primarily in the host society.

22. Waters, *Black Identities.*

23. Among Dominican respondents, 89% of those with dark skin and 75% of those with medium skin chose a national or Latino identity, compared with 73% with light skin. Among Puerto Ricans, 70% of those with medium skin did so, compared with 64% of those with light skin; of the four Puerto Rican migrants with dark skin, two identified as Black or African, one as Puerto Rican, and one as "working race."

24. See also Ana Y. Ramos-Zayas, "Racializing the 'Invisible' Race: Latino Constructions of 'White Culture' and Whiteness in Chicago," *Urban Anthropology* 30 (2001): 341–380.

25. However, they invariably include in this category White Europeans that fall outside of Anglo-Saxon culture, such as Italians.

26. See Tuan, *Forever Foreigners or Honorary Whites?*

27. See Margaret A. Gibson, *Accommodation without Assimilation: Sikh Immigrants in an American High School* (Ithaca, NY: Cornell University Press, 1988).

28. Rodríguez, "Challenging Racial Hegemony," p. 141.

29. Kasinitz et al., *Inheriting the City.* See also Portes and Rumbaut, *Legacies.*

30. Kennedy, *Interracial Intimacies;* Kroeger, *Passing;* Drake and Cayton, *Black Metropolis.*

31. See Kasinitz et al., *Inheriting the City.*

32. Howard, "Reappraising Race?"; Itzigsohn, Giorguli, and Vazquez, "Immigrant Incorporation and Racial Identity"; Waters, *Black Identities.*

33. I have translated this to what I consider a colloquial equivalent. The original expression is *al país que fueres, hacer lo que vieres* (literally, "in the country you go to, do what you see").

Chapter 7

1. U.S. Census Bureau, Overview 2010.

2. Richard Alba, *Blurring the Color Line: The New Chance for a More Integrated America* (Cambridge, MA: Harvard University Press, 2009); Van C. Tran, "English Gain vs. Spanish Loss? Language Assimilation among Second-Generation Latinos in Young Adulthood," *Social Forces* 89 (2010): 257–84.

3. Omi and Winant, *Racial Formation,* p. 13.

4. Maxine W. Gordon, "Race Patterns and Prejudice in Puerto Rico," *American Sociological Review* 14 (1949): 294–301.

5. Rodríguez, "Effect of Race," p. 80.

6. O'Brien, *The Racial Middle;* Gómez, *Manifest Destinies;* Ricourt and Danta, *Hispanas de Queens;* Oboler, *Ethnic Labels, Latino Lives;* Tanya Golash-Boza, "Dropping the Hyphen? Becoming Latino(a)-American through Racialized Assimilation," *Social Forces* 85 (2006): 27–55.

7. Harris and Sim, "Who Is Multiracial?"

8. J. Scott Brown, Steven Hitlin, and Glen H. Elder, Jr., "The Greater Complexity of Lived Race: An Extension of Harris and Sim," *Social Science Quarterly* 87 (2006): 411–31; Karl Eschbach and Christina Gómez, "Choosing Hispanic Identity: Ethnic Identity Switching among Respondents to High School and Beyond," *Social Science Quarterly* 79 (1998): 75–89; Elizabeth Vaquera and Grace Kao, "The Implications of Choosing 'No Race' on the Salience of Hispanic Identity: How Racial and Ethnic Backgrounds Intersect among Hispanic Adolescents," *Sociological Quarterly* 47 (2006): 375–96.

9. Numerous works detail the creation of new racial classification systems, e.g., Davis, *Who Is Black?;* Marx, *Making Race and Nation;* Mörner, *Race Mixture;* Roediger, *Working toward Whiteness;* Virginia R. Domínguez, *White by Definition: Social Classification in Creole Louisiana* (New Brunswick, NJ: Rutgers University Press, 1986).

10. Rogers, *Diffusion of Innovations*; Levitt, "Social Remittances."

11. E.g., DiMaggio, "Culture and Cognition"; Skrentny, "Culture and Race/Ethnicity"; Brubaker, Loveman, and Stamatov, "Ethnicity as Cognition."

12. Gravlee, "Ethnic Classification in Southeastern Puerto Rico."

13. See Vaisey, "Socrates, Skinner, and Aristotle."

14. Clara E. Rodríguez, *Puerto Ricans: Born in the U.S.A.* (Boston: Unwin Hyman, 1989).

15. For works that address aspects of their migration experiences, see Grosfoguel and Georas, "Racialization of Latino Caribbean Migrants"; María del Carmen Baerga and Lanny Thompson, "Migration in a Small Semiperiphery: The Movement of Puerto Ricans and Dominicans," *International Migration Review* 24 (1990): 656–83; Kasinitz et al., *Inheriting the City*.

16. Flores, *From Bomba to Hip-Hop*; Juan Manuel Carrión, *Voluntad de nación: Ensayos sobre el nacionalismo en Puerto Rico* (San Juan: Ediciones Nueva Aurora, 1996); Arlene M. Dávila, *Sponsored Identities: Cultural Politics in Puerto Rico* (Philadelphia: Temple University Press, 1997); Morris, *Puerto Rico*.

17. Douglas S. Massey and Brooks Bitterman, "Explaining the Paradox of Puerto Rican Segregation," *Social Forces* 64 (1985): 306–31; Lance Freeman, "A Note on the Influence of African Heritage on Segregation: The Case of Dominicans," *Urban Affairs Review* 35 (1999): 137–46; Kasinitz et al., *Inheriting the City*.

18. U.S. Census Bureau, "The American Community—Hispanics: 2004" (American Community Survey Report, ACS-03, 2007).

19. Ibid. In part, this likely reflects the concentration of Dominicans in northeastern areas with rental markets.

20. Alba and Nee, *Remaking the American Mainstream*. Since English is taught in schools in Puerto Rico, Puerto Ricans have higher rates of English proficiency than other Latino groups. See U.S. Census Bureau, "The American Community-Hispanics," p. 14.

21. See John U. Ogbu and Herbert D. Simons, "Voluntary and Involuntary Minorities: A Cultural-Ecological Theory of School Performance with Some Implications for Education," *Anthropology and Education Quarterly* 29 (1998): 155–88. This comparison is complicated for Puerto Rican migrants, however, as those who relocate to the mainland share some of the characteristics of voluntary migrants as well.

22. Grosfoguel and Georas, "Racialization of Latino Caribbean Migrants."

23. Alba and Nee, *Remaking the American Mainstream*; Alba, *Blurring the Color Line*; Kasinitz et al., *Inheriting the City*.

24. See Aranda, "Struggles of Incorporation."

25. Tuan, *Forever Foreigners*.

26. Jiménez, *Replenished Ethnicity*.

27. Alba, *Blurring the Color Line*.

28. Ibid.

29. Kasinitz et al., *Inheriting the City*.

30. Yancey, *Who Is White?*

31. Ibid; Gans, "Possibility of a New Racial Hierarchy"; Lee and Bean, *Diversity Paradox*.

32. Itzigsohn, *Encountering American Faultlines*; Bailey, "Dominican-American Ethnic/Racial Identities"; Edward E. Telles and Vilma Ortiz, *Generations of Exclusion: Mexican Americans, Assimilation, and Race* (New York: Russell Sage Foundation, 2008). This may, however, be tempered by class in later generations. See Jody Aguis Vallejo, "Brown Picket Fences: Patterns of Giving Back, Ethnic Identity and Ethnic Associations among the Mexican-Origin Middle Class" (Ph.D. diss., Department of Sociology, University of California, Irvine, 2008).

33. Lee and Edmonston, "Hispanic Intermarriage."

34. Jennifer Lee and Frank D. Bean, "America's Changing Color Lines: Immigration, Race/Ethnicity, and Multiracial Identification," *Annual Review of Sociology* 30 (2004): 221–42.

35. Lee and Bean, *Diversity Paradox.*

36. Lee and Edmonston, "Hispanic Intermarriage."

37. Lee and Bean, *Diversity Paradox.*

38. Lee and Edmonston, "Hispanic Intermarriage."

39. Zhenchao Qian, "Options: Racial/Ethnic Identification of Children of Intermarried Couples." *Social Science Quarterly* 85 (2004): 746–66.

40. Lee and Bean, *Diversity Paradox.*

41. Duncan and Trejo, "Intermarriage and Intergenerational Transmission"; Alba and Islam, "Case of the Disappearing Mexican Americans." Alba and Islam find that many of the people with Mexican ancestry who do not identify as Latino report some European ancestry in addition to Mexican, suggesting that many of them are the descendants of intermarriages.

42. While intermarriage may permit a loss in Latino identification across generations in one family, it actually produces a larger Latino-identifying population overall. Since two-thirds of their children are classified as Latino, intermarriage increases the Latino-identified population more than if Latinos only married one another. See Lee and Edmonston, "Hispanic Intermarriage."

43. Ibid.

44. Brian Duncan and Stephen J. Trejo, "Ethnic Choices and the Intergenerational Progress of Mexican Americans" (unpublished manuscript, 2004), p. 10.

45. Duncan and Trejo, "Intermarriage and Intergenerational Transmission."

46. Alba and Islam, "Case of the Disappearing Mexican Americans."

47. Degler, *Neither Black nor White.*

48. Lee and Edmonston, "Hispanic Intermarriage"; Duncan and Trejo, "Intermarriage and Intergenerational Transmission."

49. South, Crowder, and Chavez, "Migration and Spatial Assimilation."

50. Wendy D. Roth, "Are Latinos' Networks Segregated by Skin Color? How U.S. Migration Influences the Color Composition of Dominicans' and Puerto Ricans' Social Networks" (paper presented at the annual meeting of the International Network for Social Network Analysis, May 1–6, 2007, Corfu, Greece).

51. Susan Saulny, "Black? White? Asian? More Young Americans Choose All of the Above." *New York Times*, January 29, 2011, online edition (see interactive graphic). See also Zhenchao Qian and José A. Cobas, "Latinos' Mate Selection: National Origin, Racial, and Nativity Differences," *Social Science Research* 33 (2004): 225–47.

52. Roth, "Racial Mismatch." This conclusion is also clear from Mara Loveman and Jeronimo O. Muniz, "How Puerto Rico Became White: Boundary Dynamics and Intercensus Racial Reclassification," *American Sociological Review* 72 (2007): 915–39.

53. Murguia and Saenz, "Analysis of Latin Americanization."

54. Ibid.; Telles and Murguia, "Phenotypic Discrimination"; Villarreal, "Stratification by Skin Color,"; Espino and Franz, "Latino Phenotypic Discrimination Revisited"; Gómez, "Continual Significance of Skin Color."

55. Waters, *Black Identities.*

56. Murguia and Saenz, "Analysis of Latin Americanization."

57. Eduardo Bonilla-Silva, "We Are All Americans! The Latin Americanization of Racial Stratification in the USA," *Race and Society* 5 (2002): 3–16; Bonilla-Silva, "From Bi-Racial to Tri-Racial." For empirical studies relating to this thesis, see Forman, Goar, and Lewis, "Neither Black nor White?"; Frank, Akresh, and Lu, "Latino Immigrants and the U.S. Racial Order."

58. Murguia and Saenz, "Analysis of Latin Americanization," p. 87.

59. Telles and Murguia, "Phenotypic Discrimination."

60. Huntington, *Who Are We?* Deborah J. Schildkraut, *Press One for English: Language Policy, Public Opinion, and American Identity* (Princeton, NJ: Princeton University Press, 2005).

61. Alba and Nee, *Remaking the American Mainstream*; Jiménez, *Replenished Ethnicity*; Kasinitz et al., *Inheriting the City*; U.S. Census Bureau, Overview 2010; Rubén Rumbaut, Douglas S. Massey, and Frank D. Bean, "Linguistic Life Expectancies: Immigrant Language Retention in Southern California," *Population and Development Review* 32 (2006): 447–60.

62. U.S. Census Bureau, Overview 2010.

63. For example, Steven Hitlin, J. Scott Brown, and Glen H. Elder, Jr., "Measuring Latinos: Racial Classifications and Self-Understandings," *Social Forces* 86 (2007): 587–611.

64. Campbell and Rogalin, "Categorical Imperatives."

65. See Roth, "Racial Mismatch."

66. Denton and Massey, "Racial Identity among Caribbean Hispanics"; Douglas S. Massey and Nancy A. Denton, "Racial Identity and the Spatial Assimilation of Mexicans in the United States," *Social Science Research* 21 (1992): 235–60; Rodríguez, "Racial Classification"; Qian and Cobas, "Latinos' Mate Selection."

67. Luisa Farrah Schwartzman, "Does Money Whiten? Intergenerational Changes in Racial Classification in Brazil," *American Sociological Review* 72 (2007): 940–63.

68. I discuss some of the options for adding a measure of color to nationally representative surveys in Roth, "Racial Mismatch."

69. Cornell Law School, Wex online resource: www.law.cornell.edu/wex/index.php/Civil_rights.

70. Tanya Katerí Hernández, "Latino Inter-Ethnic Employment Discrimination and the 'Diversity' Defense," *Harvard Civil Rights Civil Liberties Law Review* 42 (2007): 259–316. See also Taunya Lovell Banks, "Multilayered Racism: Courts' Continued Resistance to Colorism Claims," in *Shades of Difference: Why Skin Color Matters*, ed. Evelyn Nakano Glenn, pp. 213–22 (Palo Alto, CA: Stanford University Press, 2009); Trina Jones, "The Case for Legal Recognition of Colorism Claims," in *Shades of Difference: Why Skin Color Matters*, ed. Evelyn Nakano Glenn, pp.223–35 (Palo Alto, CA: Stanford University Press, 2009).

71. U.S. Census Bureau, Overview 2010.

72. Rockquemore and Brunsma, *Beyond Black.*

73. Nobles, *Shades of Citizenship*; Bailey, "Unmixing for Race Making"; Reginald Daniel, *Race and Multiraciality in Brazil and the United States: Converging Paths?* (University Park, PA: Pennsylvania State University Press, 2006).

74. Telles, *Race in Another America*; Bailey, "Unmixing for Race Making."

75. Paschel, "The Right to Difference"; Paschel and Sawyer, "Contesting Politics as Usual."

76. Ibid; Nobles, *Shades of Citizenship.*

77. See John W. Meyer, John Boli, George M. Thomas, and Francisco O. Ramirez, "World Society and the Nation-State," *American Journal of Sociology* 103 (1997): 144–81.

Appendix

1. Some respondents were as many as five degrees removed from my original contact.

2. As I could not violate respondent confidentiality by asking respondents if they knew other respondents, I cannot guarantee that some did not know one another through connections other than the route I used to locate them. Any associations between respondents were unknown to me.

3. Two of these terms were not commonly used in their home countries and do not appear in Table 3 (in Chapter 1)—*pardo* (a Brazilian term) and *blancusino* (an outdated term found in histor-

ical documents). These terms served as a check for whether respondents would claim that they hear every term on the list. Almost all admitted that they do not hear these two terms.

4. Married respondents were generally not asked to list previous romantic partners.

5. This approach is consistent with the measures of phenotype used in most of the literature. Frank F. Montalvo and G. Edward Codina, "Skin Color and Latinos in the United States," *Ethnicities* 1 (2001): 321–41; Carlos H. Arce, Edward Murguia, and W. Parker Frisbie, "Phenotype and Life Chances among Chicanos," *Hispanic Journal of Behavioral Sciences* 9 (1987): 19–32.

6. Jorge Duany, Luisa Hernández Angueira, and César A. Rey, *El Barrio Gandul: Economía subterránea y migración indocumentada en Puerto Rico* (Puerto Rico: Universidad del Sagrado Corazón, 1995).

7. Anselm Strauss and Juliet Corbin, Basics of Qualitative Research: Techniques and Procedures for Developing Grounded Theory (Thousand Oaks, CA: Sage Publications, 1998).

Index

Italic page numbers indicate figures and tables.

acculturation. *See* cultural assimilation
affirmative action laws, enforcement of, 198
African Americans: migrants passing as, 159–60, 168–69, 171–72, 173; migrants' resistance to identification as, 78–79, 152, 160, 171, 187, 188, 189, 193–94, 240n23; movement of dark-skinned migrants into category of, 193–94; racialization of early Latino migrants as, 74–75; skin color and social hierarchy in, 139; social class and perception of discrimination in, 144
African racial heritage, phrases used to indicate, 35–36, 226n73
African traits, as less desirable in continuum racial schema, 21–22
Alba, Richard, 191, 242n41
American(s): interactions with, and diffusion of U.S. racial schemas, 122; as racial category in nationality racial schema, 66, 152–53, 161
ancestry: as basis of U.S. racial schema, 19; as source of racial identity, 2. *See also* biological/genetic concepts of race
appearance. *See* phenotype
Arizona, immigration law SB 1070, 6
assimilation. *See* cultural assimilation; structural assimilation
azulito(a), defined, 19

Balaguer, Joaquín, 26
Barth, Frederik, 27

behavior, as signal of group membership, 154
bicultural fluency: advantages of, 162–65, 171, 174; retention of in cultural assimilation, 195
bicultural interviewing, 214–15
biological/genetic concepts of race: in Dominican Republic, 33–34, 40, 41–42, 45–46, 49–50, 56–57, 186; genotype vs. phenotype in, 55–57; Latino concept in, 101–2; migrants with higher education, adoption of, 82–83; in nationality racial schemas, 34; as popular view, 57; in Puerto Rico, 33–34, 34–39, 40–41, 47, 55, 68, 186, 227n85
Blackness: and discrimination in home countries, 132–38; and discrimination in U.S., 138–49; Dominican distancing from, 11, 42, 45, 124, 182, 227n83
Blackness, criteria for: changes in, and opportunities for political mobilization, 149–50; in Dominican Republic, 5, 11, 22, 29, 131–32; dual sense of in non-migrants, 115–17; in Puerto Rico, 132; in United States, 5. *See also specific racial schemas*
Black political mobilization, increase in, 198–99
blanco(a): defined, 19; uses of term, 1, 20, 21, 22, 43, 44, 47, 49, 52, 53, 57, 69, 114
blanco-blanco: defined, 37–38; uses of term, 113, 116
blanco(a) con raja, defined, 19
blanquito(a): defined, 19; uses of term, 18, 133, 134